'Hangman Hawley' is one of the villains of the '45 and holds a prominent place in Jacobite demonology but was also held in contempt by those who hated the Jacobite cause. He is reputed to have been a man who enjoyed hanging his own soldiers, looting from his enemies, and harrying defeated foes, yet he was defeated in the only battle that he ever held command. No one has come forward to defend his reputation.

However, the Duke of Cumberland, commander in chief of the British Army in the 1740s and 1750s, declared him to be a highly capable cavalry officer. He certainly had the experience; being given his first commission when less than ten years old and fighting in Spain, Flanders, Scotland and Germany, rising from ensign to lieutenant general, being wounded in the process.

This book covers both Hawley's professional and personal life. In both he was a figure of controversy. Many hated him – especially Jacobites and civilians – but among soldiers his reputation was more mixed. Drawing on numerous sources this is the first attempt to provide a full-length study on an important and controversial figure in 18th century British history.

Dr Jonathan Oates is a historian and a prolific author on the subject of the Jacobite campaigns from 1689-1746. His focus is on military matters, the British Army and its commanders, and especially the English dimension of the period. This is his seventh book on the topic and he has also written about thirty articles on aspects of Jacobitism, anti-Jacobitism, and the associated military campaigns. He has also edited three volumes of relevant material; the memoir of a loyalist Scottish officer, the letters of the Duke of Cumberland, as well as a memoir of an 18th century Leeds schoolmaster. He is currently working on a title which will examine the sieges of the '45.

Jonathan studied history at Reading University in 1988-1991, obtaining a First Class degree with a thesis about the '15, and then a doctorate from the same place in 2001, covering responses in north-eastern England to the two major 18th century rebellions. He has been employed as Borough Archivist for the London Borough of Ealing since 1999 and has also written extensively about criminal, local, and family history, especially in and around London.

Dedicated to Dr Alastair Massie

# King George's Hangman
## Henry Hawley and the Battle of Falkirk, 1746

Jonathan D. Oates

 Helion & Company Limited

Helion & Company Limited
Unit 8 Amherst Business Centre
Budbrooke Road
Warwick
CV34 5WE
England
Tel. 01926 499 619
Email: info@helion.co.uk
Website: www.helion.co.uk
Twitter: @helionbooks
Visit our blog at https://helionbooks.wordpress.com/

Published by Helion & Company 2019. Reprinted in paperback 2024
Designed and typeset by Mary Woolley (www.battlefield-design.co.uk)
Cover designed by Paul Hewitt, Battlefield Design (www.battlefield-design.co.uk)

Text © Jonathan D. Oates, 2019
Illustrations © as individually credited
Maps drawn by George Anderson © Helion & Company 2019

Front Cover: 'Hawley at Falkirk' (Painting by Peter Dennis © Helion and Co. 2019)
Back Cover: Hawley as Colonel of the Royal Dragoons c.1748, oil on canvas by David Morier (Courtesy of the Hawley family; image courtesy of Bonhams)

Every reasonable effort has been made to trace copyright holders and to obtain their permission for the use of copyright material. The author and publisher apologize for any errors or omissions in this work and would be grateful if notified of any corrections that should be incorporated in future reprints or editions of this book.

ISBN 978-1-804515-69-3

British Library Cataloguing-in-Publication Data.
A catalogue record for this book is available from the British Library.

All rights reserved. No part of this publication may be reproduced, stored in a retrieval system, or transmitted, in any form, or by any means, electronic, mechanical, photocopying, recording or otherwise, without the express written consent of Helion & Company Limited.

For details of other military history titles published by Helion & Company Limited contact the above address or visit our website: http://www.helion.co.uk.

We always welcome receiving book proposals from prospective authors.

# Contents

| | |
|---|---|
| List of Plates and Maps | vi |
| Introduction | 7 |
| 1  Baptism of Fire 1685-1709 | 13 |
| 2  Peacetime Soldiering, 1709-1740 | 36 |
| 3  Hawley and the Theory of War | 59 |
| 4  Return to War, 1739-1745 | 73 |
| 5  The Jacobite Campaign: the First Phase, 1745-1746 | 91 |
| 6  The Battle of Falkirk | 105 |
| 7  The End of the Jacobite Campaign | 147 |
| 8  Back to Europe, 1747-1748 | 170 |
| 9  Last Years, 1749-1759 | 178 |
| Conclusion | 188 |
| Appendix: Casualties at Falkirk | 190 |
| Bibliography | 196 |
| Index | 202 |

# List of Plates and Maps

Thomas Pelham-Holles, Duke of Newcastle. (Author's collection)     55
Hawley's scheme for Light Dragoons, 1728; mounted and dismounted private.
    Drawings by Rev. Percy Sumner after coloured originals in the Cumberland
    Papers (Published in *JSAHR* Vol. 25, No.102 (Summer 1947), and
    reproduced here by the generous permission of the Hon. Editor)     67
Henry Hawley by Christian Friedrich Zincke. Enamel on copper portrait
    miniature, verso of bloodstone and diamonds, in original shagreen case.
    (National Galleries of Scotland)     72
William Augustus, Duke of Cumberland. (From Evan Charteris' *William
    Augustus, Duke of Cumberland: His Early Life and Times, 1721-1748*)     80
Charles Edward Stuart. (From R. Fitzroy Bell (ed.), *Memorials of John Murray of
    Broughton, 1740-1747*)     96
Callendar House, near Falkirk. (Author photograph)     107
The Battle of Falkirk, 17 January 1746.     116
Falkirk Moor; view west towards Jacobite line. (Author photograph)     118
The ravine on the British right flank at Falkirk. (Author photograph)     129
Falkirk battle monument. (Author photograph)     135
Tomb in Falkirk churchyard of Captain William Edmundstone (or Edmundson)
    of Blakeney's Regiment, killed at Falkirk. (Author photograph)     135
The Battle of Culloden, 16 April 1746.     159
Culloden Moor battlefield, from an old postcard. (Author's collection)     162
Hawley as Colonel of the Royal Dragoons c.1748, oil on canvas by David Morier
    (Courtesy of the Hawley family; image courtesy of Bonhams)     173
West Green House, Hartley Wintney, Hampshire. (Author photograph)     186

# Introduction

The Jacobite campaign of 1745-1746 is one of the most well known in 18th century British history and the stream of books, articles, and dramas written about it and its participants is apparently never ending. Charles Edward Stuart, 'Bonnie Prince Charlie', and the Battle of Culloden have gained the lion's share of this, but the other two major battles have not been wholly neglected and campaign histories are legion, as well as studies of the men who fought on the Jacobite side. The Battle of Falkirk, though, has only had one book devoted to it (and unlike Culloden and Prestonpans the battle is not marked by a single poem or song), and the role of the commander of the British army is but little explored.

Three of the leaders of the British army of this campaign have not been ignored by authors; with a number of studies on the victorious Duke of Cumberland, one on Lieutenant General Sir John Cope and another on Field Marshal George Wade. Biographers have treated these figures, often seen in general histories as being brutal or incompetent, sympathetically. However, of all the principal commanders involved in the Jacobite campaign of 1745-1746 there is one that has never been seriously studied, and only mentioned in passing, and he is the man who commanded at Falkirk.

The stereotype of the brutal, sadistic British officer who was also inept as a leader on the battlefield is still with us. In the 18th century this applies to those men fighting in America against the French in the Seven Years War or the rebellious colonists in 1775-1781 (think of *Last of the Mohicans* and *The Patriot*) as well as those dealing with the Jacobites in 1745-1746. Fans of the popular novels and television drama set mainly in the 18th century, *Outlander*, will recall the books' principal scoundrel, the evil Captain Jonathan 'Black Jack' Randall, who may in part have been inspired by the subject of this book, though as far as known, his real counterpart had no homosexual tendencies nor was he a rapist of women or men.

That fourth man is Lieutenant General Henry Hawley, commander in chief in Scotland for the critical month of 20 December 1745 to 30 January 1746. Usually viewed as a strict disciplinarian towards both his own men and the Jacobites, as an inept general for having lost the Battle of Falkirk, and then as one of the principal directors of the campaign against the Jacobites in the aftermath of Culloden, this is the first biography of a soldier whose active service covered half a century including Britain's three major Continental wars from the 1690s to 1748 as well as the two important domestic campaigns of 1715 and 1745.

The Battle of Falkirk, fought on 17 January 1746, was the largest battle of the Jacobite campaigns in terms of numbers of men; almost 20,000. The Jacobites were at the peak of their strength in the '45 campaign, and had the benefit of French troops as well as Scots. The battle had the potential to decide the campaign; that it did not do so is perhaps one reason for its relative neglect. Only a single book has been devoted to it,[1] compared to the many for Culloden, and even the far smaller battle of Prestonpans has had two books written about it.

Hawley's command at Falkirk tends to have gone unassessed, and there is another aspect of Hawley's character that is focussed upon. Most writers on the '45 are sympathetic towards the Jacobites and so are hardly likely to view their opponents favourably. Sir Charles Petrie refers to Hawley as 'an officer who was possessed of the same amiable characteristics of his chief'. Petrie has already labelled Cumberland as being merciless and goes on to accuse him of 'peculiar sadism'.[2] In a later book, Hawley is introduced with a brief and unflattering portrait thus:

> In the course of his 50 years service Hawley had earned an unenviable reputation for severity, and his nickname of 'Lord Chief Justice' was well merited. Quoting Horace Walpole, Lord Mahon describes how on one occasion in Flanders "a deserter being hanged before Hawley's windows, the surgeons begged to have the body for dissection. But Hawley was reluctant to part with the pleasing spectacle, 'At least' said he 'you shall give me the skeleton to hang up in the guard room'". His military capacity was less apparent, for having fought at Sheriffmuir, where his regiment was posted on the victorious right wing, he had acquired the mistaken belief that Highlanders were unable to resist a cavalry charge.[3]

More recent writers have been no less harsh; to Professor Lenman, Hawley is damned in one word 'brutal' and Dr McLynn does likewise, titling him in the

---

1   Geoffrey Bailey, *Falkirk or Paradise* (Edinburgh: John Donald, 1996).
2   Sir Charles Petrie, *The Jacobite Movement* (London: Eyre and Spottiswoode,1932), pp.209-210, 215.
3   Katherine Tomasson and Frances Buist, *Battles of the Forty Five* (London: Batsford, 1962), p.89.

index to his biography of Charles Edward Stuart, 'Hangman'.[4] Professor Black notes Hawley's extensive military service and adds, 'A notorious disciplinarian, Hawley was more energetic (and confident) than Wade'.[5]

Authors with Jacobite sympathies really go to town on the subject of Hawley and lay it on thick. According to Christopher Duffy, Hawley was 'quirky and sadistic', 'represented a pronounced strain of jocular savagery among the senior officers' and apparently had the remains of an executed deserter in his tent, either as a hide or a skeleton, and believed in no mercy towards his own soldiers and captured Jacobites. Later in Duffy's book we are again reminded about the remains of the deserter at his headquarters and added that Hawley was 'a highly professional soldier, sadist, and man of very strange private habits' and 'a devotee of floggings and executions'.[6] Presumably the story of the executed deserter derives from the Walpole tale which most historians recount, though Walpole's spy has now morphed into a deserter. In his revised work, Duffy refers to Hawley as having 'a sadistic streak and was notorious as a hanger and flogger' and as 'old and mad'.[7]

McLynn is similarly unsparing on the subject of Hawley. As with Duffy, he lumps Hawley along with a number of other British officers who displayed severity towards the Jacobites, introducing him as 'Hangman Hawley', noting his predilection for gibbets, savagery, his military incompetence, and then when referring to the severity of a French officer, comments that he was a man of 'the Hawley stamp'.[8] All that is missing is any reference to Walpole's famous remarks.

Biographers of Cumberland, anxious to defend this much-maligned man, are no less unsympathetic, perhaps to make Cumberland look better. Ewan Charteris, the first modern biographer, refers to Hawley's service, as Black was to do, and then comments on his severity,

> But his notoriety depends less on his ability as a commander than on his brutality as a disciplinarian. Amongst soldiers he was known as the "Lord Chief Justice" or "Hangman", and was credited with a passion for frequent and sudden executions. In such an age to have deserved such a reputation denotes an altogether abnormal temperament. The gibbet and the halberds, indeed, seem to have been his sole means of enforcing

---

4   Bruce Lenman, *The Jacobite Clans of the Great Glens* (London: Methuen, 1984), p.157; Frank McLynn, *Bonnie Prince Charlie* (London: Routledge, 1988), p.634.
5   Jeremy Black, *Culloden and the '45* (Gloucester: Sutton, 1990), p.137.
6   Christopher Duffy, *The '45: Bonnie Prince Charlie and the Untold Story of the Jacobite Rising* (London: Cassell, 2003), pp.126, 128, 402.
7   Christopher Duffy, *Fight for a Throne: The Jacobite '45 Reconsidered* (Solihull: Helion, 2015) pp.292, 350.
8   McLynn, *Bonnie Prince Charlie*, pp.159, 202, 465.

obedience or establishing discipline, and beyond these his ideas did not carry him.⁹

He then retails the Horace Walpole quote cited above, adds criticism from another contemporary, Major James Wolfe, and then refers to 'his coarseness of fibre and stunted imagination'. Professor Speck, on introducing Hawley, notes his long military experience and then refers to him as Hangman Hawley and repeats the Walpole quote. He adds 'Hawley clearly crossed a recognisable line, or he would not have obtained his nickname of the Hangman'.¹⁰ Whitworth writes of Cumberland, 'He remonstrated with "Hangman Hawley" for his excessive zeal with the noose and the execution squad' and refers to a 'rascally old general like Hawley'.¹¹ The present author, in his work on Cumberland, has cited Hawley's plans to execute deserters and Cumberland's pardoning of these men.¹² A recent and impartial author, when introducing Hawley, makes no reference at all to his antecedents.¹³ Even Charles Dalton, who wrote several small pieces about Hawley, was damning, 'he never did anything heroic and was a complete failure as a general'.¹⁴

There has been some less negative work about Hawley. Just after World War Two, there was a flurry of articles in the *Journal of the Society of Army Historical Research*, drawing on Hawley's own writings in the Hawley-Toovey papers. These focussed, not on Hawley's record as a hangman or as general during the '45, but on his experience at Almanza in 1707 and on his writings about the use of cavalry.¹⁵

Returning to 1745-1746, the only straw in the wind against the welter of negative historiography has been provided by, unsurprisingly, Stuart Reid, who as a former soldier is sympathetic to the British Army, in one of his ground-breaking studies of the campaign. According to Reid:

---

9   Ewan Charteris, *William Augustus, Duke of Cumberland, His early Life and Times, 1721-1748* (London: Edward Arnold, 1913), pp.241-242.
10  William Speck, *The Butcher: The Duke of Cumberland and the suppression of the '45* (Oxford: Blackwell, 1981), pp.105, 141.
11  Rex Whitworth, *William Augustus: Duke of Cumberland*, (Barnsley: Pen and Sword, 1992), pp.90, 101.
12  Jonathan Oates, *Sweet William or the Butcher? The Duke of Cumberland and the '45* (Barnsley: Pen and Sword, 2008), p.53.
13  Jacqueline Riding, *The Jacobites: A New History of the '45 Rebellion* (New York: Bloomsbury, 2016), pp.342-344.
14  Charles Dalton, 'Parentage of Lieut. General Hawley', *Notes and Queries*, 8th Series, IX, (1896), p.121.
15  Rev. Percy Sumner, 'General Hawley's Scheme for Light Dragoons', *Journal of the Society for Army Historical Research*, XXV (1947), pp.91-94; Percy Summer, 'General Hawley's Chaos', *JSAHR*, XXVI (1948), pp.63-66.

Too often dismissed simply as a boorish and vicious martinet, he was actually nobody's fool and passionately interested in the theoretical as well as the practical aspects of his profession. He was undoubtedly irascible and possessed of a black sense of humour, but if the soldiers now under his command considered him harsh, that undoubtedly reflected the crying need to take them in hand and restore discipline in what was a badly demoralised army.[16]

Reid is later critical of Hawley at Falkirk in not sending out scouting parties:

This indeed was Hawley's biggest mistake. He had an overwhelming superiority in mounted troops – no less than three regiments of dragoons – and as an experienced cavalryman he should have known how to use them…In short there was no reason at all why they should not have been allowed to build up their confidence through aggressive patrolling, and at the same time keeping their commander fully informed as to where the rebels were and what they were doing. Instead he was plainly reluctant to let them out of his sight and kept them close to his infantry with the result that he was effectively blind.[17]

A recent author noted, 'His career was built upon personal courage, royal patronage and loyalty to the Protestant succession: it was also marred by his shortcomings as a leader'.[18]

There have been relevant articles in the nineteenth century *Dictionary of National Biography* and in the more recent *Oxford Dictionary of National Biography*. The latter, original, well balanced and well sourced, provides the best biography of Hawley to date, though is necessarily concise in its coverage.

Hawley has never lacked for critics, both contemporary – Jacobite and non-Jacobite authors – and more recent. Several well-known contemporaries in published works were critical of him. These included John Home in his *History of the Rebellion*, for his defeat at Falkirk; Andrew Henderson in his, the first, biography of the Duke of Cumberland to whom Hawley is always compared unfavourably; and Horace Walpole, for his damning remarks about Hawley in his correspondence, which has been in print since the early 19th century. And that is before we proceed to the Jacobite memoirs, notably *The Lyon in Mourning*, a catalogue of indictments of the soldiers of the British state after Culloden.

---

16  Stuart Reid, *1745: A Military History of the Last Jacobite Rising* (Spellmount: Staplehurst, 1996) p.92.
17  Reid, *1745*, p.98.
18  Ira D. Gruber, *Officers and their Books* (University of North Carolina Press, 2010), p.89.

Hawley's only celluloid depiction has been very brief, in one scene of the film *Chasing the Deer* (1994) in which he is (contrary to fact) shown on horseback adjacent to the Duke of Cumberland towards the latter stages of Culloden, where he is used as a sounding board for Cumberland's comments about dealing with the Jacobites after the battle is over. The character is played by John Claudius as a middle-aged man and his single line is 'My congratulations your Royal Highness on your victory' and Cumberland replies, 'Not yet, Hawley…'. He is earlier mentioned in this film and in the 1948 *Bonnie Prince Charlie* as having been defeated at Falkirk. A rather peripheral character compared to his fellow generals, Sir John Cope and Cumberland.

What is certain, in history as in film, is that Hawley has only been treated in a most marginal way. There has been no systematic examination of his life and his stated atrocities. He is deemed a peripheral figure and has been unexplored. Fortunately, there are a number of important primary sources that show a light on his career. The Cumberland Papers and the Hawley-Toovey papers in the Royal Archives include letters to and from him, as do the Newcastle Papers in the British Library, the State Papers for Scotland and the State Papers Domestic held at the National Archives, principally for 1745-1746. Newspapers often refer to him, as do accounts by Jacobite officers and propagandists, all of which have been published. The Royal Archives also holds his unpublished autobiography, a hitherto overlooked source.

This book covers the whole of Hawley's life and military career, which spanned over half a century. There is space devoted to his time when he was not facing the Jacobite forces of 1745-1746, which covered eight months of his life. More of his soldiering took place on the European Continent; whether in the Low Countries, Germany and Spain, from 1697-1748, as well as soldiering at home, both in his early years between the major European wars, and in later life, in the run up to the Seven Years War. His personal and family life were of less importance than his military career, but he took his non-military interests seriously and was as much attached to the women in his life as any bachelor soldier could be. These show an additional side to his character and reveal him as less as a two-dimensional villain – even the fictional 'Black Jack' had a humane side when dealing with his brother. However, the central episode in Hawley's life, as in this book, is the Battle of Falkirk, correctly the second battle (the first being the defeat of William Wallace by Edward I in 1298), fought on 17 January 1746. This was Hawley's first and last experience of independent command in battle. His life hitherto was to be a preparation for this moment.

# 1

# Baptism of Fire 1685-1709

Hawley's military experience was certainly longstanding compared to almost any other participant at a senior level on either side in the Jacobite campaign of 1745. This was not just because he was one of the oldest (not the most elderly as that was Field Marshal George Wade), but because he received his first commission in the 1690s. Virtually all his life had been spent as a soldier and this may have resulted in a belief that he was a master of the profession.

There is a great deal of mythology about Hawley's birth and antecedents; it has been alleged that his birth was in about the year 1679 and this has been repeated in print until fairly recently.[1] This 'fact' can still be found on the internet, even on reputable sites. It has also been alleged, as Ewan Charteris noted without comment in 1907, 'Popular rumour alleged that he was a son of King George [II], and that on this account his brutalities were condoned'.[2] In March 2018 a fellow researcher at the National Records of Scotland related this story to the present author on learning of my interest in the man. Given that George II was born in 1683, this popular rumour is palpable nonsense; the mystery is why it lasted so long. These points were scotched many years ago by military historian and genealogist, Charles Dalton, but this research does not seem to have become well known.[3]

Hawley's lineage can be traced back to country gentry in Tudor times. His great grandfather was Sir Henry Hawley (1586-1623) of Wivelscombe, Somersetshire, an active justice of the peace and married to Elizabeth, daughter of Sir Anthony Poulett. His eldest son was Francis (1608-1684), who raised a regiment of cavalry to fight for the King in the Civil War. Charles I made him first Earl Hawley of Duncannon, of the Irish peerage, in 1644. One of Sir Henry's younger sons was

---

1    Reid, *1745*, p.92.
2    Lord Elcho (ed. Ewan Charteris), *A Short Account of the Affairs of Scotland, 1744-1746* (Edinburgh: David Douglas, 1907), p.362.
3    Dalton, 'General Hawley's Parentage', p.121.

Robert Hawley (Hawley's grandfather), who was the second husband of Susanna Erle, mother of Thomas Erle (and of he, more anon) and fourth daughter of William Fiennes, first Viscount Saye and Sele. Robert fought for the King, too, and was elevated to major. After the restoration he was a cavalry officer; as a younger son he would not inherit much, and died in Wivelscombe on 4 May 1682. Robert and Susanna had a daughter, Elizabeth, baptised 19 October 1653, a son, Francis, born in the following year, and another son, Henry.[4]

The Henry Hawley that this book is concerned with was the firstborn child of the 30-year-old Captain Francis and Judith Hawley (nee Hughes, 1659-c.1737), born on 4 January 1685 and baptised eight days later at the church of St. Martin's in the Fields in Westminster. His parents, both of the parish of St. Martins in the Fields, had married at the newly rebuilt church of St. Nicholas Cole Abbey, in the City of London, on 22 January 1684 by licence. Little is known about his mother, but his father was a young yet experienced soldier in the relatively new English standing army.[5] Given that his father had chosen a career as a soldier, it is unsurprising that Francis did likewise. On 7 April 1675 Francis Hawley had been commissioned as second lieutenant in Captain Hudson's company of infantry.[6]

Francis Hawley then switched to Captain Berkeley's company in Colonel Russell's Regiment of Foot Guards, at the rank of ensign, the lowest grade of a commissioned infantry officer, but in a far more prestigious unit, where officers were of a higher social class than in other regiments and with possible access to the monarch. Yet he applied for, on 24 November 1676, permission for leave of absence for 12 months overseas. This could have been in order to fight in the ongoing War between France and the Dutch Republic which had been raging since 1672. England was not then taking part in the war, having been fighting the Dutch Republic on the seas in 1672-1674, but many ambitious British soldiers chose to fight in the war to gain experience, be noticed by their superiors and hopefully gain promotion. A licence for leave was granted on 13 December of that year.[7] Francis became a captain in the Duke of Monmouth's newly raised infantry

---

4 PCC Wills, Durston parish registers, Wilvescombe parish registers, via Ancestry.co.uk; Charles Dalton, *English Army Commission Registers 1661-1685* (London: Eyre and Spottiswoode, 1892), Vol.I, pp.4-5, 60, 76.
5 Marriage registers of St. Nicholas Cole Abbey, London and baptism registers of St. Martin in the Fields, London, via Ancestry.co.uk.
6 Royal Archives, Hawley-Toovey Papers (hereafter RA, HT), 7411-24-101, p.1.; F.H. Blackburne Daniell (ed.), *Calendar of State Papers, Domestic series, of the reign of Charles II*, 1675-6 (London: Longman, 1860-1947), p.57.
7 Blackburne Daniell (ed.), *Calendar of State Papers, Domestic series, of the reign of Charles II*, 1676-1677 (London: Longman, 1860-1947), pp. 431, 451.

regiment on 10 February 1678. According to his eldest son 'he began the worlde a volunteer with the Duke of Monmouth in France'.[8]

However, once he was home again, Francis soon ran into trouble by wounding one William Boone, who later died of these injuries (this may have been a duel). Francis faced a manslaughter charge. On 29 April 1679, he petitioned the Recorder and the Sheriffs of London, pleading that he had 'being assaulted and highly provoked', presumably suggesting that he had killed in self-defence. On 10 July of that year he was pardoned, presumably by the King as the pardon emanated from a royal palace, Hampton Court.[9] He also served as a lieutenant in the grenadier company of the Foot Guards, being commissioned on 14 June 1680 in Tangiers later that year at the end of English occupancy, which had begun on Charles II acquiring it as part of his dowry on marriage with Catherine of Braganza. Its possession had involved much fighting with the Moors and very little benefit, so it was evacuated in 1683.[10]

Promotion came on 20-21 April 1684, with Francis being able to purchase a captaincy in the Foot Guards that he had served in for about four years.[11] In the following year Charles II achieved his ambition to die peacefully as King and was succeeded by his younger brother, James II. This sparked off two attempts to dethrone him, from both Scotland and England, on the grounds that James was openly Catholic in a very largely Protestant country. On 5 June Charles II's eldest illegitimate son, the Duke of Monmouth, the same man that Francis Hawley had served under in the previous decade, arrived at Lyme Regis in Dorset with a few followers and arms and began to gather support, in a bid to become King. Hawley later stated of his father's campaign, 'In Monmouth's rebellion he did a very great action'.[12]

James sent troops to the West Country whilst maintaining forces around London, too. One of the regiments sent westwards under Louis de Duras (1641-1709), second Earl of Feversham, was the First Foot Guards, Francis's regiment (a recent historian has confused Captain Francis with his son as having taken part in this campaign). Feversham was not a particularly capable officer and on Saturday 27 June 1685, on hearing musketry emanating from the lane leading to the village of Phillip's Norton in Somersetshire, his subordinate, the Duke of Grafton, ordered 20 Horse Guards and the 45-strong grenadier company of Foot

---

8   RA, HT, 7411-24-101, p.1.
9   Blackburne Daniell (ed.), *Calendar of State Papers, Domestic series, of the reign of Charles II, 1679-1680* (London: Longman, 1860-1947), pp.132, 195.
10  Dalton, *English Army Lists and Commission Registers, 1661-1685*, Vol.I, p.275.
11  Blackburne Daniell and F.L. Bickley (eds.), *Calendar of State Papers, Domestic series, of the reign of Charles II, 1683-1684* (London: Longman, 1860-1947), pp.392.
12  RA, HT, 7411-24-101, p.1.

Guards forward. Despite coming under fire from the rebels, the troops advanced, exchanging fire and then charging the rebels with bayonets. It was not a successful action for the royalists, with at least eight or nine men, and possibly as many as 20, being killed and about 30 wounded. However, it was noted in a newspaper that 'Captain Hawley who commanded the Grenadiers did all that a good officer could do'.[13] Furthermore, Hawley was captured as the men with him were killed. Yet he managed to escape by killing his two guards using a dagger hidden under his coat which they had not seen. Apparently 'for some time after' this led to a fashion for concealed weaponry.[14]

However, on 5-6 July the decisive action of the campaign occurred at Sedgemoor. Monmouth's army made a night march to surprise Feversham's army but the element of surprise was lost and a shooting match developed between both sides. On the next day the rebels were utterly routed, and as an officer in the Guards we can safely assume that Francis Hawley played his part in the triumph. Less than three weeks later, on 26 July Francis became major in Berkeley's Dragoons (its colonel had previously served with Hawley in the Guards). [15]

Three years later the kingdom was in turmoil yet again. Mounting domestic opposition and the falling away of James II's natural supporters together with an impending invasion by the forces of the King's son in law, William of Orange (1650-1702), meant that the army was potentially in action again. Francis was, in November 1688, promoted to lieutenant colonel in the same cavalry regiment, termed the Princess Anne of Denmark's Regiment of Dragoons. According to his son, he was promoted by the King personally at the army camp at Hounslow Heath.[16] When William's troops arrived in Torbay on 5 November, the British army was centred on Salisbury as a prelude to battle, but several high-level defections led to James' nerve failing and he ordered a retreat. In the following weeks he left the country and by the next year William was crowned King. Francis Hawley's part in the revolution are unknown but clearly he was no stalwart supporter of James.

The Crown was not yet settled. In 1689 Viscount Dundee led a rebellion in Scotland against William III, and troops were sent from England to reinforce those in Scotland led by Major General Hugh Mackay (1640-1692). One regiment of cavalry sent northwards was Berkeley's, which was led by Lieutenant Colonel

---

13   *London Gazette*, 29 June-2 July 1685; Anon, *Ninth Report of the Royal Commission on Historic Manuscripts, Part II: Appendix and Index* (London: Eyre and Spottiswoode, 1884), p.3.
14   RA, HT, 7411-24-101, p.1.
15   Blackburne Daniell and Bickley (eds.), *Calendar of State Papers, Domestic series, of the reign of Charles II, 1685* (London: Longman, 1860-1947), p.278.
16   RA, HT, 7411-24-101, p.1.

Francis Hawley. Berkeley 'being no military man' was an absentee commander and operational leadership fell to the lieutenant colonel.[17] The regiment took part in a skirmish in the Highlands in early June, fighting alongside Livingstone's Dragoons against the men of the MacLean clan, who were marching to join Dundee's army. Diverse accounts give the fighting as a victory for both sides.[18] Dundee was later killed at the Battle of Killiecrankie on 27 July, in which his army gained a costly victory, and his army was defeated at Dunkeld a month later. Berkeley's was present at neither action.

Little is known about Francis's actions in the following year, but he obtained passes for travelling in Lincolnshire and Grantham in March and June respectively.[19] His unit was about to serve on the Continent in the following year in William's war against the French (the Nine Years War, 1688-1697), and perhaps this prompted him to make his will on 25 February 1692. This document shows that he held property in the parish of Wivelescombe in Somersetshire, and that he now had three more children; Edward, Charles, and Anne as well as Henry. His wife was still alive after four pregnancies, too, and his will left all his property to her as well as in the event of his death, some to be spent on 'the educating and upbringing of my children'. After her death the property should pass to Henry and he was to give Charles and Edward £100 each with £400 to Anne. The witnesses to the will were Sir Francis Ware and Colonel Thomas Erle (1650-1720).[20]

On 3 March 1692 Hawley took ship from Harwich. The regiment, with Francis Hawley in charge as brevet colonel from 10 May, fought at the Battle of Steinkirk on 30 July. It was more than a bloody battle, with numerous casualties among the officer corps as well as 3-4000 men among the allied forces. These included was colonel Francis Hawley, not quite 40 years old, killed by a bursting grenade. Of the regiment, only the quartermaster, four sergeants, and a few troopers escaped the fighting unscathed. Apparently, Francis had also been shot through his left shoulder. He thus left a widow and four children all aged under ten, 'in a bad way'.[21] It is not known how this affected his eldest son, but in his memoir, he writes of his father with respect.

17  RA, HT, 7411-24-101, p.1.
18  Jonathan Oates, *The Battle of Killiecrankie* (Solihull: Helion, 2018), pp.43-44.
19  William John Hardy (ed.), *Calendar of State Papers, Domestic of the reign of William and Mary, 1689-1690* (London: Stationery Office, 1895-1906), p.513; Hardy (ed.), *Calendar of State Papers, Domestic series, of the reign of William and Mary, 1691-1692* (London: Stationery Office, 1895-1906), p.39.
20  TNA, PROB11/418/451.
21  Hardy (ed.), *Calendar of State Papers, Domestic series, of the reign of William and Mary, 1691-1692*, pp.168, 391-392; RA, HT, 7411-24-101, p.1.

Following Francis' death, the family had to sell his properties in Wivelscombe to pay his debts. Francis had acquired West and East Whitfield and property named the Jewes in that parish. These were sold for £1,950 to settle what he owed with the remainder left for his family. The residue was to go to Henry, but as a minor, it had to be assigned to the two executors of the will.[22] However, within two years of their father's death, both Edward and Henry were commissioned officers in the English Army. The former (aged six) became a cornet in the Earl of Essex's Dragoons (his father's old regiment) on 1 August 1692.[23] The youngest son was Charles, who became an ensign on 15 November 1695 in John Mere's company of Sir James Lesley's Regiment of Foot.[24]

On 10 January 1694 Henry was appointed as an ensign (being paid three shillings a day with a further eightpence as his servant allowance) in Captain Thomas Phillips' company in a regiment of infantry commanded by Brigadier Thomas Erle, a staunch supporter of the new King.[25] The lieutenant colonel from 1691-1709 was his uncle Henry. This was very fortunate for a young man, for to progress in the army an influential patron was very important indeed. In 1697 he joined his uncle abroad, aged 13, acting as his aide, and taking two horses with him. He recalled, 'being so young he did no duty in the regiment, but in the quarter ground and the gentlemen on guard'. He was also aide to Colonel William Cadogan (1671-1726).[26] It should be noted that it was not unknown at this time for children to be given junior military commissions, though they would not see active service until reaching their later teens, but it was not commonplace. The habit had begun under Charles II and was used by the monarch to reward brave soldiers. The 12-year-old Hugh Mackay was commissioned onto his late father's regiment following the latter's death at Steinkirk, too, and another child was commissioned aged three.[27] As the son of a deceased army officer, Hawley's being placed in the army was not at all out of keeping at the time.

Because this is a book which studies an 18th century British soldier, it is worth spending a little time considering the army in which he was an officer, from ensign to general. The army was divided into regiments of infantry and cavalry, the latter comprising both regiments of horse and the more numerous, cheaper, and lighter dragoons who would be expected to fight on foot as well as mounted. The infantry

---

22 TNA, C8/539/14.
23 Charles Dalton, *The Army of George I* (London: Eyre and Spottiswoode, 1910), Vol.I, p.331.
24 RA, HT, 7411-24-101, p.1.
25 William John Hardy (ed.), *Calendar of State Papers, Domestic series, of the reign of William III, 1694-1695* (London: Stationery Office, 1913-1937), p.5.
26 RA, HT, 7411-24-101, p.1.
27 Charles Dalton, 'Child Commissions in the Army, 1661-1714', *Notes and Queries*, 8th Series, VIII, 1895, pp.421-422.

regiments were divided into 10 companies, each commanded by a captain with a lieutenant and ensign as well as NCOs. The regiment's three 'field officers', the colonel, lieutenant colonel, and major, would also be company commanders as well. Cavalry regiments were divided into six troops, with a captain, lieutenant, and cornet as the officers. Regiments were known after the colonel's name. The colonel could often be a general officer as well and so day-to-day (and battlefield) command was often delegated to the lieutenant colonel. There were also three battalions of Foot Guards plus four troops of Horse Guards and two of Horse Grenadier Guards. From 1716 there was the Royal Regiment of Artillery.[28]

To become an officer in peacetime depended on two attributes; money and influence. A man or boy had to start with the most junior position, but also had to have the ear of the commanding officer as well as enough money to purchase the next commission above his. To advance he needed there to be a vacancy in the rank above him, perhaps created by death, retirement, or disgrace. This vacancy would be offered to the man with the longest service and if he could not buy it, it would be offered to the next man in seniority and so on. Purchasing of a new commission could be offset by the sale of a man's current commission. As ever the commanding officer had to approve and this had to be confirmed by the commander in chief and sovereign, though the government was also consulted on promotions. In wartime, progress through the ranks was faster than in peacetime, when death or disabling wounds in action created vacancies. When an officer stepped into a 'dead man's shoes' he did not have to buy that commission. Powerful friends and money were important, but so was talent.[29]

It should be stated that there is nothing that is known about the first decade of Henry Hawley's life. Presumably he lived in Westminster with his mother, though whether he received any formal education we do not know. He would have been too young to have attended any school, such as Westminster School. As any army officer's son his upbringing would have been comfortable but probably not opulent. He may well have received some instruction in reading and writing by a tutor and learned to ride. Army officers had to be Anglican and so Hawley would have been brought up as a member of the Church of England.

It seems that Hawley went overseas in 1697, for on 26 April 1696 a pass was granted to Mrs Francis Hawley to go to the Dutch Republic.[30] Here Hawley was under Erle's supervision, for the brigadier 'took him every where with him, by which he was soon known to ye King and all the gentle officers'.[31] The latter

---

28   Reid, *1745*, pp.183-194.
29   Reid, *1745*, pp.183-194.
30   William John Hardy (ed.), *Calendar of State Papers, Domestic series, of the reign of William III, 1696* (London: Stationery Office, 1913-1937), p.145.
31   RA, HT, 7411-24-101, p.2.

included Prince Charles Henri de Lorraine of Vaudemont (1649-1723) and his wife, Princess Anne Elizabeth. He was commander in chief of the Spanish army in the Netherlands and a confidant of William III. His wife was active in hospital provision for the British army in the Netherlands. He also saw his first action near Brussels in the war's final year. There was a general forage and Hawley, on his uncle's orders, accompanied a number of volunteers, men wanting to become officers but lacking the funds to purchase commissions, who marched with the men but messed with the officers and hoped to obtain a commission by death in battle of a junior officer. It is not known what happened on this occasion. Yet Hawley was unwell with 'Bloody Flux' (dysentery) and was returned to Brussels. The Prince of Vaudemont 'ordered great care to be taken of him'.[32] It seems that his life was despaired of, because the Princess sent a priest to give him the last rites, though he could not have been a Catholic. In any case he recovered and was able to accompany his uncle to the Dutch Republic.[33]

They then went to England as the fighting had come to an end as peace talks had begun at Ryswick in the summer. They had a good passage to the Downs, where the ship anchored. There was then a fierce storm and the vessel lost its anchor and was driven over the Goodwood Sands. Fortunately, a spring tide helped the ship off the sandbank. That night, however, 16 horses which were in the hold, broke free. Hawley recalled 'everybody gave themselves up for lost'. Eventually, it was possible to have the horses killed by their throats being cut, presumably to avoid damage to the ship and those aboard it.[34] For the next few days the ship was tossed by storms, but eventually reached Norway, where the storm began to abate. For Hawley and his shipmates, it was an abysmal experience, 'they had neither water or provisions on board, and were in a miserable condition for two days'. To top it off, they were captured by a French privateer, which put a prize crew on board, but at least provided the hungry men with provisions. They were taken to Dunkirk, and en route it was then found that the articles of the peace treaty had been concluded in September, the news being relayed from another French ship. The ship which Hawley was in then sailed to Helvoetsluys, though their condition was still wretched, 'half starved, and the horses stinking in the hold'. Back home, 'when they landed Hawley was so near starved he had not strength to stand, having had but one small mess of very bad oat-meal for four days'.[35]

Peace, albeit of a temporary nature, broke out at the end of 1697 with the Peace of Ryswick where Louis XIV had to surrender his territorial gains made since

---

32   RA, HT, 7411-24-101, p.2
33   William John Hardy (ed.), *Calendar of State Papers, Domestic series, of the reign of William III, 1696* (London: Stationery Office, 1913-1937), p.145.
34   RA, HT, 7411-24-101, p.2.
35   RA, HT, 7411-24-101, p.2.

1678. This led to a general disbandment of much of the British Army, including Erle's Regiment, which was reduced to a mere three companies. Hawley was then put on half pay, which would have given Hawley less than two shillings a day to subsist on.[36] Mrs Hawley then petitioned William III thus:

> her husband, Colonel Francis Hawley, was killed at Steinkirk, leaving her in charge of four children, with no other fortune but the hopes of His Majesty's royal favour, which he had been graciously pleased to promise to the petitioner's brother Major General Erle…petitioner by her endeavours to fit her children for His Majesty's service has engaged herself in great difficulties.

This was on 11 October 1699 and she received a gratuity of £40, though her eldest son later recalled that it was £300 per year, continued until her death in 1737.[37]

Erle had two other infantry regiments in his proprietorship and offered his nephew the first vacancy for an ensign that would arise. He took the lad to London to meet the King, whose hand Hawley kissed. William remembered Hawley 'and told him he would take care of him for his father's sake'. Yet, with the regiment completely reduced, Hawley was unemployed as a half pay officer, so returned to dwell with his mother.[38] However, fortune shone on him. At the end of 1697, Prince George of Denmark (1653-1708), husband of the King's sister-in-law, Anne (1665-1714), who was heir to the throne, remembered him. George had served in the Danish army, as John Evelyn noted in 1683, that he was 'reported valiant, and indeed he had bravely rescued and brought off his brother, the King of Denmark in a bataile against the Swede'.[39] The prince had known Hawley's father and asked John Churchill, Earl of Marlborough (1650-1722), in charge of the Prince's Bedchamber 'if he [Colonel Francis Hawley] had left any sons, he should be glad to take one of them into his family'. Churchill called for Hawley and introduced him to the prince, who made him a page of the Bedchamber. This involved his sharing a room with the prince's surviving son, the 10-year-old William Henry, Duke of Gloucester, born in 1689 and after his mother the next in line to the throne, and other pages.[40]

Being a page was not without its disadvantages. Apparently, the young Duke, 'upon some little provocation drew his little sword in a passion, and making a full

---

36   RA, HT, 7411-24-101, p.2.
37   Dalton, *Army Lists*, Vol.III, p.374.
38   Dalton, 'General Hawley's parentage', *Notes and Queries*, pp.121-122; RA, HT, 7411-24-101, p.1.
39   John Evelyn, *Diary* (London: Everyman, 2005), p.673.
40   RA, HT, 7411-24-101, p.2.

thrust at him [Hawley], ran him through the hand and arms and almost thro' his side, but no great hurt being done'. The Duke gave Hawley presents to the value of '10 pieces' (guineas?) and begged him not to speak of this incident. No other page spoke of it, so Hawley recovered from his wounds and became a little richer. However, on 30 July 1700 Gloucester died, aged only 11; which meant there were now no heirs to the throne following William and Anne. This was a problem that Parliament solved by designating George, Elector of Hanover, as the next monarch.[41] Doubtless, though, Hawley had other worries as he would have lost his place at court and reverted to living with his mother on his meagre pay.

Hostilities in Europe recommenced in 1701, in what was known as the War of the Spanish Succession. Britain, the Empire, and the Dutch Republic, with some German allies, fought France, Spain, and Bavaria over who would inherit the vast Spanish Empire now the childless Carlos II of Spain was dead. Hawley became an ensign in Sir Richard Temple's newly raised infantry regiment on 10 May 1702.[42]

The troops embarked for Flanders in 1703 and Hawley begged Prince George to let him go on campaign; he was now in his late teens, an age when many junior officers fought in battle. George said no and promised him a better position. By the end of the summer, he gave him a lieutenancy in the Foot Guards, a far more prestigious regiment and which gave officers access to the court. However, a difficulty arose as the Captain General of Britain's armies, Marlborough, asserted that he had promised the commission to James Allen and so Hawley was disappointed.[43]

In order to compensate for this setback, the Prince gave 'him a very good horse, and ordered him to be always at Windsor with him'. He had a place at the royal table and spent his days hunting in the Prince's retinue, a sport that was to be a favourite pastime of his for many decades to come. It did, however, have its dangers, as Hawley soon found to his cost as he broke his collar bone whilst out hunting. There were other ways to pass the time at court. One was gambling and on 6 January 1704 the prince was playing at hazard and won 'a hatful' of money. He gave this to Hawley to carry up to his apartment in the castle and then for the young man to stay in his (the prince's) closet. When the prince returned, he gave Hawley 100 guineas and told him to stay quiet about it. That winter saw Hawley sustain another injury whilst out fox hunting; breaking a rib and the last joint at the bottom of his backbone. He was unable to leave his bed for two months.[44]

---

41   RA, HT, 7411-24-101, p.2.
42   RA, HT, 7411-24-101, p.2.
43   Dalton, *Army Lists,* Vol.III, p.374.
44   RA, HT, 7411-24-101, pp.2-3.

Once recovered, Hawley was promised by the prince another military position, and on 11 September 1704, Hawley, now aged 19, was made a cornet in Captain George Fielding's troop in the Duke of Northumberland's Regiment of Horse, later the Royal Regiment of Horse Guards or Blues.[45] This did not initially lead to service overseas, but attendance with the Queen and Prince at Newmarket, as he remained a royal page as well as a cornet. Whilst riding by the side of the royal coach, the prince asked him whether he was riding his best horse, presumably because he did not like what he saw. When they were in London again, the two met and the Prince gave Hawley 50 guineas 'and bid him buy a horse that was more fit for an officer and ordered it should be a black one'.[46] Again, Hawley was sworn to secrecy as to the source of his money. He was, however, seeking more than a new horse. What he wanted was another commission. He was pleased to learn that there was the possibility of a vacant lieutenancy in Ross' Dragoons, available for £500. The regiment was currently serving in Flanders under Marlborough, too. He realised that he could sell his cornetcy for more than £500 because it was in a prestigious regiment of horse and so commanded a higher price, despite being of a lower rank, than a line dragoon regiment. Yet his uncle opposed the move because Ross' Dragoons was on the Irish establishment (at this time there were three different military establishments in Britain – the English, the Scots and the Irish and though the first two merged in 1707 the third remained separate until union in 1800) and because Erle and Ross did not get on together.[47]

Although much of the campaigning in the war of the Spanish Succession took place in the Low Countries and Germany, at the end of 1703 a treaty had also been made between England, Portugal, and the Dutch Republic. The three countries were to take the war to Spain on the Emperor's behalf. There were to be 28,000 Portuguese troops and 12,000 to be provided by England and the Dutch, who were also to pay for half of the Portuguese troops. These forces arrived in Spain in 1704, and by 1705 Barcelona had fallen and Catalonia rose in their support. In the following year, success seemed in the allies' reach as Madrid was taken in May by an Anglo-Portuguese force under Henri de Massue de Rouvigny, first Earl of Galway (1648-1720), a Huguenot. Archduke Charles, the Austrian claimant to the Spanish throne was even crowned as Carlos III there. However, by the end of the year they had had to retreat to Valencia. In the following year, with Franco-Austrian hostilities in Italy coming to an end, additional French forces could be

---

45  RA, HT, 7411-24-101, p.3.
46  C.S. Knighton (ed.), *Calendar of State Papers, Domestic series, of the reign of Anne, 1704-1705* (London: Boydell Press, 1916), p.89.
47  RA, HT, 7411-24-101, p.3.

released to the Spanish theatre and the allies needed to send more men there to combat the rejuvenated French strength in Spain.[48]

In 1706 there was an expedition to Spain to be led by the Marquis de Guiscard to consist of 10 regiments of infantry and two squadrons of cavalry together with Dutch and Protestant French troops. Captain George Collings, a veteran of Steinkirk, of Essex's Dragoons (Hawley's father's old regiment) was unable to accompany his regiment because of his poverty and he wanted to sell his commission. He offered it to Hawley for £1,000 and Hawley agreed, but he needed the prince's permission to sell his cornetcy in the Guards. On asking him, the prince seemed to agree and told him that he would help to arrange it with the Queen.[49] Hawley then looked to find a buyer for the cornetcy and found an elderly lady who wanted it for her son, Edward Bird. They agreed on a price of £1,075, so Hawley would make a slight financial profit in the transactions. Next day, on telling the Prince, he found that the Queen would not allow anyone who was about to depart for foreign service to sell their commission, 'it had a very ill look' as it was 'a desperate piece of service they were going for'. In fact, Anne declared that she would have Collings thrown out of the service for desiring to leave when ordered abroad and so Hawley could have his commission gratis in that circumstance.[50]

This did not please Hawley and he pleaded that Collings' fate be averted. This was not purely disinterested charity in favour of a fellow officer, but because had Hawley taken the vacancy in the way that his royal mistress desired, then 'What a figure should he make to be the cause of Captain Collings' ruin who had been a particular friend of his father', and, wounded as he had been at Steinkirk, 'a very brave man'? Collings had a large family and was much in debt; this was the reason for wanting to sell up, not any form of reluctance to fight, as the Queen may have imagined. Hawley begged the Prince to intercede with the Queen to change her mind, to forgive Collings and appoint Hawley as a volunteer with the regiment to serve under Collings and Prince George agreed to do so. A volunteer was a man who could not obtain a commission by purchase or influence, but aspired to do so; he would march with the men but socialise with the officers in the hope that when a vacancy occurred on campaign caused by death he could then pick up a free commission if the colonel agreed.[51]

Prince George advised Hawley to wait on the Duke of Northumberland, when he was next at Windsor. As Hawley's colonel, he would allow the young man to sell the commission he held in the regiment. So, Hawley went down to Windsor

---

48   RA, HT, 7411-24-101, p.3.
49   RA, HT, 7411-24-101, p.3.
50   RA, HT, 7411-24-101, p.3.
51   RA, HT, 7411-24-101, p.3.

and met two other important men; Brigadier Robert Wroth (1660-1720), the regiment's lieutenant colonel, and Captain Fielding, Hawley's immediate superior. Northumberland asked Hawley why he wanted to leave and 'he very innocently answered he had a mind to go into the army again, meaning the service'. Fielding and Hawley went into the castle yard and the former took the latter by the sleeve and let Wroth walk ahead whilst they could talk confidentially. The two turned into Windsor Park 'for he had something to say to him'.[52]

Fielding told Hawley he had been reflecting on the regiment he wanted to leave and said 'it was not of the army, and that one of them must fall'. Wroth then came up to the two men and ended the conversation, he was clearly angry for he 'used him very roughly'. However, George now had the Queen's consent for Hawley to sell his commission to Mrs Bird and buy the captaincy in Essex's Dragoons at the prices earlier discussed. Hawley therefore made a £75 profit in the deals, though apparently Edward Bird was 'hanged some years after', for the murder of a waiter in a brothel in 1719.[53]

So, on 27 May 1706 he became captain of a troop in the Earl of Essex's Regiment of Dragoons (previously Berkeley's) with the pay of 15s 6d daily. This was the same regiment that his brother Edward was serving in, who was raised from cornet to lieutenant on 25 June 1706.[54] As the wording went, 'His Royal Highness does think fit that commissions be presented to Her Majesty for Henry Hawley Esq. to be captain of a troop in the Earl of Essex's Regiment of Dragoons in the room of Captain Collins'.[55] There was also royal favour; on 24 June Prince George appointed Hawley as a royal equerry, with the additional income that brought with it.[56] With his spare money he bought a tent, a bed, two good horses 'and very little baggage'. He also employed a valet.[57]

Hawley and his servant left to join the regiment at Chichester, Hawley leaving behind him £100 worth of debts. Arriving there he learnt that the regiment was now in camp on the Isle of Wight prior to embarkation. However, presumably after Hawley had been officially presented with his new rank, the men remained on the island for three weeks. Hawley had a letter from Erle, now a lieutenant general, to meet him at Portsmouth.[58] Erle explained on meeting that he had been given sudden orders to accompany the expedition with Lord Rivers and wanted Hawley,

---

52   RA, HT, 7411-24-101, p.3.
53   RA, HT, 7411-24-101, p.4.
54   C.S. Knighton (ed.), *Calendar of State Papers, Domestic series, of the reign of Anne, 1704-1705* (London: Boydell Press, 1916), pp.875, 1005.
55   TNA, WO4/513, p.67.
56   RA, HT, 7411-24-101, p.4.
57   RA, HT, 7411-24-101, p.4.
58   RA, HT, 7411-24-108, p.25.

as in 1697, as his aide, adding that the salary of ten shillings a day 'would not hurt him'. He was also offered, from the Prince, a present of 100 guineas, which Hawley accepted, using the money to pay off his debts and to buy another horse and a few other items with his remaining half guinea. They then set sail on HMS *Lennox* from Spithead.[59]

On board, along with Erle's retinue, was one Sir William Trumper who 'loved drinking, musick and hazard from morning till night'. As Mr Wensley, MP, who had been Erle's other aide, left, presumably for Parliamentary duties, Hawley was made 'the Drudge for all errands'. Yet the voyage turned out to be pointless. The weather in the Channel was foul, so the fleet was dispersed by storm. In any case, Guiscard's expedition was 'all cut to pieces'. After 11 weeks the fleet had returned and arrived at Torbay. The young man's hopes had been disappointed yet again.[60]

There was to be a new hope, however. There was a new expedition planned to reinforce the troops on the Continent. Galway was leading allied forces in Spain and was to be reinforced. It was a difficult journey from England, with many men dying aboard ship in the seven weeks they were at sea. Initially this mixed force of English, Dutch, and French was meant to go to France, but orders came to divert them to Spain to join Galway.[61] Again, bad weather disrupted the voyage. The ship they travelled in was the *Lennox* and it was scattered from the others in the Bay of Biscay. It nearly foundered and all the officers on board gave her up for lost. The storm led to the admiral putting what ships he had with him into Lisbon harbour for repairs and provisions for the horses. Hawley had at least profited by the journey; beginning it with half a guinea but 'had the good luck to be a winner of Sir William Trumper's hazard table and landed at Lisbon with a hundred moidores'.[62]

Once in Lisbon, Hawley used his new found gains to buy new equipment and so began the campaign on land with 'as good an Equipage as anybody'. He had to remain in the city for some time because his two horses had been in another ship and apparently that had been forced to Ireland by a storm. Meanwhile he was put in charge of the disembarkation that went on until late at night as stores were taken from the Tagus onto land. He had the misfortune to eat fruit in Lisbon and this gave him the 'bloody flux', which he endured whilst travelling by ship from Lisbon to Alicante. He recovered whilst at sea, but was in danger again when a Dutch naval vessel crashed into the *Lennox*, which destroyed part of the galley

---

59   RA, HT, 7411-24-101, p.4.
60   RA, HT, 7411-24-101, p.4.
61   RA, HT, 7411-24-101, p.4.
62   RA, HT, 7411-24-101, p.4.

where Hawley was, but 'he had just time to throw himself back into the cabin'. They finally arrived at Alicante at the end of January 1707, NS.[63]

Hawley evidently viewed this expedition, his first real taste of action, as being important. So important was it to him that he kept a journal of the time he was in Spain, focussing on the month of April which was the lead up to his first major battle. It is a day-to-day account of what happened, focussing on the battle. He only did the like for another occasion; that of the expedition to Spain in 1719. In both he concentrates on a top-level picture of what happened, rather than a worm's eye view, and does not refer to his own part in proceedings overly much, but does give occasional opinions as well as providing a framework of events and dates.

Erle took his men into Oriel and Guastalla, stopping at the latter for a week, before journeying to Valencia to meet up with Galway. It was on 5 April that the force, about 1,000 strong and including dragoons as well as infantry, arrived at the valley of Pollope. Next day they were in Consintina and halted for a day on the 7th. Hawley was sent ahead to Galway's camp at Fontalaquerra and on the 8th he visited the forces at Alicante. Erle's main body was at the valley of Fontineras on the 9th and next day they met with Galway's army at Carbiras.[64] On 11 April the combined force marched in three columns, with the artillery and the baggage on the right, and camped that night at Goidette. Galway's plan for battle, which Hawley evidently was aware of, was that the British forces would be on the left, with the Dutch in the centre and the Portuguese on the right. Galway would not alter this tactical disposition, even though he knew that the army would not be joined by any Spanish. Yet he believed his plan would keep the Portuguese in the ranks 'in good humour', but Hawley disapproved, stating 'and for this he deserved to be hanged'. Others were unhappy, too, 'This caused great discorde, and difference amongst the General officers of the English and a general dislike to everything my Lord Galway did'. Galway was resolved to attack the enemy wherever he found them, however.[65]

The army then marched in two columns on 12 April to Yecla. They found that the Duke of Berwick, James Fitzjames (1670-1734), an illegitimate son of James II and a young marshal of France, had recently left there with a small force of four battalions of infantry and 11 regiments of cavalry, who were clearly an advance guard and incapable of resisting attack by the main allied army. His abandoned camp, however, offered many spoils for the allies. Attempting to catch up with Berwick, the allies marched on the following night at 8:00 p.m. to Montalegre, but

---

63 RA, HT, 7411-24-109, p.2. NS signifies New Style, that is to say the Gregorian Calendar then in use on the Continent but not adopted in the British Isles until 1752.
64 RA, HT, 7411-24-101, p.5
65 RA, HT, 7411-24-109, p.2.

Berwick had left an hour previously, but once again had been forced to relinquish stores in the abandoned town to the allies.[64]

On the 15 April the allies marched back to the deserted camp at Yecla and on the 17th were at Villena. Here there was a town with a castle, the latter 'very strong by nature'. It was garrisoned by 150 French troops with six cannon. One Monsieur Grosseteste was in command and naturally he was summoned to surrender. On his refusal, the allies opened batteries, which on the night of the following day, they commenced firing with their six 12-pounders. The bombardment continued for the next few days, when a French deserter informed them that Berwick and a sizeable French army of 55 battalions of infantry and 101 squadrons of cavalry was on its way and would be there in two or three days' time.[66]

By 23 April the Portuguese guns were obliged to cease firing because their ammunition had run out, but more was on its way from Alicante. Galway, however, was more concerned with Berwick's army and hoped he could find a stronger camp. He heard that Berwick was at Almansa and held a council of war, resolving to attack Berwick before the French could attack them. On 24 April the army was arranged into three columns and the camp was on the left of Goidette, marching at night towards the enemy.[67]

At daybreak on 25 April, Hawley was with the brigade majors. He was instructed to stay and count the number of men in the allied army who were about to go into battle. He estimated that there was a maximum of 13,400. Between 10:00 and 11:00 that morning the French camp was sighted. Galway ordered his army to form into battle lines as soon as possible. Yet the infantry were tired, having marched over rocky and rough ground. Hawley was sent forward by his uncle to find Galway, who was presumably to the fore of his main body of troops, and to give him an account of how matters stood.[68] Hawley rode a league forward and found Galway on a hill overlooking the French camp, which was over half a league away. He told the commander about the troops' condition, 'very much fatigued'. Yet Galway did not seem to pay heed to this remark, but said, 'We must make what haste we could to attack them'. Hawley was unable to distinguish the French infantry from the French cavalry, but noted that they were present in great numbers. Berwick was putting his French and Irish troops on the right, to face the British and Dutch, and had the Spanish on his left, to face the Portuguese forces. Both sides were marching towards each other, and when the British were on top of the hill where Galway was,

---

66   RA, HT, 7411-24-109, p.2.
67   RA, HT, 7411-24-109, p.2.
68   RA, HT, 7411-24-109, p.2.

'The men were all quite blown', noted Hawley.[69] It was hardly a hopeful way to start a battle.

The allied army marched onto the plain, whilst the French were standing outside Alamansa. The allied cavalry was conventionally on the wings of the army, but was thereby forced to be positioned in broken ground, hardly suitable for offensive action. On the right was the Marques Das Minas with the Portuguese cavalry and 22 battalions of infantry. Erle was in charge of the five Dutch and 13 British battalions on the left, but the British and Dutch horse and dragoons on the far left were outflanked by Berwick's army. On the left the troops were all in one line, two ranks deep, presumably in order to extend the line as much as possible to minimise the extent of the outflanking. To strengthen that wing were placed three veteran British battalions and two Portuguese squadrons taken from the right, these were commanded by Colonel James O'Hara, Lord Tyrawley (1682-1774). Galway was unhappy with these dispositions and told Erle so, 'our disposition seems to me to be very wrong, our Foot being all in the plain, and our Horse upon the Hills'. To which Erle replied, 'you should have thought of that before, or not to have come here at all'. Galway had no reply to that, so rode off, and Erle thought 'he looked upon us to be beat before we began'.[70] The French had a considerable advantage in numbers.

In his memoir, Hawley elaborates a little on his own role in the preliminaries of the battle, referring to himself, as 18th century writers invariably did, in the third person, 'The captain having been employed very often in carrying orders and having tired out two horses'. There was a volunteer with the army, one Sir Charles Hotham MP (1663-1723), and at one point he offered to take a message but Hawley 'always went and did not mind him, and till the last time before the fire began to grow a little tired and peevish and said "Where would you go? Nobody will mind what you say"' for Hotham had never previously been given orders as an aide.[71] Unsurprisingly, Hotham was angered by such a remark and 'met him with a pistol and told him they must have a battle, for what he had said to him'. Given that there would soon be more than enough fighting against the French, an adjutant of the Guards stopped them and told Erle of the incident. The latter called them over and 'scolded the knight', before Hotham left the battlefield as hostilities were about to commence.[72]

The left wing of the allied army was first to fight and was initially pushed back, but rallied and drove off the enemy, who then brought up their artillery. The

---

69    RA, HT, 7411-24-109, p.2.
70    RA, HT, 7411-24-109, p.2.
71    RA, HT, 7411-24-109, p.2.
72    RA, HT, 7411-24-101, p.6.

British cavalry on the left charged twice, with Erle at their head on at least one occasion. A barrel of gunpowder exploded in the French lines, which was no accident but the signal for a general French advance. Despite the fact that the French artillery 'began to play very warm' and two battalions of the British left giving way, the fortunes of battle changed. The British battalions in the second line advanced and rallied those before them. The French began to retreat 'their whole Body of Foot that were before the British and Dutch all gave way, and were driven as far as the Town'. Yet the Portuguese troops in the right did not engage the enemy but 'stood still and threw down their arms and called for quarter'. Only one squadron of the Portuguese Horse charged – that of Das Minas' Troop of Guards – the others fled and rode to the allied camp, killing the servants there and plundering the baggage.[73]

Although the British infantry had been victorious, the rout of the Portuguese meant that Berwick had to transfer fresh troops from his left, which 'soon broke all the English and Dutch infantry (who believed for some time that they had got the Day)'. Erle clearly had Hawley with him, so presumably the young man had taken part in the British cavalry charge, and at this point had him send a message to Count Dohna on the right to tell him of the British retreat and so entreated him to retreat likewise as well as he could.[74] Hawley reached Dohna, and stayed some time with him, because it was a lengthy business to call the cavalry to retreat. Retreating from an enemy in battle is dangerous and Hawley later related how three of Berwick's orderlies chased him. They fired and shot his horse through the neck 'but he being a better horse than theirs and fresh he got off'. Hawley then attached himself to the remnant of Portmore's Regiment, which came under attack and was taking increasing casualties, Hawley escaped again and found his uncle with two Dutch squadrons of Drimborn's Horse. Near to them were three battalions of French infantry. Hawley wanted the cavalry to charge, but they refused, wheeled around and fled. Erle then ordered Hawley to tell Colonel Jasper Clayton, who was in charge of Hill's Regiment of Foot, to hold his ground, keeping a pond to their fore, telling them that he would use his remaining cavalry, now reduced to two squadrons of Harvey's Horse, to charge the flank of the French battalions who were advancing towards their position.[75]

Hawley gave Clayton his orders, but the advancing French fired, hitting Clayton and many of his officers. As he was about to return to Erle, he found the battalion's senior surviving officer, Major Francis Collingwood, who was on the left of the battalion. He told him of Clayton's death and so relayed the orders to

---

73   RA, HT, 7411-24-101, p.6.
74   RA, HT, 7411-24-109-2.
75   RA, HT, 7411-24-101, p.6.

him. However, the French fire was heavy and both Collingwood and his drummer were shot dead. Meanwhile, Erle's counter attack was defeated by the fire of an Irish battalion and the charge of two French squadrons on their flank. Yet despite the infantry, made up of deserters from Galway's army, calling on Harvey's cavalrymen by name 'asking them if they were made and that they would gave them good quarter', the cavalry still rode over three or four of their platoons before the French cavalry demolished them. Hawley later wrote 'every one gott off as well as he could' and he did not know of Galway's fate until nightfall. Several days later Major General John Shrimpton and 3-4000 men who had retired to a mountain pass surrendered on terms.[76]

Hawley's first experience of a set-piece battle had been a sobering experience, for it was his lot to have been on the defeated side though he had had but a peripheral part in it. It had been a dismal performance. Hawley was at Xativa for five days after the battle. It was at this point that he ceased his campaign journal, yet included further material in his autobiography. He referred to the remainder of the campaign as 'a continual retreat'. He was reunited with Erle, and implored his uncle to let him stand in line in action 'to learn his duty as a captain'.[77]

Hawley's next taste of action came in the form of a skirmish. He was on picket duty one night, posted near a sheepfold, when he was told that the French had captured a cornet's guard, so, at midnight, Hawley was ordered out with 60 horse and dragoons to march to where the cornet's guard had been and take possession of it from the enemy. If the latter were gone, then he was to send word back and to pursue at day break, towards Lerida, and take prisoners to obtain intelligence of the enemy.[78] They took a guide with them as 'it was so dark he [Hawley] could not see his horse's ears'. A sergeant and a dozen men were sent ahead to locate the enemy, which they did. Hawley asked Lieutenant William Wood of Harvey's Horse, the second-in-command, what was to be done on meeting the enemy, 'if we don't charge, they will charge us for they have not answered the sergeant's challenge'. Hawley decided to charge and the enemy turned out to be 100 Portuguese horse who were plundering corn without permission. Nine were killed, other wounded and the remainder fled. Hawley had three men wounded, whom he sent back to the main camp.[79]

Hawley marched on and reached Lerida, but found that the castle's British garrison under Major General Charles Wills (1666-1741) had surrendered. The French camp was only three miles away, by the river. Galloping ahead to a hill

76  RA, HT, 7411-24-109-2; 101-1, p.7.
77  RA, HT, 7411-24-101, p.7.
78  RA, HT, 7411-24-101, p.7.
79  RA, HT, 7411-24-101, p.7.

overlooking the camp, whilst being careful not to show himself, Hawley saw 10 squadrons of cavalry on the move, and another 40 below. Returning quickly to his men, he sent the best-mounted troopers back to the allied camp to give notice of the cavalry threat to them.[80]

His task now was to delay the enemy, with but a fraction of their strength. He marched his men to a ridge, lined them up two-deep but only allowed their heads to be seen by the enemy. He also had two standards to be made from muskets and handkerchiefs to give the impression that there was at least a whole regiment there, not just two squadrons. The 10 French squadrons stood and waited for a quarter of an hour before sending two squadrons to within a quarter of a mile of Hawley's position. Hawley sent one man back to camp and retired his squadrons from the ridge and crossed a plain.[81] When 30 French cavalrymen crossed the ridge and deployed on the plain, Hawley had his men about face and told Wood to take half the men and attack them, which they did, beating the French back and taking two men and a horse captive. The prisoners told them that the castle had fallen and their army was on the march. Hawley had his men retreat at a trot. Returning to the guard post at their camp he learnt that the main force had marched two hours ago. Eventually re-joining them he learnt that it was thought that he and his men had been lost. Galway was impressed, and as Hawley was senior captain in his regiment he was made a brevet major on 1 November 1707.[82]

Later in the Peninsular campaign, Hawley was shot in the leg on a scouting expedition. A piece of his bone was broken off and he had to convalesce in Barcelona for a month. By the year's end, Erle returned to England on HMS *Falcon*, with Hawley in tow. In the Gulf of Lyons the ship was chased by six French men of war, and despite the *Falcon*'s captain hauling up French colours, the chase continued until they were off Toulon on the following day.[83] The ship's captain, Delavall, was determined to fight 'as long as he could swim' and that Erle 'must prepare the share the same Fate with him'. There were six other officers along with Erle and Hawley and they and their servants, 26 men in all, were given guns and posted on the poop 'with orders to fire upon the Frenchman's deck as soon as the *Falcon* began with her cannon'. They fired together and the Frenchmen ran from their guns. Subsequent French fire did little damage and they veered off, which none on board the *Falcon* could understand.[84]

That night, Hawley, lying in a hammock in the gun room, 'no very sweet place', and could not sleep, so walked the deck with the ship's lieutenant in order to

---

80  RA, HT, 7411-24-101, pp.7-8.
81  RA, HT, 7411-24-101, pp.7-8.
82  RA, HT, 7411-24-101, pp.7-8.
83  RA, HT, 7411-24-101, pp.7-8.
84  RA, HT, 7411-24-101, pp.7-8.

exhaust himself so he would sleep. At about midnight he saw 'a very black cloudy weather gathering a head' but took no notice. Fifteen minutes later he asked the lieutenant 'a good humoured young fellow' what was that that he had seen. The lieutenant made no answer, but dashed to the ship's head and sounded the alarm. Cries of 'all hands upon deck the ship is lost'. Yet half an hour later all was well. Delavall explained to Hawley that what he had seen was the great bluff head west of Toulon bay which had their course been maintained, would have sunk the ship; he had believed that they were 60 leagues from it. Hawley had saved the ship and all their lives.[85]

Two days later they were at Genoa. Hawley and Erle travelled via Turin, Milan, the Tyrol and so on to Holland, returning to England by the end of January 1708. Once in London, Hawley found that there had been changes, and not for the better, among the officers of his regiment, at least according to him. Richard Lucas was now lieutenant colonel, 'who knew nothing at all about the service'. John Knox was the major, 'an old gouty man of no use'. At the end of February, Hawley was ordered to go to Derbyshire recruiting and by the end of May the regiment had a full complement of men and horses again.[86] He then returned to London and learnt that Erle was put in command of a major expedition of 9,000 infantry (11 battalions from England and five from Ireland) and Essex's Dragoons against France. His regiment was to sail from Portsmouth but Hawley was to be his uncle's aide yet again. They sailed at the end of June with ships commanded by Admiral Sir George Byng (1663-1733) as escorts.[87]

Hawley commented that 'This expedition was to harass the coast of France, to make them draw some troops down that way to make a diversion'. The fleet sailed to Etaples and anchored in sight of Montreuil. The grenadiers were landed there first, but the fleet were advised to land at Bullon Bay, so did so and on the next day the generals, with their aides and the brigade majors met on the *Greyhound*. The council of war had to decide what to do because they thought they could see 'a regular body of troops both Horse and Foot & Cannon drawn up along the shore', which would prevent any landing.[88] During the hour and a half discussion, mortars from a French fort fired at the fleet, but without hitting anything. Erle called for Hawley and ordered him to take the pinnace and be rowed as near to the shore without being shot 'to bring him the best account he could of the Troops there'. He did so and found that there were about 9,000 infantry and 3,000 cavalry. There was also artillery there. They did not fire at him at first, but on passing them

---

85 RA, HT, 7411-24-201, pp.7-8.
86 RA, HT, 7411-24-101, pp.7-8.
87 RA, HT, 7411-24-101, pp.7-8.
88 RA, HT, 7411-24-101, pp.7-8.

all, a mounted officer rode out into the water towards them. He rode out further and fired at him, and other officers joined him and did likewise. Hawley turned the boat around and told Erle what he had seen, and then it was thought best to not land. The grenadiers were recalled and a few days later the fleet arrived back at Portsmouth.[89]

Essex's Dragoons were disembarked at Portsmouth, but Hawley stayed on board with Erle and they sailed with the infantry to Ostend. The *Greyhound*, on which they still travelled, struck rocks and 'the thought she had beat her bottom in, but she went on though much damaged'. They then went to Fort Albert and encamped what men there were, less those who were ill at Ostend, between there and Leffinge. Hawley took up a post there. An advanced guard of 30 French soldiers camped nearby. Erle decided to give Hawley a command; he was to take charge of 80 men, assemble them at night and then attack the French at daybreak, 'Which he accordingly did, and killed twelve of them'.[90]

There then came news that the French were marching 10,000 men to force through Leffinge. Hawley was sent by Erle to give a message to Major General William Seymour who was there, that if the fort was in good order, he was to leave a colonel and 1,000 men to defend it. Hawley had to navigate with his guide along the flooded areas as the French had opened the sluice at Nieuport which had led to a great rise in the waters. The guide missed his way and Hawley's horse fell into the dike on one side of the causeway & he was very near being drowned'. The message delivered, Hawley returned with 200 dragoons from Lille who would now assist Erle.[91]

The fort was now under siege by the French who had dug trenches and mounted batteries against it. Erle sent Hawley with 300 infantry to reinforce it at night time and then to return at night to let him know what was happening there. Major Solomon Rapin, of Mohun's Foot, at the fort, led a sally against the French and captured two officers. Hawley escorted these two to Erle. Meanwhile Leffinge was surrendered by Colonel Thomas Caulfield, 'shamefully' without firing a shot. However, Lille fell to the allies under Marlborough's leadership, and Ghent was retaken. Once these had happened, in October and November 1708, Hawley and Erle returned to England, though the news there for the former was mixed. His patron, Prince George, had died on 28 October, but his post of equerry worth £300 annually, and possession of a house, was continued by the Queen.[92]

89   RA, HT, 7411-24-101, p.10.
90   RA, HT, 7411-24-101, p.10.
91   RA, HT, 7411-24-101, p.10.
92   RA, HT, 7411-24-101, p.11.

This marked the end of the war as far as Hawley was concerned, though Britain's role continued until 1711 and included a major battle at Malplaquet on 31 August 1709; a costly victory for the Dutch and German troops under Marlborough's command. Hawley had survived a major battle and several skirmishes, whilst acting as Erle's aide, and was still a captain. However, his youngest brother Charles was less fortunate, having been fatally shot in the upper body at the siege of Aire in the autumn of 1710.

2

# Peacetime Soldiering, 1709-1740

Whilst Hawley was abroad, his regiment had been transferred to Scotland where it remained for the duration of the war, possibly due to the fears caused by the attempted French invasion of 1708. Once Hawley re-joined it, he found that the major, Knox, wanted to sell his commission. Yet Hawley lacked the money to be able to buy it. Fortunately, Erle, now in Ireland, as lieutenant governor of Kinsale, was willing to come to the rescue of his relative and would give him the money needed. Apparently, he intended to leave Hawley £1,000 in his will and was able to give this sum to him now rather than later. As Hawley was the captain in the regiment with one of the longest number of years' service, it was natural in the ordinary course of military practice for him to want to acquire the commission of major.[1] However, when Hawley applied to Lord Essex, who as colonel had the power over commissions in his regiment, he was turned down. This was because Essex had promised it to Captain Collings, who had been a captain in the regiment since 1694 whilst Hawley's captaincy only dated from 1706. Hawley, perhaps unreasonably, 'thought this was very hard'. He applied to the Queen, as ultimate head of the armed forces, and with the final decision on the bestowal of army commissions. On receiving his petition, the Queen 'ordered that the Major Knox should have leave to sell to no other but him'. Essex was clearly adamant to block Hawley and so persuaded Knox not to sell at all.[2]

The matter reached deadlock. In the spring of 1709 Hawley went with the regiment's lieutenant colonel, Richard Lucas, to Scotland and found the situation disagreeable, as 'the greatest part of the Officers were sett against him'. Unlike many officers at the time, he took the business of soldiering as being deadly serious, but, as a professional surrounded by amateurs, he was likely to ruffle feathers.

---

1    RA, HT, 7411-24-101, p.11.
2    RA, HT, 7411-24-101, p.11.

His way was not one to court popularity. Lucas, 'who lived at Edinburgh minded nothing but drinking' was uninterested. The regiment was merely a collection of six independent troops. Hawley lived in his quarters 'having nothing more to do at Court'. Yet he did pay attention to his troop 'and got his Troop in order as soon as he could, tho' he found it the best of the six, all the rest did as they pleased' as their master never cared to inspect them.[3]

At the summer's end, the regiment was to be inspected by Lieutenant General David Melville, third Earl of Leven (1660-1728) the commander in chief of the troops in Scotland, who, despite being a veteran of the first Jacobite campaign of 1689, Hawley thought 'was but one degree above a fool'. Captain John Cage, who had served in the regiment as captain since 25 October 1707 and as a lieutenant since 1694, brought his troop to the rendezvous at Linlithgow, a few miles to the west of Edinburgh. As it, in comparison with the two other troops of the regiment already there, was 'in miserable order', he went to Edinburgh and asked Leven that the troop be excused from review, without Lucas' (or Hawley's) knowledge. At the same time, Hawley ordered the three troops to be ready to march. Next day Cage sent his sergeant to Hawley to inform him that his troop was not to be reviewed and therefore did not need to march.[4] Hawley had his brother, Edward Hawley, inform Cage that he was under arrest and that the lieutenant of Cage's troop attend Hawley. The latter did so and Hawley 'asked him if he intended to mutiny too' and he said no, he was ready to obey orders. So, the three troops marched to be reviewed and Hawley told Lucas what had happened, as he had come to see his three troops. Hawley gave it as his opinion that Cage had principally insulted him, Lucas, and Lucas replied that Hawley had acted correctly. After the review, the men were sent back to Linlithgow and Cage would be court martialled, though he was not arrested prior to that hearing.[5]

Hawley remained at Edinburgh that night in case Cage would send him a message. As he did not Hawley wrote to him, to let him know what Lucas had said, and it was delivered by Hawley's servant. That night, whilst abed, Hawley received a letter written by Cage, where he said he 'thought there was a shorter way than a Court Martial if he would meet him the next morning before the Troops marched to their Quarters'. What he was implying was a duel, which was illegal but not uncommon among officers and gentlemen. Prior to gaining his commission, Cage 'had been originally a Fencing master, and from thence had ever been over troublesome'.[6]

3   RA, HT, 7411-24-101, p.11.
4   RA, HT, 7411-24-101, p.11.
5   RA, HT, 7411-24-101, pp.11-12.
6   RA, HT, 7411-24-101, p.12.

The two officers met that morning with their seconds and drew swords. According to Hawley's later account:

> the Captn. The first thrust run the Major [Hawley] who had his coat open through the side of the Coat, but his sword was so long he could not disengage it. The Major at the same time run into him, and wounded him, his sword breaking half off – They then parted again, and the Captn made two thrusts at him tho' he had no sword – He did not know then that he had wounded the Captn: Then came two officers and seized them both. The Captn said he was killed & was sorry for what he had done, he died two days later'.[7]

Hawley stayed in the vicinity until noon, when he and his cornet went after his troop to Glasgow. On the next day, the Earl of Islay, brother to the powerful Duke of Argyle, head of Clan Campbell, told him of the severity of the Scottish laws and that he had committed a capital offence. He recommended going to England to sort out his problems. Hawley went next day to Berwick and remained there for two months. In that time the Queen made enquiries to Robert Walpole (1676-1745), secretary at war, to find out the truth of the matter. When she got to the bottom of it she told Erle that she was pleased that Hawley was in the right 'because she knew the Prince had always a kindness for him and she knew the laws of Scotland were very severe; therefore as the shortest way she ordered a Pardon as she believed he was not very rich an she had ordered the fees to be paid'.[8]

By now it was early 1710 and on 10 January the regiment's colonel was dead. Sir Richard Temple succeeded on 24 April 1710. Once pardoned, Hawley rode south and was able to visit the Queen to thank her in person. She was glad to see him, 'she made him some compliments, then wept and said he put her in mind of the Prince'. About to retire, the Queen recovered and bid him stay and asked for an account of the matter. She listened and then said that she hoped he would have no such misfortunes and that he would 'behave himselfe well and that he would always find her his friend'.[9]

Hawley bought his major's commission on 27 January 1711, with a daily pay of £1 6d. When Lucas bought himself the colonelcy of an Irish regiment, he offered Hawley the lieutenant colonelcy of the dragoon regiment, but, lacking the necessary funds, Hawley had to turn it down. There was a possibility that another might buy it instead, but when Anne was asked to confirm the appointment, she asked about

---

7     RA, HT, 7411-24-101, p.12.
8     RA, HT, 7411-24-101, p.12.
9     RA, HT, 7411-24-101, p.12.

whether Hawley was still the major in that regiment and when being told he was, she learnt he had not the money for it, so she consulted the secretary at war, now George Granville, about it.[10] Anne then conferred with Major General John Hill (died 1735), one of Hawley's best friends, a fact she was aware of, as well as being a protegee of Anne's because he was brother to the Queen's favourite Lady Abigail Masham (c.1674-1734). Hill had been a groom to the Duke of Gloucester and page to Prince George; he and Hawley had served together in the war in Spain and both fought at Alamansa, and Anne had wanted to give him the vacant colonelcy of Essex's Dragoons but was thwarted by Marlborough. Citing her esteem for any who had had her late husband's favour, she gave Hill a bank bill for £1,000 to give to Hawley. Wasting no time, he purchased the commission of lieutenant colonel on 4 April 1711, and now earned £1 4s 6d a day. His brother, Edward, became a captain in the regiment on 13 May 1712.[11]

This was not all that Anne bestowed on Hawley. She confirmed his possession of property in London, a house, stables and coach house on Hedge Lane (now the lower part of Whitcomb Street, Soho, to the west of St. Martin's in the Fields where he had been baptised; the house is long gone) adjacent to a mews owned by her. However, it was in such a ruinous condition that Hawley had to spend £300, which he could probably little afford, to make the place habitable.[12]

Hawley then returned to Scotland; he was never again to see the woman who had helped him so much. Charles Lanoe was now the regiment's major, Knox having left. Yet it was for Hawley to administer the unit and this was the first time that he had had to put his imprint on a whole regiment. It was quartered in the environs of Glasgow and Hawley thought his 'own troop was worthe any three of the others for goodness and he was resolved to shew the captains he knew how to command'. Whilst he had spent money to improve his troop, they had not and had even laughed at him for doing so whilst they made a profit at the expense of military efficiency. He began by laying off half of the men and did not replace them until the following spring. One of the 'mutinous Captains' (John Liard or Lyard) died on 10 March 1712 and so he filled the vacancy with 'a young Lord [Edward Lord Hinchingbrooke, created captain on 13 May 1712] who never came near it for a long time'. He also went to England to buy nearly 100 horses.[13]

In Lanoe, Hawley had an ally in his quest to improve the regiment, but 'there was still one very mutinous Captain left, a very illiterate brutall fellow, who could not digest receiving no more than his pay'. He had not filled vacancies but instead

---

10   RA, HT, 7411-24-101, p.12.
11   RA, HT, 7411-24-101, p.12, *Oxford Dictionary of National Biography* online, https://doi-org/10.1093/ref.odnb/3280, Dalton, *Army Lists,* Vol.VI, p.37.
12   BL, Add. Mss. 61603, f.97r.
13   RA, HT, 7411-24-101, p.12.

pocketed the money that should have been paid and 'had long looked on his troops as his estate' and was always grumbling.[14]

Then there came an incident which shows Hawley dealing with a very difficult officer. It was in the June of 1712 when Hawley and the adjutant, James Walsh (appointed 5 December 1711, left 11 July 1712), went to Carlisle to see the new horses he had put to grass near there. On the first night they were staying at an ale house on Douglas Mill. A sergeant interrupted them to tell them that Captain John Farrar of his regiment had arrived and wished to see Hawley. The latter exclaimed, 'Why don't he come in?' and the sergeant reported that the captain seemed unwell. The adjutant went to see him and was away for a long time.[15] On his return, he locked the door on the inside and told Hawley that he had had Farrar arrested. This was because 'the Captain he believed was mad…he told him he was there to put the Coll. to deathe'. Armed servants were posted at Farrar's door and on the next day, Lanoe arrived from Glasgow. By now Farrar 'had growne coole…and wanted to ask pardon'. Hawley wanted to see the man cashiered. Lanoe discovered that when Farrar heard that Hawley was to go to Carlisle, that 'he came the same morning to wait for him on the road, designing to attaque him, and how he missed him he could not tell'. Farrar was taken by Lanoe back to Glasgow the next morning. When Hawley returned there too, Lanoe interceded on Farrar's behalf, 'at last the Coll. agreed to forgive him upon condition he would fall on his knees at the door before all the officers and repeat all he had told the Major and owne his crime & beg to be forgiven, all which he did'.[16] Farrar served in the army for at least another decade and fought bravely at Sheriffmuir in 1715. Farrar could have been cashiered for so grave an offence.

Despite Marlborough's victories, the country was becoming increasingly war weary with no end to the wear in sight and a change of government in 1710 led to Britain's withdrawal from the conflict. Peace was signed at Utrecht in 1713. Part of Spain's empire had been assigned to the Habsburg Empire, with Gibraltar and Minorca to Britain; France recognised the British succession and Louis XIV's grandson gained the Spanish throne. The balance of power had been preserved and French ambitions checked. Hawley's regiment was stationed in Ireland following the end of Britain's involvement in the war of Spanish Succession, arriving there in the summer of 1713. His new colonel, replacing Temple, on 12 October 1713, was Major General William Evans (died 1740). Evans had been soldiering since 1690 when he obtained a commission in the Foot Guards and served in both the Nine Years War and that of the Spanish Succession, becoming a brigadier in 1707 and

---

14  RA, HT, 7411-24-101, p.13.
15  RA, HT, 7411-24-101, p.13.
16  RA, HT, 7411-24-101, p.13.

major general in 1740.[17] Yet Hawley had to wait before going to Ireland until he had recovered from a fall, perhaps whilst out hunting, which broke a collar bone and two ribs.[18]

Little is known of the regiment's duties in Ireland, but presumably they included police operations; keeping the peace, deterring and suppressing rioters, smugglers and other criminal groups that were beyond the capabilities of the militia and constables. They probably also took part in ceremonial duties in celebrating the King's birthday and providing guards for civic dignitaries and for castle garrison duties. Regiments were usually scattered about the country and so rarely had an opportunity in taking part in drill and exercises as a regiment.

However, although the international scene was quiet enough in western Europe, it was not so in Britain. In 1714 George, Elector of Hanover, was crowned King, following Anne's death. The title to the throne was contested by James Francis Stuart (1688-1766), the late Queen's half-brother and only legitimate son of James II. Many in Britain thought he was the rightful King, especially Tories and Catholics in England and, in Scotland, Episcopalians and those opposed to the Union of the kingdoms in 1707. These people were known as Jacobites and in 1715 there were major military attempts in Scotland and England to assert James' rights, though Catholic Ireland remained quiet.

The major military thrust was in Scotland. On 6 September, John Erskine, sixth Earl of Mar (1675-1732), once Secretary of State for Scotland and aggrieved that he had lost the power and wealth that went with being a senior politician, raised forces in Scotland to fight for James. The number of British forces in Scotland at that time was limited to four battalions of infantry and a regiment of dragoons; little more than a thousand men. The Jacobites seized Perth on 14 September and began to amass further support. John Campbell, second Duke of Argyle (1680-1743), took command of the British troops gathered at Stirling and was slowly sent reinforcements.

As prior precautionary measures, the government had already decided to send troops to Scotland. On 30 July Hawley was told to make the arrangements to have Orrery's, Forfar's and Hill's Regiments sent there from Ireland. In the previous month he had been told to receive Colonel Hamilton into Ireland and to review any subsequent troops sent there.[19]

On 14 September, Argyle suggested to his political masters that Evans' Dragoons be sent to Scotland.[20] On 24 September, Viscount Townshend, one of the principal

---

17　Dalton, *Army of George I*, Vol.I, p.331.
18　RA, HT, 7411-24-101, p.13.
19　RA, HT, 7411-24-108, pp.23, 22.
20　TNA, SP54/8, f.68.

Secretaries of State, assured him that Evans' would be one of the units sent as reinforcements.[21] By 19 October, though, there was no sign of the regiment or the two infantry battalions promised from Ireland and Argyle was beginning to become anxious.[22]

Evans' Dragoons eventually arrived in Scotland on 25 October and was stationed at Glasgow. Argyle was impressed with them, writing that they were 'the very best without exception that ever I saw in my life and their cloathing and accoutrements in perfection'.[23] This reflected well on the regiment's officers and especially Hawley as lieutenant colonel, who was in day to day command. The regiment was just under 190 men strong; divided into six troops, each with a sergeant and a drummer, as well as up to three officers, and a total of 170 troopers and corporals.[24]

On 11 November, Argyle learnt that the Jacobite army was marching south west from Perth and on the next day marched his forces northwards to Dunblane. He viewed the Jacobite army on the morning of the following day and decided to advance his army in column so as not to be outflanked by the Jacobite army. Argyle was at the men's head, and the second regiment behind him was Evans', with the plan that the regiment would be the second of the dragoon regiments on the right flank once the army formed up against the Jacobites. Argyle's plan was to use his cavalry and infantry on his right flank to attack the Jacobite left and to destroy/rout it. The Jacobite army outnumbered his by over two to one, the worst odds ever faced by a British general in dealing with the Jacobites, though in Mar the Jacobites had a novice commander whilst Argyle was a seasoned soldier as were most of his men. The Jacobite troops put up stout resistance, however, as one of Argyle's officers later noted, 'the enemy kept up their fire longer than could have been expected, the fire was very hot upon Evans' regiment for a quarter of hour they had a deep stripe before them which they could not well pass which made them run about in some disorder'.[25] It was the terrain in front of Evans' men which was the problem, 'tho Evans' dragoons were in some little disorder, it was not throw occasion of the enemy, but through the deepness of the marsh ground, which was near to have bogged their horses'.[26]

Evans' Dragoons were able to wheel round, found better ground and then 'performed as could be desired'.[27] Initially this unit had reeled back from the

---

21 Leeds University Library, Special Collections, Townshend Manuscripts, f.7r-8v.
22 National Library of Scotland, Manuscripts, 7104, f.114.
23 TNA, SP54/10/39.
24 TNA, SP54/11/2b; 9/92.
25 National Records of Scotland, GD220/5/787a.
26 Anon., *Report on the manuscripts of the Duke of Roxburghe…14th Report, Appendix III* (London: Royal Commission on Historic Manuscripts, 1894) p.168.
27 Anon., *14th Report, Appendix III*, p.168.

weight of a Jacobite volley (and suffered the highest casualties suffered by any of Argyle's cavalry regiments that day – nearly a third) and had disordered the volunteer cavalry to their rear, but both soon rallied and entered the fray. One reason for Evans' men rallying was because 'Rothes' volunteers call out for Shame to them…[and] took a terrible vengeance'.[28] Sir Robert Anstruther later gave a graphic account of this part of the battle:

> At the time that Evans' Regiment came amongst us my horse got on and his hind part stuck in the marshy ground where we were formed which made him fall back upon me and I concluded that he had been killed dead but he immediately got off me, I kept the reins and got him mounted again with great difficulty for the balls were flying so thick that the horse did not stand long in one posture and I had the good fortune to escape with some bruises occasion'd chiefly by the fall and was so well as to continue on horseback all the pursuit.[29]

Apparently in the pursuit, Evans' Dragoons 'made them give little quarter'.[30] They also took seven of the Jacobites' standards.[31] Cavalry often turned a victory into a rout of their fleeing opponents if the latter was unsupported or was unable to make an orderly withdrawal. This was not the first time, nor was it to be the last, when the routers suffered serious casualties in flight, and it should not be it classified as a war crime by the standards of the day. The pursuit of the Jacobites took some time, but, by the afternoon, it was clear that not all had gone well for Argyle because when he rallied his cavalry and returned with the infantry battalions to the battlefield he learnt that the Jacobite right wing had defeated the troops on his left and so he faced the remnant of Mar's army with the troops he had with him. Again, he was outnumbered and Evans' Dragoons were placed to the left of his remaining infantry. The attack never came, for Mar was unsupported by a key subordinate, and by the day's end the Jacobite army began its march back to Perth. Argyle had thus succeeded in preventing Mar's army from marching south and thus had won a strategic victory in what was otherwise a tactical draw.

On the 14th the cost of the day's fighting was assessed. Evans' Dragoons had certainly been badly hit; of less than 200 men, 20 were dead and another 33 wounded. Thirteen horses had been killed and 44 injured. Over a quarter of the men had become casualties and these included several officers. One of these was

---

28   NRS, GD220/5/787a.
29   NRS, GD220/5/489/4.
30   NRS, GD220/5/787A.
31   TNA, SP54/10/48.

Hawley. According to Henry Fletcher, writing on 21 January 1716, Evans and Hawley 'were blamed for being mounted on horses of a quite different colour from those of their Regiments, which drew the shot upon them… Haly's [sic] horse had 4 ball in him, and was shot in the body, but is recovering'.[32]

It is not certain whether or not Hawley withdrew from the battle immediately due to his wounds, but he may have been rendered hors de combat for the remainder of the campaign, as one of his colleagues certainly was. Captain John Farrar later wrote 'that Unfortunate Day I had the Misfortune to receive a Musquett shott into my left thigh which broke and shattered all the bone to pieces I lay madam 24 weeks on my back end'.[33] Hawley was deemed important enough to be mentioned in the press, and though the wound was serious, a few days later it was reported 'there is hopes of his recovery'.[34]

This was Hawley's first role in commanding men on the field of battle. However, he did not see it as being particularly significant, perhaps because he was wounded early on and saw relatively little of the action. Hawley alloted a mere paragraph to it in his autobiography. The main point that he made was that he was shot in the same place as his ancestors had; his great grandfather had been shot likewise during the civil wars; his grandfather, killed similarly whilst fighting under Turenne, presumably in the 1660s, as well as his father and brother.[35] It had been fairly short and inglorious for him personally.

Sheriffmuir was also the first time that he had fought against the Jacobite Highland army. The lesson that he may have learnt from Sheriffmuir was that the Jacobite infantry could be defeated by cavalry even if the latter were outnumbered (several hundred had put to flight several thousand). However, he would not serve again in battle for almost three decades as Britain fought no major war until the 1740s. Hawley's regiment itself remained in service and in the following year, when Argyle, now reinforced by Dutch and Swiss troops as well as two more British dragoon regiments, advanced against Mar, Evans' Dragoons was part of that army. It was reduced in number, though, with little over 150 men, due to 20 being sick, wounded, or prisoners of war. As it happened there was no more fighting. Most of Mar's army had deserted and the Jacobites decided to retreat rather than fight; Mar left Scotland and by February the Jacobite army was no more. The regiment stayed in Scotland awhile, garrisoning Montrose and Brechin, prior to returning to Ireland.

---

32   Irene J. Murray (ed.), 'Letters of Andrew Fletcher in 1715-1716', SHS 4th series, Miscellany, X, (1965), p.154.
33   NRS, GD45/14/263.
34   *London Gazette*, 5383, 19 Nov. 1715.
35   RA, HT, 7411-24-101, p.13.

After the campaign was over, Hawley took ship to London whilst his regiment marched south in the spring. They met at Newbury where they undertook recruiting to make up the losses suffered at Sheriffmuir. At the end of the summer they were reviewed by the Prince of Wales, later George II, a veteran of the Battle of Oudernade (1708). He later accompanied them to York, where they were quartered for the winter of 1716-1717. Whilst at York, Hawley received a letter from Argyle, asking him why he did not come to London and offered him the colonelcy of Major General George Wade (1673-1748)'s regiment of horse.[36]

Hawley thanked him but declined the suggestions on the grounds of poverty; John Ducros, the regimental surgeon since 1692, having absconded 'with a great deal of money'. However, Argyle sent him a bank bill for £300, as authorised by the Prince, swearing Hawley to secrecy. In the spring of 1717 he went to London and stayed until summer. He then re-joined the regiment at Durham under Major General Charles Wills' command. There a letter from Erle awaited him, informing him that the King offered him an Irish infantry regiment that had been Wade's and that this offer had been opposed by Lieutenant General Lord William Cadogan – right hand man to the Duke of Marlborough and a prominent supporter of the Hanoverian Succession, who had jointly put an end to the Jacobite Rebellion of 1715 – but that the King had insisted.[37] On 19 March 1717 Hawley replaced Wade to become a regimental colonel of infantry – the regiment, now Hawley's, would eventually become the 33rd Foot.[38] However other letters sent to Hawley told him that it was Cadogan who obtained the regiment for him and that he should thank him. Visiting Wills at Newcastle, he asked who his benefactor had been. Wills believed it was the King. Hawley pressed him several times to ask who had spoken for him. It could not have been Cadogan because of Hawley's antagonism towards him because of his treatment of Erle.[39]

The troops had returned to Ireland by the end of 1717, but the Continent of Europe was about to be troubled once more. This time it was due to the ambitions of the Spanish Court. In 1713 they had lost their provinces in Italy to the Empire and to the House of Savoy. They had never agreed to these losses, which had been confirmed to the Empire by France. In the summer of 1717 the Spanish took Sardinia: the Empire, engaged in a war with the Turks and in any case lacking a navy to speak of, was unable to stop them militarily. Both France and Britain were opposed to this disturbance of the Utrecht settlement, and despite James Stanhope, Secretary of State for the Southern Department and Britain's de facto first

---

36  RA, HT, 7411-24-101, p.14.
37  RA, HT, 7411-24-101, p.14.
38  Dalton, *Army of George I*, Vol.I, p.179.
39  RA, HT, 7411-24-101, p.14.

minister, leading diplomatic missions to Paris and Madrid, hostilities developed. The Spanish fleet was destroyed by the Royal Navy at Cape Passaro and hostilities were officially declared in December 1718. This led to an attempted invasion of Britain by Spain, but most of the ships were blown off course and those few troops which did land were defeated, along with a number of Highland clansmen who had again risen for the Stuarts, at Glenshiel on 10 June 1719.

There had already been a French incursion into Spain led by Marshal Berwick, as well as combat in Sicily between newly released Imperial troops and the Spanish. The British government decided to increase the pressure on Spain by sending a force of its own to the Iberian Peninsula, as they had in the previous decade, but with a less ambitious remit. The decision had been made by July but was shrouded in secrecy as troops began to assemble that summer on the Isle of Wight. One of the regiments to take part in this was Hawley's.

At the time Hawley believed that it was an important campaign and wrote a daily account of the expedition, as he had for the previous Spanish campaign in 1707. However, in retrospective he dismissed it, writing in the perspective of 1752, 'the colonel was in the expedition with his regiment under Lord Cobham [1675-1749], who as Richard Temple was his former colonel, when nothing extraordinary happened'.[40] Yet much happened to Hawley from 1720-1752 and these events clearly overshadowed this Spanish campaign of 1719. At the time, as a less experienced and younger soldier, he clearly did see it as important enough to record it in some detail.

On 27 August the four battalions from Ireland, including Hawley's, arrived at the Isle of Wight for Spithead. Orders for embarkation began to be made on 2 September and by the next day all were on board. They sailed to Spithead on the 4th and by the 5th the whole flotilla were ready to sail. Yet there were many delays. Limited wind on 10 September was the first. It was then decided to transfer men to the fireship and bomb ships in order to ease crowding on the transport ships and another 200 grenadiers were put on board.[41] Yet it was some weeks before the fleet arrived off Spain, and Hawley meticulously recorded these weeks, with frequent remarks about the winds and other meteorological issues which held them up. Meanwhile the officers had to deal with court martials and provisioning whilst gales in the Channel prevented them sailing until the last week of September. They were still off Plymouth on the 23rd.[42]

Cape Prior, Galicia, was sighted on 25 September, and a French vessel sighted on the next day as the remainder of the fleet was awaited. The squadron of Vice

---

40 RA, HT, 7411-24-101, p.14.
41 RA, HT, 7411-24-111-1.
42 RA, HT, 7411-24-111-1.

Admiral James Mighells, and the transports, reached the coast of Galicia and there cruised for three days, waiting for Captain Johnson's ships to join them. There was no news of him, so, given it was dangerous to lie stationary with transport ships full of troops, they decided to act without him. The wind set fair for Vigo and so Cobham set sail for there.[43]

On 29 September OS, the convoy entered the harbour of Vigo. It was seven in the morning. The fireship in the fleet was despatched first, but the water there was found to be good and by eleven the whole fleet anchored. The only sign of opposition was that a gun from the castle of Vigo was fired throughout the day to warn the countryside of the invaders.[44] As was customary with siege warfare and other difficult tasks, the grenadiers were the first to land on shore, as planned. It was now four in the afternoon. This was three miles from Vigo itself. The only opposition was some long range shooting from some peasants in the mountains. They did the grenadiers no harm. Cobham had gone ashore with the grenadiers and the other troops followed as quickly as the landing boats could take them. By midnight all the infantry save three companies were landed, as had two guns. Both that night and the subsequent one, the troops had little sleep, resting on their arms in case of attack. The grenadiers were posted ahead, on the rising ground a mile from the castle. On that night there were some random musket shots from the Spanish peasants. Provisions for four days campaigning was unloaded over the next days. Advance parties were sent out above a mile from the bridgehead and posted on a number of routes.[45]

On the following morning, 30 September, the advanced guard of grenadiers moved forward and came across a settlement. They found cellars full of wine and meanwhile burnt all the houses nearby. Other soldiers arrived and 'by turns ran into the Guards, and gott drunk, several wounded and missing'.[45] Little else happened on the 30th, in order 'to let our men get sober'. At three in the afternoon, however, there was a march inland for one and a half miles. Tents arrived from the ships and Lord Hinchingbrooke, who had left Hawley's old regiment in 1717 to become a colonel of his own infantry regiment, was sent back in a French ship to Lisbon with the news of the force's disembarkation.[46]

The force marched towards Vigo on 1 October and made their camp with their left flank to the sea, near the village of Boas. Their right was extending towards the mountains. Advance parties were also sent forward towards Vigo. All this movement demonstrated to those in Vigo that preparations for an attack were

43   *London Gazette*, 20-24 October 1719.
44   RA, HT, 7411—24-111-1.
45   RA, HT, 7411-24-111-1.
46   *London Gazette*, 10-14 November 1719, p.1; RA, HT, 7411-24-111-1.

taking place.[47] The carriages and cannon in the town that could not be moved, about 60 large iron cannon were destroyed or spiked in order to deny them to the British. An outer fort, St. Sebastian, was also given up. It seemed that the town was to be abandoned to the magistrates and citizens (who despatched two envoys to Cobham that day), whilst the regular troops retired into the citadel. When Cobham summoned the town to surrender, the magistrates there did not hesitate to do so.[48]

The Spanish garrison in the citadel consisted of seven companies of the Regimiento de España and four companies of the Regimiento de Valencia, apparently almost 800 men in all, although Hawley stated that it was 907. They had 43 guns, of which 15 were brass, and two large mortars. They were also equipped with 2000 barrels of gunpowder and chests containing 8,000 muskets. These latter had been on board the invasion force which had sailed for Britain earlier in the year, as had some of the garrison.[49]

That evening Cobham sent Brigadier Philip Honywood (c.1679-1752) and 800 men to take up positions in the town which had by now been abandoned by the Spanish regulars. They also took over the fort of St. Sebastian which had been evacuated. That night the castle's guns fired several shots at the besiegers, with presumably little effect, and the two bomb ships, which had been towed into the harbour by two naval vessels, threw 20 large bombs, some of which went into the castle. As it was firing at a long distance, presumably to be out of range of the citadel's artillery, it did little damage. That evening, though, heavier guns were landed on shore and about 40-50 large mortars and smaller coehorn mortars were established in a battery under the protection of Fort St. Sebastian.[50]

On 2 October Honywood marched along the coast with 800 men to take the town of Vigo and the fort. However, danger came from another source. Some of the 'marauders' from the British camp were killed by the Spanish peasantry.[51]

The British guns began to fire on the same night and continued their bombardment for four days with 'great success'. Apparently over 300 men were killed or wounded; counter fire was limited and only killed two officers and three or four men. On the fourth day, 3 October, additional artillery, 44 coehorns and mortars, were brought to bear, with battering cannons being landed. These, with the addition of some cannon salvaged from the town, were placed alongside the mortars at the fort of St. Sebastian. Disciplinary measures were taken, presumably

---

47   RA, HT, 7411-24-111-1.
48   RA, HT, 7411-24-111-1.
49   RA, HT, 7411-24-111-1.
50   RA, HT, 7411-24-111-1.
51   RA, HT, 7411-24-111-1.

on those who had been drunk a couple of days ago, Hawley referring to 'whipping all day at the head of every regiment'.[52]

The camp was moved a mile closer to Vigo on 4 October and its left was moved down to Boas. There was further firing, with ships in the bay also firing at the citadel at night time, presumably because they would present too vulnerable a target in the daylight. Firing continued on the 5 and 6 October. Action against the Spanish peasants persisted, with a captain from the 3rd Guards amongst a number of men killed and wounded, whilst parties were sent out and succeeded in taking peasants back to the British camp. On 6 October Lord Mark Kerr (1676-1752), a brigadier, marched with a picket around the castle to Bedondella and burnt it, in the next few days his expedition seized a Spanish ship in the harbour and captured more peasants. Meanwhile, an Irish cadet of the Coldstream Guards led some deserters to the castle.[53] Yet the traffic in deserters went both ways. An Irish sailor left the castle on 7 October and gave the besiegers 'a pretty good account of 'em'. At ten that morning, a message was sent to the governor, to inform him that if he did not surrender the citadel by the time that the new battery of cannon was ready, there could be no quarter.[54]

Colonel Jean Ligonier (1680-1770) was sent with the message, but on arrival at the fort he found that the governor, Don Joseph de los Cereros, had been carried from there, wounded. In his absence, the lieutenant colonel, Don Gonzales de Sotto, who was now in charge, desired time to consult with the Marqués de Risbourg, Captain General of Galicia, who was at Tuy, for his instructions. Artillery fire continued that day, with a captain from Barrell's grenadier company being killed from fire from the castle. At five that afternoon, Colonel George Whitmore, of the 3rd Guards, and Hawley, marched with 1,000 men to relieve Honywood's 800 who were stationed in the town. Despite heavy rain that night, the besieging batteries continued to fire.[55]

Rain continued on the morning of 8 October, but at eight two officers from the castle came out under a flag of truce, to let them know that they had no answer from their Captain General, so could not surrender. The guns and mortars opened fire again and the four 24-pounders that had been found in the town were also ordered to fire, having been repaired after the Spanish had put them out of what turned out to be an only temporary condition. At 11:00 p.m., however, the Spanish wanted to discuss terms. They had had 80 officers and men killed and 225 wounded, so were reduced to two thirds of their initial strength. Their governor had been

---

52  RA, HT, 7411-24-111-1.
53  RA, HT, 7411-24-111-1.
54  RA, HT, 7411-24-111-1.
55  RA, HT, 7411-24-111-1.

wounded in six places (and died by 11 October) and they asked for a cease fire as a prelude to a capitulation. Cobham agreed, but had hostages exchanged and gave the Spanish until seven the next morning. Major Paul Gually, Cobham's adjutant, brought Cobham's answer to the garrison and told them that they must formulate their terms that night.[56]

Gually and Hawley took Cobham's demands to the garrison on 9 October and 'after a long while they consented to deliver up a port upon ye terms my lord gave 'em'. The articles of capitulation were as follows. The garrison was free to leave with arms and baggage, drums beating and flags flying, flasks full of powder and ball, without hindrance. Carriages would be allowed for the transportation of officers' baggage and tents. They would march to the bridge of St. Payo with enough provisions for four days. All these were granted, though the garrison had to find their own carriages. At four that day Fort St. Phillip was garrisoned by 40 grenadiers from the Guards battalions.[57]

Not everything went so smoothly. The Spanish wanted to be allowed to take six brass cannon and two mortars with them, with a dozen balls each. If there were insufficient land carriages, the guns could be taken by water as far as Ullo. This was refused. They also wanted carriages to be granted for the wounded and those too ill to move could remain at Philip IV's expense. Again carriages had to be found by the Spanish. The militia wanted to march out with arms and baggage and go where they chose without molestation, but they were not allowed to take their weapons. Foreigners working in the artillery and elsewhere wished to be allowed to go free and this was allowed, unless any were deserters from the British Army. The Spanish also wanted to retrieve any possessions left in the town; they had to specify what and where it was and it would be brought to them.[58]

For the British the benefits were: 'This capitulation being granted, all Magazines of Ammunition and Provisions shall faithfully be delivered to the Person of His Excellency the Lord Cobham shall appoint, and the gate of St. Philip shall also be delivered up'.[59] So, on the morning of 11 October the Spanish garrison marched out of the citadel. It was seen as 'strong enough to give a great deal more trouble'. The town was divided into cantons for the quartering of troops, according to the quartermaster's plans. A detachment of 50 grenadiers were placed into the castle in case there was an accident because of the quantity of gunpowder there. When the rest of the army came to Vigo on 12 October, 100 men relieved the grenadiers

---

56   RA, HT, 7411-24-111-1.
57   RA, HT, 7411-24-111-1; *London Gazette*, Oct. 1719.
58   *London Gazette*, 20-24 Oct. 1719.
59   *London Gazette*, 20-24 Oct. 1719.

in the castle. Several soldiers and sailors were killed or wounded by the peasants on this day.[60]

Meanwhile, Cobham summoned the adjacent countryside to supply provisions and make cash payments 'on pain of military execution'. Many people had fled away to Portugal. The few regular troops there had been drawn up by Risbourg at Tuy which was within three or four leagues of Vigo. Some of the Spanish officers spoke to the British officers before marching off and told them that the Jacobite Duke of Ormonde was raising an English regiment at Valladolid. Efforts were made to ascertain the truth of these stories.[61] Cobham was also able to seize seven ships in the Vigo harbour, three of which were being fitted up as privateers, one being of 24 guns. The other ships were trading vessels.[62]

On 13 October, the brass cannon from the castle were taken on board the British ships. On the next day, stores from the castle, the 24-pounders, four 12-pounders, six 4-pounders and two mortars, all brass, were also taken on board. Major Defysher was sent to England with the news of the fall of Vigo.[63] On the same day, 1000 men under Wade were taken by transports and convoyed by the *Speedwell* ship to the nearest landing stage near Pontevedra, setting sail on the 14 October. They reached there and found no opposition. Cannon (two 4-pounders, four 24-pounders, six 8-pounders) and four mortars, all brass, 80 iron cannon and 2,000 small arms and many stores were also found. The transportation of all this artillery carried on until 17 October. He also took a fort four miles from the town, again with no opposition. Apparently, the captain and his men left by jumping over the walls and abandoned it on Wade's approach. The British seized 18 cannon of various calibre, all newly mounted, and stores. A ship, the *Bideford*, was sent up river to transport Wade's captures.[64]

The Spanish peasants on the 15 and 18 October killed and wounded several soldiers, presumably by musket fire. So, on 19 October, a detachment of Guards was sent against them, 'and burnt all the country rounde and where the paysans sheltered themselves, to fire at our sentrys'. Much firing took place all day long between outposts of soldiers and the peasants, killing and wounding several men. Another punitive expedition took place on 20 October, with 150 soldiers in parties marching out to kill and burn all they could find 'they did for a league or four rounde but could not follow ye paysans to catche 'em'. This day, being the fifth anniversary of George I's coronation, what guns there were, were fired at noon.

60   RA, HT, 7411-24-111.1.
61   RA, HT, 7411-24-111.1.
62   *London Gazette*, Oct. 1719.
63   RA, HT, 7411-24-111-1.
64   RA, HT, 7411-24-111-1.

Boats from Vienna also arrived, with an English consul and goods to sell. They learnt that Colonel Hinchingbrooke was still at Lisbon.[65]

The end of the expedition was in sight. On the 20 October, the few dragoons were re-embarked, but in the town, with sailors setting fire to a house on the waterside, they nearly blew up far more as 200 barrels of gunpowder were nearby. On 21 October the last of the stores from the castle were embarked, as were the horses belonging to the artillery and the officers. Gunpowder and shells were loaded into the castle to destroy it, whilst the iron cannons there were spiked.[66] Wade's command of 1,000 men were the first to be re-embarked out of the infantry, though 15 men deserted from the Guards and six from the other units he had with him. Otherwise he could report no casualties. Those remaining soldiers were supplied with five days of bread and dried fish from the castle stores. Another loss was Colonel Whitmore, who died suddenly.[67]

On 24 October the ships from Pontevedra returned with all the brass cannons Wade had found, though all the iron cannons and 7,000 small arms had been blown up. The bishop's palace there had been burnt and Fort Marvine, with its guns and stores, had been demolished. Near Vigo, the baggage and some of the troops were re-embarked, whilst others, including Barrell's Regiment, were stationed in the town and in outposts to cover the departure.[68] More men went on board ship on the next day and by noon only the rear guard remained. The castle was then blown up. That night the peasants came into the remains of the castle and all around the town, but did not molest the rear guard. At 11:00 a.m. on 26 October, the rear guard embarked, without a further shot being fired. Most of the town was now ablaze. When the fleet was departing, they could see Spanish coming into view. The fleet sailed for England on the following day and on 1 November were in the Channel, and off Plymouth on 10 November. Five days later, six regiments, Grove's, Barrell's, Howard's, Chudleigh's, Hinchingbrooke's and Hawley's, were sent to Ireland again. Cobham and Kerr went to London on 17 November.[69]

Hawley's life was not wholly taken up in soldiering. His memoir states that in 1720 'he was going the next day from his house in the country'.[70] This is the first reference to West Green House, a house near Hartley Wintney in Hampshire. On 10 June 1720, Hawley leased the property for five years from the estate of late William Shipway, who had died in 1718. On 27/28 April 1722 it was conveyed by

---

65   RA, HT, 7411-24-111-1.
66   RA, HT, 7411-24-111-1.
67   RA, HT, 7411-24-111-1.
68   RA, HT, 7411-24-111-1.
69   RA, HT, 7411-24-111-1.
70   RA, HT, 7411-24-101, p.14.

Mary Shipway to Hawley.[71] The house had been a farm house in the seventeenth century and under Hawley's ownership it underwent considerable remodelling. Stone vases were put on the corners of the roof and porch. There was a stone tablet over a glazed door on the west front which read 'Fay ce que Voudras', the motto of the Hellfire Club, though it is not known if Hawley was a member; if he was not it is not certain why he should have this here.[72]

Hartley Wintney was a small village near Basingstoke in northern Hampshire, but within a day's journey of London. According to the diocesan visitation of 1725 it had a population of between 400-500 people, of whom none were Catholics, but a few were Dissenters. There was a small school, a post house and one parochial charity. The vicar, the Rev. Charles White, wrote, 'There is no nobleman, gentleman, or person of any considerable note of either sex, except Colonel Henry Harvey [sic], now in His Majesty's service, lately settled amongst us'.[73] It is not known why Hawley chose this rural backwater, but perhaps its geographical situation and perhaps its probable cheapness provide the answers. He was to have it as his home when not on service for the remainder of his life; another four decades, so it clearly appealed to him.

It seems he spent time in England and Ireland at this time. At some stage he petitioned the Lords Commission of the Treasury to complain about the house the late Queen had given him; he had had to pay another £100 to have it repaired and so desired that it could be leased to him for 31 years.[74]

In about 1720, Hawley was given the regiment that had formerly been Gore's Dragoons, as Brigadier Humphrey Gore had become colonel of the Royal Regiment of Dragoons now that their former colonel, Sir Charles Hotham, was dead. This meant a trip to London to kiss the King's hand to officially sanction his new post. However, in 1721 Hawley was advised to resign his new post for another man, a friend of Sir Robert Walpole, the new first minister, and would be made an aide with a daily pay of 10s and would be offered the next available vacancy for a colonelcy of a dragoon regiment. Hawley initially refused, but 'he was told to consider the consequences of disabling the first Minister' and eventually yielded 'the foolishest thing that he ever did in his life'.[75]

Hawley was also made a member of the privy council, on 1 October 1724. Following the death of George I, he was re-appointed on 14 September 1727. As

---

71 Hampshire Record Office, 20M50/194.
72 David Gorsky, *The Old Village of Hartley Wintney* (Hartley Wintney: Hartley Wintney Preservation Society, 1973), pp.44, 46.
73 W.R. Ward (ed.), *Parson and Parish in eighteenth century Hampshire* (Winchester: Hampshire County Council, 1995), p.67.
74 BL. Add. Mss. 61603, f.97r.
75 RA, HT, 7411-24-101, 14.

part of the duties recumbent on this office, he was also invited to the new King's coronation at Westminster Abbey on 10 October.[76] On the accession of George II, following his father's death in 1727, Hawley kissed the new King's hand and returned to his regiment in Ireland. The new king decided to make Hawley one of his aides and then summoned him to Windsor. There the Duke of Dorset bid Hawley to kiss the King's hand for the colonelcy of Harrington's Dragoons, Lord Harrington being the new Secretary of State. George II told Hawley that this was the best regiment of dragoons in the army 'and will no doubt that he would keep it so'.[77] Yet as Gardiner's Dragoons in 1745, its performance at the Battle of Prestonpans was abysmal.

When Hawley went to his new regiment in Ireland, he 'found it had been farmed out for some time to a Scotts Lt. Coll. who had made the most of it and had done so many dirty things he was forced next year to take the command of the regiment from him'. This was Lieutenant Colonel John Ramsey. Officers had horses that were of little value; none being worth over £6: 7s, and were then sold for a pittance. Hawley returned to England to tell the King what he had done and that the regiment would be complete next year. He learnt that Harrington had no idea of what had happened previously.[78]

Away from soldiering, one of Hawley's major passions was horses, and he was an enthusiastic member of the Charlton Hunt, founded in 1721 and one of the most socially important of gatherings outside London. Master of the Hunt from 1731 was Charles Lennox, the second Duke of Richmond (1701-1750), who was also a soldier. Among the members during Hawley's time were several of the political and military elite. They included Thomas Pelham-Holles, first Duke of Newcastle (1693-1768) and Secretary of State, the Dukes of Grafton and St. Albans, Lord James Cavendish, Sir Henry Liddell MP, and Generals Honywood, Churchill, and Kirke, Colonel John Huske (1692-1761) and Henry Pelham MP (1694-1754), Paymaster of the Forces and Newcastle's half-brother.[79] These were important contacts for Hawley to have made and to maintain, just as Erle, Prince George, and Queen Anne had been earlier in the century.

Entry to the hunt was by ballot only, seven or more days after application had been made. At least nine existing members were needed for a legitimate ballot. A single black ball would exclude any prospective new member. One nomination a year was allowed. Clearly for Hawley to become a member he must have been

76   RA, HT, 7411-24-101, 113, 108, 24.
77   RA, HT, 7411-24-101-1, pp.14-15.
78   HT, RA, 7411-24-101, p.15.
79   T.J. McCann (ed.), *Correspondence of the Duke of Newcastle and Richmond, 1724-1750* (Lewes: Sussex Historical Society, 1983), p.25; The Earl of March, *Records of the Charlton Hunt* (London: Elkin Matthews, 1910), pp.40, 42.

Thomas Pelham-Holles, Duke of Newcastle. (Author's collection)

held in esteem by the voting members.[80] When he could, Hawley attended meets regularly. He was there on 12, 21, and 25 February 1738 at Charlton, but active service on 25 February 1745 debarred his presence.[81]

A significant hunt that was participated in by Hawley took place on Friday 26 January 1739. The fox was first seen at a quarter to eight in the morning at Eastdean Wood, Chichester. The hounds took up the scent and the chase began. Near Herring Dean, Hawley changed his horse for one that could be wholly depended on, as did Brigadier Ives. It was a long chase, lasting 35 miles, with many of the huntsmen dropping out along the way. By the time Houghton Wood was reached, only Richmond, Hawley and one Mr Pauncefoot remained. Finally, the fox was run to earth near South Stoke, near Arundel at ten to six in the evening, and 23 hounds 'putt an end to the campaign'. There at the death were Ives, Richmond, and

---

80 March, *Records*, p.41.
81 March, *Records*, pp.43-44.

Hawley. It was thus a tribute to his skill that he was able to keep up throughout the chase; apparently he had changed horses only the once.[82]

Hawley shot as well as hunted, and for many years was accompanied in his shooting with his favourite spaniel, Monkey, to whom he clearly felt great devotion and on the dog's death he had cause to erect a tombstone to her in his garden, which read as follows:

> Oh Poor
> Monkey
> Come, all yee shooters, come my losse bewaile
> The best black spaniel that ere wag'd a taile
> Of questing kinde and royall breed shee came.
> Great was her science, and as great her fame,
> 15 hard winters she did hunt, and last
> This stone in memory of service past
> Anno = 34
> I say no more.[83]

Notwithstanding these pursuits he was also a portly fellow, weighing 17 stones in 1739.[84]

Meanwhile, his career progression was slow. However, he accrued additional posts. In 1723 he was an aide to a general, for which he received an additional £173 10s per annum, as well as his pay as a colonel of £3,147 5s 1d.[85] Movement through the ranks was slow in peacetime as new openings are not created by deaths in battle, nor was the army expanded to meet wartime needs, but was kept small to keep taxes low, which was a political necessity. Had the country fought in the War of Polish Succession in 1733-1735, matters would have been different and doubtless many officers would have welcomed this; certainly George II, himself a soldier, did, but was persuaded by Sir Robert Walpole, his chief minister, averse to the multitudinous costs of warfare, not to involve Britain.

On 26 December 1726 one John Toovey became a lieutenant in the regiment; he had been an ensign since 19 July 1719.[86] This was an important event for Hawley, because Toovey's mother was to become the woman in Hawley's life, though it is unknown when they first met; possibly prior to Toovey's appointment, though possibly afterwards. She will be considered in Chapter 9. On 25 August 1740,

---

82 March, *Records*, pp.63-64; RA, HT, 7411-24-114.
83 Gorsky, *The Old Village*, p.46.
84 Charles Lennox, *A Duke and his friends* (London: Hutchinson and Co, 1910), p.51.
85 Dalton, *Army of George I*, Vol.II, pp.430, 153.
86 Dalton, *Army of George I*, Vol.II, p.411.

Toovey's younger brother, William Henry, was appointed as quartermaster of Captain William Wentworth's troop in the same regiment; on 1 July 1741 he was made cornet and on 23 April 1742, lieutenant.[87]

On 18 December 1735 Hawley was made a brigadier general, as were a number of other colonels.[88] On 17 July 1739 he became a major general.[89] Many other officers, such as Ligonier and Sir John Cope (c.1690-1760), were promoted to brigadiers and major generals at these times, as elderly officers died or sold their commissions and some older officers such as George Wade gained higher ranks.

Hawley wrote, 'he thought there was one end of his hopes and he was resolved to get into some other service and accordingly went to worke and trusted but two people with it. There was one in England then with whome he treated and that person had an answer to his proposals and a very good bargain he had made and it was ripe and he wanted nothing but to get leave to quitt'. This would seem that the middle-aged Hawley was planning to leave the army but does not say what his alternative was; perhaps a business venture? However, the colonelcy of the Royal Regiment of Dragoons became vacant again and 'his friends were dayly at him to ask for it but he persisted never to ask again'. Despite the government's nominating others for it, George II was steadfast in his control over patronage and gave this to Hawley. On 12 May 1740 he became colonel of the Royal Regiment of Dragoons.[90]

Hawley gained from two wills in this period. General Erle made his will in 1717, which proved in the year of his death three years later and he included the following clause, 'I give to my brother [sic] Henry Hawley, esquire, the sum of £100 and to each of the children of my brother Francis Hawley, esquire deceased, viz Henry, Edward and Anne, the sum of £50'. When the former Henry Hawley died in 1724, he left much to his nephew Captain Edward Hawley, but also wrote, 'I give and devise unto my nephew Colonel Henry Hawley my right title and interest in Sterminster [Sturminster] in the county of Dorset, where in I have an estate, and moreover I give and remit unto him the said Henry Hawley all the sums of money and debts he owes me'.[91]

Not all went well for Hawley's family in these years. His brother Edward became a captain in the Royal Irish Regiment on 24 December 1720. He transferred to Harrison's Foot on the British establishment on 7 April 1726. He also married, perhaps after his inheritance in 1724, now he had the money to marry. His bride was one Elizabeth, possibly Elizabeth Colleton, daughter of Robert, son of John

---

87   RA, HT, 7411-24-400, 1-3.
88   *London Gazette*, 7464, 16-20 Dec. 1735.
89   *London Gazette*, 7823, 17 July 1739.
90   *London Gazette*, 7940, 12 May 1740; RA, HT, 7411-24-101, p.15.
91   Dalton, 'Parentage', p.122.

Colleton, baronet, but he was was dead before 1735; his widow having a pension of £26 per year. There may have been a son by the name of Richard, to whom Anne Hawley refers in 1769.[92]

Finally, their mother, Judith, died in 1737, still resident in the parish of St. Martin's in the Fields, at the grand old age of about 78. Her will, made in 1724 and proved at the Prerogative Court of Canterbury on 5 July 1737, gave all her property to Anne as her sons 'being already sufficiently provided for'. The unmarried Anne was now Hawley's dependant. On her mother's death, Hawley, as her only remaining brother, petitioned the King and Walpole that half of his mother's pension be bestowed on his sister. They refused. Hawley petitioned Queen Caroline and when the King returned from Hanover he said it was not unreasonable to allow Anne £150 a year. Hawley thought this was reasonable as he had lost the £300 a year equerry post bestowed on him by Anne, in George II's accession. Yet it seems this was stopped, so Hawley, who was receiving £200 per year as an aide, gave this to his sister. After that Hawley resolved never to ask for anything again.[93] It seems that she adopted one Anne, later Mrs Ciprani, 'who hath lived with me from her infancy and been very faithful and tender to me' and had various servants.[94]

Soon, though, this middle-aged officer's career was about to change as European affairs erupted again.

---

92   Dalton, *Army, of George I*, Vol.I, p.331; Vol.II, pp.306, 303.
93   Dalton, *Army of George I*, Vol.I, p.44; RA, HT, 7411-24-101, p.15.
94   TNA, PROB11/953.

# 3

# Hawley and the Theory of War

Hawley was not involved in any war for over two decades after 1719. Yet his mind was not far from the subject. He gave considerable thought to how the army could and should be run and how it could perform even better in campaign and in battle.

Soldiers are often seen, historically at least, as being men of action rather than thought. Few 18th century soldiers attended university and not many attended school, for soldiering was a profession that was entered into in youth. Hawley, as noted, was no exception. Yet some soldiers did think about their profession and some even wrote down their thoughts on paper for publication. Lieutenant General Hugh Mackay certainly did, and, later in Hawley's time, Major General Humphrey Bland (1686-1763) did likewise and his work, *A Treatise on Military Discipline* (1727), became one of the best known in the 18th century, undergoing a number of editions. Despite his reputation as being a brutal disciplinarian, Hawley was also a man who used his mind, though whether he always drew the right conclusions is another question.

Hawley knew that few other officers were students of war, and that they should read and study the art of warfare. They should attend courses on siege and fortifications. He believed that exams should be taken for promotion. Caesar's *Commentaries* and Saxe's *Traite des Legions* were among his favourite books, explaining as they did discipline and the co-operation between infantry and cavalry. He also read the campaigns of Turenne, Marlborough and Eugene, as well as those of Bland and Feuquieres.[1]

In the long peace of the 1720s and 1730s Hawley had time on his hands and took pen to paper to write down his opinions on the subject of soldiering. His comments were never published, however, so are not well known. We will now

---

1   Gruber, *Officers and their Books*, p.91.

examine his manuscript notes for they cast a light on his character and philosophy as well as his views on the military life.

Hawley gave an explanation as to why he wrote:

> Being born and bred in the army, from after the death of my father… having been a commission officer now [1725] thirty five year, I have come through almost all the military gradations. When I was a subaltern I thought very little of learning my trade, any more than the cannon you fire, one fault I find to general among the youth of the army. When I came to be Capt [1706]…I began a little to think, and being then in service I had frequent occasion of practice and experience butt I began to find more & more that occasion & experience only, was a very slow way to come at science…and began to reflect and study and to write and consider things that I had either read or heard or seen. And I still sett them down in a rough way…with thoughts and remarques of my owne.[2]

Education was an ongoing process, he thought, 'I am of opinion that a man can never be perfect in war, but may always be learning'.[3] He added that when he had been a cornet of horse 'which there was nothing of what wee call discipline now' and that this fell short of what was set out in 'Coll. Blands treatise', which dealt with encampment, exercise, and evolution. 'I thinke his booke a very usefull one for young officers who first come into the army…but I can't help thinking even that teaches ane officer but very little'. The information that Bland presented about the cavalry only taught how a regiment should be ordered and how it should be prepared for it to be reviewed by the King. Yet officer readers who must then embark for Flanders and take the field 'woulde they not be as ignorant and as awkward as can be imagined…in every part of their duty'. Few are born inspired, he thought. When generals die those who are left may not have had much experience in all the aspects of military service.[4]

Hawley noted that there were different classes of 'old officers'; a few had had commissions in William III's time who had not forgotten how to stand fire. Then there were those who had served under Marlborough, and finally there were those who are called 'old' because they had received pay for years. Many infantry officers were in cavalry units and vice versa; which Hawley thought was ridiculous and he made the following comparison: 'a man who has served his time and learned to be a good gunsmith is not to pretend to be sett up for a good sword cutter' (Hawley

---

2    RA, HT, 7411-24-123-6.
3    Sumner, 'General Hawley's Chaos', p.91.
4    RA, HT, 7411-24-123-6.

had been a cavalry officer and was now colonel of a regiment of infantry, but his focus was on the former). Many infantry officers serving in cavalry would only become good cavalry officers if they were given time and sufficient effort. There were differences in pay of dragoons and horse but no other major difference.[5] He recommended that the King offer older officers money to retire with and a small reward for past services. Otherwise regiments would become 'marching hospitalls' that is to say, full of elderly officers.[6]

It was not just elderly men who caused a problem for the army. Other officers were also 'a prejudice likewise than any good to the service'. Those who bought commissions and then grew weary of them, and 'never mind their business' have 'no pleasure to them in serving, no emulation, no ambition in short no spirit'. They were a bad example to young officers at home and on active service and 'the consequences may be worse'. They did not want to venture their lives and were not as bold as they could as they took no pleasure in their calling and so were no particularly efficient. He also wrote, condemnatory, of his fellow officers 'moste of them likewise have foolishly marryed, and have familys and as they most commonly marry for love and not to better themselves, so when they dye along with them, thers a wife & children left a starving'. Hawley never married, but as we shall see he was no misogynist.[7] Some soldiers were men 'who never can nor will be officers as nature never designed them for the trade'. They could not help it but 'these are very soon found out by the men, as soon by them despised'. If the King could clear the army of these men, they would be better pleased and thus 'I need not explain the great advantage it would be to the service'.[8]

Hawley wrote a number of other essays on numerous military subjects. It is not known whether any of these ever reached a wider audience, but they do show that he thought about these topics and they probably informed his thinking and actions. Unfortunately, most of them are undated, but presumably all post-date the mid-1720s.

One of them concerned advice to young men entering the army in the rank and file, who were not usually considered as being worthy of the attention of senior officers, who had very little interaction with them. It is in the form of an address to a new recruit, giving advice as to his conduct (conduct books in the early modern period were a common form of superiors addressing their inferiors with 'advice' as to their conduct; whether any of the intended audience, assuming they were literate, read them is unknown). He wrote 'I will suppose every Recruit actuated

---

5  RA, HT, 7411-24-123-6.
6  RA, HT, 7411-24-123-6.
7  RA, HT, 7411-24-123-6.
8  RA, HT, 7411-24-123-6.

by ambition when they enlist for it will scarce prove himself deserving of military subsistence whose indolence and profligacy incapacitated him from gaining a livelihood as a Labourer or Mechanic. The Reward of Industry will be Respect & Promotion if Idleness, stripes & Ignominy'.[9] Attention to appearance was an important facet of army life. Neatness in dress and an upright carriage indicate 'a good old soldier'. Therefore, it would be to gain the golden opinions of an officer if a new recruit could copy this example. They must take pride in themselves, but not exaggeratedly so, to be not be above doing any type of work that a superior may order them to do. To disobey the youngest corporal is to disobey the colonel 'this is the most unpardonable of all crimes & strikes more directly as the foot of good Discipline it cannot be too soon checked'.[10]

No man is an island, so there was the question of the young man making a 'prudent choice of companions'. Many young men are 'so infected with the vicious habits of bad comrades & some they are in every regiment'. In this case, the young man becomes more attentive to rules laid down by 'them in their drunken conversations, than to the advice of their officers' who care for the men by duty and inclination. The 'very good & feeling officer is highly gratified when he commends diligence & is no less hurt when obliged by his duty to inflict punishment on idleness & obstinacy'.[11] Since it was commonplace that 'troops [were] quartered apart from one another', they were easily led into 'snares which old abandon'd offenders will use to inveigle you into their society' with 'profligate Discourses'. The soldier must be diligent and sober and avoid being 'in the Society of a drunken Rabble which are the constant Inhabitants of an ale house kitchen'.[12]

He suggested that the young man spend much of his time in cleaning weapons, but also in presenting himself to lessons given by a sergeant, in basic literacy and mathematics; reading, 'casting accounts' and writing in a 'fair & legible hand, which above all things will advance your future interests'. Such basic literacy was crucial for a man to become a sergeant, with the added responsibility, pay, and status. Hawley's regiment had a writing master to benefit those inclined to learn, and it was deemed shameful if this opportunity was neglected.[13]

The recruit would be deemed as a superior kind of soldier if he paid attention to the drill sergeant or corporal and when he did well he would be shown up as an example to the indolent soldier, 'who is treated like a dog & taught his business after the same fashion by hard words & harder blows'. Another vice was highlighted: 'Avoid any species of gaming, it ill suits the pocket'. Officers

9   RA, HT, 7411-24-127.
10  RA, HT, 7411-24-127.
11  RA, HT, 7411-24-127.
12  RA, HT, 7411-24-127.
13  RA, HT, 7411-24-127.

did it (Hawley noted having done so as a young officer in the War of Spanish Succession) but could usually easily extricate themselves; for privates, it was 'a misdemeanour worthy of punishment' and for the non-commissioned officers it was an 'unpardonable crime'.[14]

The Articles of War, governing the soldiers' lives, which spelt out what was against the rules and how it was punished, were often read out to the assembled men. The recruit must heed these. He could also obtain a copy by memorising them and so will know them off by heart.[15]

Hawley concluded that 'If you follow your directions in a few weeks the adjutant will recommend you to the commanding officer will & take a pride to point you out in the ranks standing with such a firm manly [bearing] as would not disgrace a much older [man] proficient in the service'. Then the man would be regarded as a disciplined soldier, but he must not slacken for more will be expected in proportion to his experience. Faults must be avoided in order to not let the adjutant in his confidence in the man.[16]

As already noted, Hawley deemed appearance to be very important. A cavalryman, Hawley paid particular emphasis on the role of the cavalry. A trooper had additional work to the infantry private. He had to keep his horse clean and trim, with bit polished, no rubbish in his horse's mouth, and the saddle well placed. As for the man, his hat must be well cock'd and smartly set on his head, hair neatly hid making him look like a gentleman. His belts must be whitened, his sword and gun polished until bright and his spurs well fitted. He added 'People seeing such a comely young man take post in his troop will be very out to a form a good opinion of the Regt he belongs to'.[17]

When the regiment was reviewed by a general or other senior figure, the soldier must wait for the word of command in silence and pay attention to the general. The inspecting officer would notice who the best men were and they would also attract his admiration, 'But it was also important not to have airs & attitudes on such an occasion or the soldier will appear to be a coxcomb'. Manoeuvres must be practised carefully, for it would be a mistake to think that the regiment will look good before an enemy if they do not do their exercises well. Embarrassment, hurry, and confusion would result and must be dealt with.[18]

Hawley concluded with two additional observations: 'It would be endless to quite examples from History, to prove that undisciplined multitudes have always been the most despicable enemies' and that 'constant practice and severe

---

14  RA, HT, 7411-24-127.
15  RA, HT, 7411-24-127.
16  RA, HT, 7411-24-127.
17  RA, HT, 7411-24-127.
18  RA, HT, 7411-24-127.

discipline…alone will give strength and energy to an army'.[19] It is probable that he was to see the Jacobite army in 1746 at Falkirk as such a rabble, as he had at Sheriffmuir in 1715, and thus underestimated their capability despite their victory at Prestonpans. Likewise, he had a high opinion of the troops under him, writing: 'The weight of British Cavalry & incomparable spirit of the horses has justly given them the Superior to any that can be brought against them' and so it would be shameful to sacrifice this to carelessness and indolence. These points are noteworthy and certainly Hawley applied them during his command of the army in Scotland in 1745-1746, as shall be demonstrated in subsequent chapters.[20] The duty of the trooper in battle was simply 'implicit attention to the officer who leads the squadron troop he belongs to'. He must obey orders, never suffer his horse to have its own will, and should observe silence in the ranks so as to hear instructions. His initiative in battle was limited: 'The Duty of a Private soldier in the field is in within the Reach of a very moderate Capacity'. What was important was 'implicit attention to the officer who leads the squadron'.[21]

Care of the dragoon's horse was also stressed, 'A Dragoon cannot have too great a Confidence in his horse'. Control was needed to prevent a horse going at full speed until the climax of a charge. However, a unit's speed should be regulated by that of the slowest, and racing and dashing of horses should be avoided. 'If your horse is justly to be considered as your friend & comrade in the field, you should treat him with the same attention and regard, when he returns to his stable'. Man and horse must respect one another. A horse could show his gratitude to his rider by 'saving your life or at least preventing you from walking on foot, for the last month or two of a long wearisome campaign'. Horses must be attended to, so that they do not develop a sore back, 'it should be guarded against as a pestilence' and should be an offence that Hawley would deem punishable.[22]

Marriage and money was also touched upon. Hawley was a bachelor and approved of that state for the soldier, and this applied to the rank and file as well as officers, He wrote:

> I would strongly recommend it to a young soldier to continue single, by marrying he will plunge himself into a dismal state of distress, which will in the end damp his spirit, destroy his appearance & extinguish every spark of emulation. I remember no instance of any dragoons being the better for marriage, nor can I suppose any capable of showing alacrity

19  RA, HT, 7411-24-127.
20  RA, HT, 7411-24-127.
21  RA, HT, 7411-24-127.
22  RA, HT, 7411-24-127.

& spirit in the performance of his Duty, whose mind is continually hampered with the thoughts of a starving wife & naked family.[23]

As to money, 'many advantages will proceed from an exact economy'. Properly managed, a dragoon's pay should maintain him in necessaries. Debt was to be avoided, though 'some of his more thoughtless & dissolute comrades who have squandered away their money in drinking will look up to him with envy'. Pay of sixpence a day could be managed by saving a penny each day, which if done, 'you will be a richer & more independent man'.[24] A dragoon should seek out the company of the good NCOs who would be pleased to encourage him in his ambition. Their example and instructions would help. If the man thought himself 'capable of doing the duty of a corporal, let not bashfulness prevent you soliciting the interest of your officer's recommendation'. He would be 'delighted with your spirit' and impressed by 'Diligence & attention' and each would be useful to the other.[25]

Once a man became a corporal, his responsibilities increased. It was now no longer enough to 'pay an implicit obedience to the orders of your superior', but 'to insist on the execution of your directing'. On promotion he would probably be moved to another troop in order that his previous familiarity with his comrades not affect his attitude towards them. He might 'be often timorous at first of carrying out discipline…and may be induced to desire than enforce discipline amongst his intimates & old mess mates'. Favour and friendship had better be 'absolutely annihilated' once a man became an NCO.[26] For a corporal to rise, he must strictly resolve against 'idle amusements & Diversions' and he was to take pleasure only in 'doing his duty well & being diligent…in the execution of whatever he is entrusted in…the slave to his troop'. Drink must be avoided. He must be a 'regular visitor to the stables' to ensure the horses were well cared for and their temper ascertained in order to have the troop 'appear in a uniform condition'. Any problems must be immediately reported to his superiors.[27] As for himself, the corporal must be well dressed and punctual. He must regularly inspect the men's quarters and report any absentees. This will all ingratiate himself with his superiors by showing that he is worthy of their confidence. Arms, accoutrements, dress ,and the hair of all under his supervision must be

---

23   RA, HT, 7411-24-127.
24   RA, HT, 7411-24-127.
25   RA, HT, 7411-24-127.
26   RA, HT, 7411-24-127.
27   RA, HT, 7411-24-127.

exact before being presented for inspection. In all, Hawley demanded that the NCOs promote discipline among the men as well as themselves.[28]

There were also other essays, mostly about the cavalry, as might be expected. One was titled, 'Proposal for a very cheap and expeditious way of augmentation to the Dragoons, which would not anyways hinder the Raising the Marines or filling up the Foot and would not be of great service at this present juncture'. This was to add one troop to each of the eleven existing regiments, or 10 men per troop or 20 to a squadron, if three squadrons. The troop was not to have cornet or drummer, only a captain, two lieutenants, a quartermaster, six sergeants, six corporals, six farriers and 60 troopers. £9 per horse was to be provided from the government. Officers should not be paid until all the men were recruited. All these men were to be as small as possible. Their uniforms were to be green, not red. They were to use short carbines as there were many of these in the Tower of London, which were unused. They were to wear a cap not a hat, not to have bayonets, but to wear short coats not skirts, and be armed with sword, pistol and axe. They were to practice fire on horseback, though little drill was necessary: they only needed enough to be able to load quickly and manoeuvre. The horses could be of any colour except grey, were to be of 14 to 14 ½ hands in size, of moderate age; no young horses were wanted, but they had to have some speed and strength. The horses were to have a hunting saddle only. These troopers would march in the vanguard at the head of column, to examine the flanks and to safeguard the army in case of a retreat. There were to be four men vacant from the unit in order to recruit horses. He finally added that 'How a little fellow can be expected to marche at all, on foot, with a long scimitar and a long bayonet'.[29]

There was another essay about cavalry which was titled, 'Heads of the first articles for Drilling the Troop or Troops of Carabiners'. Carabiners were light cavalry armed with carbines who had originated in the French army in the late seventeenth century. In this, Hawley advised that there was little need for exercise as the troop must be prepared to 'go thro' it with the rest of the Regt theyr different accoutrements wont allow it'. Their carbines should not be shouldered, but carried on the left arm. In his opinion, 'The chief thing is to teach them to load quick and fire', to 'marke ready and fire' as there would be no firing by platoon or regular firings, but that they should fire in two deep lines as quick as possible.[30] The troop would not undertake any evolutions, except for opening and closing files only. There was to be no regularity on horse back, only forming forward again as soon in as possible. When dismounted, 'they must march handsomely', with carbine

---

28  RA, HT, 7411-24-26.
29  RA, HT, 7411-24-26.
30  RA, HT, 7411-24-26.

and bayonet on left arm in review. They should ground arms as dragoons used to. Carbines should be slung to the trooper's belt and thrown over on left side to mount their horse; his bayonet should be drawn from his cartridge box and fixed with his carbine on his left hand. On horseback, the trooper should never draw his sword but make ready his carbine in brackets on his thighs, and swivel them and march by.[31]

Then there were Hawley's articles for drilling men of the light troops. They should never shoulder carbines but carry them on their left arm, but that they may rest on them on some occasions. What was crucial was that 'the chief thing is to teach them to loade and fire as quick as possible, no platoons nor any regular firings'. There was to be no evolutions, whilst on foot, where they would be in but one or two deep in rank. They were to saddle and accoutre themselves as soon as possible. They had to mount and dismount quickly, never more than two deep, with one word of command, advance alternate horses to the rear and then link them as fast as possible, and to load as fast as possible on horseback.[32]

Hawley's scheme for Light Dragoons, 1728; mounted and dismounted private. Drawings by Rev. Percy Sumner after coloured originals in the Cumberland Papers (Published in *JSAHR* Vol. 25, No.102 (Summer 1947), and reproduced here by the generous permission of the Hon. Editor)

31   RA, HT, 7411-24-26.
32   RA, HT, 7411-24-26.

When perfect in loading, and firing quickly on horseback, the men had then to break and practice on a gallop, firing mostly to the left, turning short and loading again and when perfect in this, to turn to priming standing. After all the motions had been performed, they were to then load with cartridge and practice but only when their horses were stationary. They would fire with cartridge, disperse upon a gallop, then wheel singly to the right and load again and go together but in no great order. When necessary, they would drop their carbines and draw swords and had to practice pursuit after the broken enemy.[33] The troops should practice pursuit again with swords in their left hand and pistols in right, fire, disperse, return pistols and take sword again. When the enemy retreated in disorder, the pursuers should halt at proper distance, load carbines and pursue again with speed. They should learn to gain left flank of enemy squadron, fire over their left arm, and disorder the enemy so that the regular cavalry could then charge them.[34]

Once fired, they should drop their carbine, draw their swords and 'gett into the rear of the enemy's squadron and upon the flank' and with their colleagues, help to break the enemy 'if the light troops do their duty'. They were then to pursue the enemy with sword and pistol, but not too far to entangle themselves in a second line. If pushed back, they should retreat towards the regular squadrons and pass through them at intervals.[35]

Little parties were to be sent out to harass the enemy and to pick up stragglers but in this they would need support from their dragoons and they by the infantry in case of the need to retreat. They should encamp on the wings of the main force or in their rear. They could escort convoys, level down ditches and hedges at front of the main marching columns. They should have minimal camp equipage. Each man should receive a guinea on enlisting and if a dragoon introduced him, there should be five shillings for him 'to encourage the men to look out and be assisting this'.[36] Hawley did not approve of basket hilted swords which would deprive a man of the use of his right hand in case of his bridles being cut or broken. 'No officer is supposed ever to fight himselfe any more than to defend his head, his chief business is to see the men fight and do well as that was sufficient'. Once the men charged, they must shorten their bridles.[37]

These ideas for light cavalry, it should be emphasised, predated the adoption of such troops by the British Army during the Seven Years War.

---

33  RA, HT, 7411-24-26.
34  RA, HT, 7411-24-26.
35  RA, HT, 7411-24-26.
36  RA, HT, 7411-24-26.
37  Sumner, 'General Hawley's Chaos', p.94, Sumner; 'General Hawley's Scheme for Light Dragoons', pp.64-65.

There were other thoughts about cavalry. Hawley was very positive about the dragoons, 'The Dragoons in England are certainly the finest troops in the world'. This statement is worth bearing in mind when we see what use he made of his cavalry at the Battle of Falkirk, and presumably his belief is due to his being a dragoon officer at this time. He composed a scheme 'for reviving a regiment of original Dragoons'. Dragoons had their origins in the early seventeenth century as soldiers who rode into battle and then fought on foot, rather than ones who just fought as cavalry. The regiments would be made up of twelve, rather than six troops, of 50 men apiece. He claimed that they would be able to march 30 miles per day instead of a mere ten, and that they would be effective against smugglers and could fight intertwined with infantry. They could wear blue coats, instead of the conventional red.[38]

Hawley was not satisfied with the British Army's regiments of horse. He thought that the Horse Guards should be turned into a regiment of cuirassiers, that is to say, armoured cavalry. The other horse regiments should be turned into dragoon regiments, as at present they were useless and expensive. He thought that cavalrymen's swords should be another six inches longer and that the men should have skull caps under their hats for protection as well as back and breastplates. He advocated that cavalry should be rid of carbines.[39]

Although most of his writings were directed towards the cavalry, Hawley also threw in his penny worth about the new metal ramrods for the infantry's muskets: 'The iron ramrods that the Foot are coming into are very ridiculous…for if they have not steel they snap like glass; in wet weather or in fog they rust and won't come out, as always by standing in the bell tents where arms always rust a little by the dew'.[40] However, these comments appear somewhat perverse in the light of the iron ramrod was to be later used in the Prussian army and being one of the reasons for their successes in the battles of the War of Austrian Succession. Hawley's knowledge and experience did not concern the infantry and perhaps this is the reason for this comment. However, he made more remarks about topics which were outside his particular remit.

He also made other statements about infantry weapons. One was that he favoured the selective reintroduction of pikemen with 10 feet pikes among the musket armed infantry (pikes had been totally discarded from the British Army at the beginning of the century, as bayonets became universal for the infantry). It is not known whether Hawley was aware that Marshal de Saxe was making similar

---

38   Sumner, 'General Hawley's Chaos', pp.91-92.
39   Christopher Duffy, *The Military Experience on the Age of Reason* (London: Routledge & Kegan Paul, 1987), p.211.
40   Sumner, 'General Hawley's Chaos', pp.91-93.

suggestions, as that officer's Rêveries at this time existed only in manuscript form. Another of Hawley's beliefs was that swords for the infantry were useless, being heavy to carry on the march, and were a hindrance in exercise as well as being used by the men during drunken brawls. He thought that the mitre caps of the grenadiers were inconvenient, being too hot in the summer, as well as being heavy, though he acknowledged that they were handsome.[41]

Hawley was also concerned that infantrymen would become too unused to exercise in peacetime and have to be transported by wagons. To combat this, he recommended that they be used to build roads, as had occurred in Scotland under Wade. As well as the work being useful in itself, the men could earn an additional sixpence a day, as well as it preventing them from being slothful and idle, improving discipline, rather than undergoing twice weekly manual exercises. Once the roads were complete, the soldiers could patrol them to deter crime.[42]

Apart from all these military strictures, there was a piece about the civil constitution and the army's relation to it. This seems like a piece of Tory or opposition 'Country' Whig philosophy, which is of interest as one would expect an army officer to be aligned to the Court Whigs and approve of a standing army. Unlike some officers, Hawley never served as an MP and his politics are otherwise unknown; in 1746 he claimed to be politically unaware. The former factions were opposed to standing, professional armies in peacetime as being detrimental to civil liberty, as shown by the rule of James II and, earlier, Cromwell, in the 17th century, as well as the militarised 'absolutist' states of Continental Europe, notably France. Hawley titled this essay 'Constitutional queries', which were 'Earnestly recommended to the serious consideration of every true Britton'. These were made up of rhetorical points. The first was whether London should be beset by troops to render King, lords, and commons precarious in their power and where laws would be subject to military regulation. He was concerned that military rule would entail the disgracing or dismissing of veteran officers, who were men of family and property, and that 'boyes, slaves and beggars' would replace them, to the detriment of the army.[43]

He believed that the setting up of alarm posts and the appointment and assignment of officers bearing a martial air was by 'no means becoming the British Constitution'. These terrifying dispositions would only serve to alarm a free people that an impending blow would be struck against them. There was also the risk that the younger son of the King could be invested with absolute control of an army and be master of fleet and thus rule the lives and fortunes, and this would

---

41   Sumner, 'General Hawley's Chaos', p.93.
42   RA, HT, 7411-24-26.
43   RA, HT, 7411-24-26.

mean that the Crown's descent would have no security but his want of ambition. If this was written in the early 1750s, following the death of George II's eldest son, Frederick, in 1751, then this diatribe is clearly directed against the King's remaining son, the Duke of Cumberland, who was seen, wrongly, by his enemies of hoping to stage a military coup. Yet as far as we know, Hawley had no animus against Cumberland.[44]

Hawley was concerned about the sole direction of army being bestowed upon the cabinet 'likewise may not give...dictatorial authority'. There was the fear that the army in peace time could usurp the law, which had been a real danger in the 17th century. This would mean that troops could execute the law without civil power concurring. If part of the country fell to military domination, there would be the danger of rule by a faction backed by the Army. Hawley gave the fatal examples of York and Lancaster and Richard III in the fifteenth century; with the latter seizing power following the death of his brother and a young son being the legitimate and vulnerable successor. He ended with the hope, 'God preserve the Succession'.[45] This comparison was also seized on by Cumberland's enemies after the death of his elder brother, who left a young son as heir.

Hawley also wrote down 'Questions on French formations', asking how deep their infantry were in line, whether they fired by platoons, and what the officers did using firings. There were other notes about cavalry in 'Comments on dress of light horsemen or rangers'. Hawley felt they should wear short leather gaiters with a spur, full length breeches, short waist coat no pockets, hunting frock coat no gloves, cravat, no powdered hair, leather cap with contour, short carbine, hanger, pistol. Their horse should have a half hunting saddle.[46]

He also composed a 'Regimental book of the Royal Dragoons' that all men now enlisting from 24 April 1751 were to be entered into, with ages. Likewise, horses were to be included, with ages on purchase.[47]

It is not known what impact any of these writings had on the army as they were never published. Yet they do show a side of Hawley's character. He clearly thought that discipline and order were paramount in the army. He disapproved of marriage for soldiers. He thought that the British cavalry could be improved by the introduction of light cavalry. It is perhaps interesting to note that he was concerned that military power might usurp civil government and that he was as opposed to this as any opposition spokesman in Parliament would be. At some point prior to 1745, he, with Generals Campbell and Honywood, put his name to

---

44  RA, HT, 7411-24-26.
45  RA, HT, 7411-24-26.
46  RA, HT, 7411-24-26.
47  RA, HT, 7411-24-26.

a document concerning the regulation of pay of non-commissioned officers in the dragoons; with sergeants to receive 2s 3d less six pence deductions; corporals and drummers 1s 9d less six pence.[48] This would represent a cut of three pence for the sergeants and a three pence rise for the others.

It is not known if Hawley shared any of his knowledge with anyone else. They do show some of his thoughts, about his sense of cavalry's superiority over irregular troops, and this was to have a decisive bearing on his command in battlefield.

Henry Hawley by Christian Friedrich Zincke. Enamel on copper portrait miniature, verso of bloodstone and diamonds, in original shagreen case. (National Galleries of Scotland)

48   BL.Add.Mss. 35453, f.88r.

# 4

# Return to War, 1739-1745

Britain, after two decades of peace, returned to war in 1739. The initial adversary was Spain, this time over commercial rivalry, before the conflict became part of a wider war fought over several continents (though the scenes of the bulk of the fighting was in Europe). In 1740 Frederick II of Prussia invaded the Austrian dominions and defeated the Austrian army at Mollwitz. George II had previously signed the Pragmatic Sanction to support the heir to the Imperial throne, Maria Theresa, daughter of the Emperor Charles VI, after the latter's death. Yet the French backed the rival claim of Elector Charles Albert of Bavaria on the grounds that only a male heir could inherit. This war was to be known as the War of Austrian Succession. Initially France and Britain fought as auxiliaries on the side of Charles Albert and Maria Theresa, respectively.

The first intimation that Hawley might be involved took place in 1741 when George II appointed him as a staff officer. The Lords Justices ordered him to have his regiment prepared for foreign service, serving under Wade, now a lieutenant general. There was a long delay in embarkation, so he stayed at home for most of the summer. One night he was awoken by a King's Messenger with a letter from the Lords Justices to offer him the command of the expedition to Spanish held Cartagena in the West Indies.[1]

As the Duke of Richmond wrote to Hawley on 18 August, 'your name was pick'd upon as the most proper person' and Richmond was asked 'if it would be agreeable to you'.[2] On 21 June 1741, Richmond had suggested to Newcastle that following the disagreements between Vice Admiral Edward Vernon (1684-1757) and Major General Thomas Wentworth (c.1693-1747) at Cartagena, that the latter should be replaced '& some good officer sent in his place', suggesting Ligonier or Hawley,

---

1    RA, HT, 7411-24-101, p.15.
2    RA, HT, 7411-24-112, p.11.

for both were 'fitt for command'.[3] Hawley was clearly unenthusiastic, as a letter from Richmond on 20 August reveals, 'your modesty was greatly commended & the refusal allowed to be an exceeding handsome one'.[4] Richmond persisted in trying to persuade Hawley; they met and discussed the matter at some length at the latter's seat at Goodwood on 23 August 1741 and he reported this to Newcastle:

> he speaks just in the same handsome manner he writ, that he has no notion of hesitating a moment where he shall go if it is for the King's service, butt he still insists upon it that it is not for the King's service to send him upon this great command for the reasons he mentions in his letter to me which your Grace saw. That he owns (butt that is only in his private conversations with me) that he should dislike it extreamly, firstly from the great uncertainty of getting any honour, & the great danger of losing it by ill success which may not be his fault, secondly the difficulty there may be in Agreeing with Mr Vernon, & the impossibility of doing anything right in concert with Mr Wentworth.[5]

Hawley suggested that Lieutenant General Jasper Clayton, lieutenant governor of Gibraltar, Lieutenant General William Hargrave, and Lieutenant General Robert Dalzell (1662-1758) were better possibilities than him; the last being the least worst. Hawley was concerned that his turning down the appointment 'may not hurt him with the King, or in any bodys opinion'. Richmond assured Hawley that this would not be the case and that there was no problem with the Lords Justices accepting Hawley's declining it and that the King would not be unhappy either. They also discussed whether Major General James St. Clair should be given the post, but Hawley thought that he should not be because he had never held a high command.

According to Hawley's own memoir, the main issues were that despite his long service, 'he had never seen a siege nor ever been in a place besieged and though he was of the rank of Major Genll he never commanded above 500 Foot'. Despite being 'pressed very hard by them to take the command, he still persisted'. His private reasons were that Vernon would be in charge but that he as commander of the troops would bear the responsibility for any failure; that most of the officers under him had limited experience; that there were no engineers for the expedition; that that he felt Wentworth was inadequate; and that he knew that the first man offered the command had been junior to him. The West Indies expedition turned

---

3   McCann (ed.), *Correspondence*, p.65.
4   RA, HT, 7411-24, 113, 10.
5   McCann (ed.), *Correspondence*, pp.70-71.

out to be a fiasco, the objectives not being seized and many men dying of sickness. Hawley had been fortunate not to be involved in it.[6]

On the domestic front, Hawley was in correspondence with a Cornet Gallatia of his own regiment, about horses. Apparently, Newcastle was looking for a hunter and Hawley had heard that a friend of Gallatia's, one Lister, had an appropriate bay. Hawley recommended that Newcastle's groom be directed to Lister's house.[7]

In March 1742, Hawley's regiment was ordered to be ready for foreign service. Instead of the West Indies, Hawley was destined for Europe. Field Marshal John Dalrymple, the second Earl of Stair, (1673-1747) was in command of the British army on the continent and Hawley was to accompany him.[8] Yet William Yonge, the secretary at war, informed him that his pay as major general would only begin from that time (though he had been appointed to the rank three years previously). He was also told that along with Ligonier and Major General Sir Charles Howard (c.1696-1765) he would have to quit being one of the King's aides. Ligonier had already been on a major general's pay for a year as well as having other posts and Tyrawley likewise and he remained a royal aide. As Hawley was senior to him he was evidently disgruntled. With nothing else to do at court he readied his regiment. Allowed one aide of his own, he designated Captain John Toovey, of his former regiment of dragoons, a clear mark of personal favour.[9]

Hawley's command was the most substantial that he had ever had; two brigadiers under him and two regiments of dragoons (Honywood's and his own), four battalions of infantry (Onslow's, Bligh's, Huske's and Ponsonby's), a train of artillery and the hospital. They needed 38 ships to take them to Ostend and were convoyed by two men of war. Once there, the infantry was ferried to Bruges as were the guns and the hospital, whilst the cavalry marched to Ghent.[10]

Once the troops were all disembarked, they were initially put into garrisons. Artillery from the Dutch Republic and the Empire arrived and there was news that George II was to arrive to lead the troops in person. Yet orders given for marching along the Lys with the right flank at Dixmuide and the left at Courtrai were cancelled as the King was not to come after all. Stair called a council of war to propose an attack on the French at Dunkirk. This was unanimously rejected as being impracticable and steps were taken to put the troops into winter quarters, with the British in Flanders and the Hessians and Hanoverians in Brabant.[11] There were, on paper, 16,335 British, 16,000 Hanoverians and 6,000 Hessian troops, the

---

6   RA, HT, 7411-24-101, pp.15-16.
7   BL. Add. Mss. 32698, f.425r.
8   *London Gazette*, 8112, 24 April 1742.
9   Dalton, *Army of George I*, Vol.I, p.43; RA, HT, 7411-24-128, 33.
10  RA, HT, 7411-24-101, p.16.
11  RA, HT, 7411-24-101, p.16.

latter two contingents being paid for by Britain. Hawley was with them and at Ghent on 16 September 1742 he complained bitterly about the state of affairs there, 'If I could describe the way wee are in you would not believe it. The truthe will be known some day'. There was a lack of supplies and the troops were reduced to eating rye bread only. Of the British troops, only 8,810 were in a fit state to fight, and 4,612 were sick.[12]

Yet as late as 10 November, a message came through for the whole army to march towards Frankfurt. The order of battle was settled, with the British forces on the right. Hawley was to command the second line of the British cavalry, with Lieutenant General James Campbell in over all charge of the British cavalry. Stair and the leader of the Hessian contingent, Prince Frederick, made representations against the march at so late a time of the season, especially with poor weather. Clayton came from England and stayed for a month, whilst the camp remained where it was.[13]

It was not until February 1743 that the army began to move, with the Hanoverians in the vanguard, followed by the first division of the British. Hawley marched on the 23 February, in charge of the fifth of nine divisions of the British forces, with his own regiment (376 men) and the infantry of Howard's (591 men) and Handasyde's (565 men). When he reached Aix with these forces, he heard news that a number of British major generals had been promoted. In part these promotions were because there were many Dutch lieutenant generals who had only just been young colonels and George II wanted 'to do them [his officers] justice'. Ligonier was one of those promoted, as was Cope. However, Hawley, 'finding himself left out though equally hurte with the rest by the Dutch promotions, he the next day writ my Lord Stair a letter setting forth his equal pretension and deigned he intercede with His Majesty either to do him justice or recall him'. Hawley told Stair he could not serve as a major general whilst others were promoted and said he would rather serve as a colonel to his own regiment to convince the King of his desire to serve him and obey Stair.[14]

Stair thought that Hawley's case was a good one and he sent a courier to Lord Carteret (1690-1764), Secretary of State, in England. Meanwhile Stair and the Duc d'Aremberg met to plan the campaign, which was to march and cross the Rhine. This was put before the senior officers. Initially Campbell and Hawley were to remain at Aix with 18 squadrons of cavalry until the infantry had made a bridgehead over the Rhine. By the end of the month the infantry was advancing, strategy being in part determined by the needs of supply, with the grenadiers

12   RA, HT, 7411-24-101, p.16.
13   RA, HT, 7411-24-101, p.17.
14   RA, HT, 7411-24-128, 69, 74-75.

at the head, through Andernach and to Mayence. There was another council of war at Aix in early April. A letter had arrived with the King's instructions from Carteret.[15] From Hawley's view point, the letter contained a most important message. Carteret informed Stair that the King 'upon consideration of the major General's case had ordered him to be included in the promotion of Lt Genlls'. This was the highest rank Hawley was to achieve. The only fly in the ointment was that he and the others would only be remunerated as major generals for the remainder of the year and would only be allocated one aide each. His commission arrived a fortnight later, dated 30 March OS. Hawley further complained, 'which did no ways do him justice as to the promotion of the younger officers in the Dutche service made Lt Genlls, over his head, as well as the rest of the English officers of his rank who were older than him'.[16]

Towards the end of April Hawley marched with the army's last division; six squadrons of dragoons, a battalion of infantry, and the artillery. They joined the rest of the army at Höchst on the Maine. Whilst there, Stair had a message from London, that as Marshal Noailles had passed the Rhine and was camped on the other side of the Maine, three leagues away, 'he had positive orders to attaque the army of the Allies'. Stair put four bridges across the Main and marched all the British and Hanoverian infantry, as well as the British horse and all the Hanoverian cavalry. Clayton and Campbell were in charge. A field of battle was chosen.[17] Whilst the allied army awaited the French, Stair had an express from Hanover from the King which forbade him not to cross the Main and that he would join the army on 18 May. So, he marched the army back across the Main. Two days later there was another council of war as to whether they should remain where they were, march to Aschaffenburg or march to Hanau and wait there for the King. The latter option was decided on, which was carried out, before marching to Aschaffenburg up the Main, but food and water were becoming scarce and the men being exhausted. Villages were plundered for bread. The French army appeared on the other side of the river and so the British moved back from the Main to avoid exposure to the French artillery.[18]

There was no respite from the day to day administrative work of a regimental colonel. On 23 June, Hawley wrote to ask permission for Cornet Francis Rainsford to be lieutenant in his regiment as Lieutenant Gaile was now dead. In his place was to be Danby Heartwell, now adjutant, and for Mr Samson Barber to become adjutant.[19]

15   RA, HT, 7411-24-101, p.18.
16   RA, HT, 7411-24-101, p.18; *London Gazette*, 8211, 5 April 1743.
17   RA, HT, 7411-24-101, p.18.
18   RA, HT, 7411-24-101, pp.18-19.
19   TNA, SP41/14, 56.

In the evening of 24 June, the King arrived. On the next day the army's supply situation worsened; leading to additional disorder and plundering. The order of battle was 'in the greatest confusion'. The King called a council of war and it was decided to march back to Hanau to alleviate the supply crisis and link up with the 6,000 Hessians and the eight Hanoverian battalions there. On 26 June the army marched in two columns, with Hawley's regiment at the fore. They learnt that the French had put two bridges over the Main at Seligenstadt and marched five battalions and eight squadrons over them.[20]

On the morning of 27 June, the army marched at daybreak, expecting to be attacked in the rear. Cope and Hawley were to lead the second line of British cavalry; Hawley leading the cavalry on the left, closest to the Main. It should have been a French victory as the allies were trapped between the Spessart Hills and the river Maine, but the Duc de Grammont made the mistake of moving his portion of the army across the bridge at Dettingen with the swamp behind them. The allied forces formed from column to line, with the cavalry covering the infantry. The elite French Maison du Roi cavalry attacked and were met by Bland's Dragoons and both suffered heavy losses. Clayton had the Blues and Honywood's and Ligonier's Regiments of Horse enter the fray, with the result that both sides retired. Hawley's cavalry attacked the French Mousquetaires Noires and stopped their advance. Elsewhere, the British infantry were able to prove their superiority in firepower and inflict twice the number of casualties that they suffered in return. It was therefore an unexpected allied triumph, though the cavalry did not pursue the fleeing French to turn the victory into an even greater one. However, it gave George II considerable glory. A sergeant of Hawley's Dragoons won fame by capturing a French standard.[21] Hawley's role in the Battle of Dettingen is unknown and he does not refer to any personal action in it in his memoir.

The army carried on its march to Hanau, where they remained throughout July. There were celebrations for the victory on 6 July. George II wanted to revive an ancient order of knighthood and to knight a dozen of his officers, 'of whiche number the Lt Genll was to have been one'. Yet most turned this honour down, believing knighthoods were commonplace. Yet some appointments were made to the Order of the Bath. Apparently Hawley 'might have been one of them but the expense was to be £800; he not having so muche to throw away, he declared he could not afford it'.[22] Soon after he was 'violently ill of a flux and vomiting which brought him near deathe'. Within 12 hours his feet and lower legs were 'dead

20  RA, HT, 7411-24-101, p.19.
21  *London Gazette*, 8240, 12 July 1743; 8237 2-5 July 1743; Michael Orr, *Dettingen* (London: C. Knight, 1972), pp.58-61, 66.
22  RA, HT, 7411-24-101, p.20.

and cold and he had strong convulsions'. Yet with repeated doses of laudanum, he recovered.[23]

The battle had been inconclusive; the French army had not been destroyed and there had been no strategic result. Later in that year's campaign, Hawley was posted to the army's first division, composed of his own, Bland's, and Campbell's Dragoons and Sempill's Highlanders, as they made their way to winter quarters in Brabant and Flanders, reaching Schwalbach on 24 October and halting at Dueren on 4 November.[24] Hawley wrote 'Nothing more was done that campagne'. By November they were in winter quarters in Flanders, where Hawley remained and commanded in Ghent with Campbell.[25]

It was likely in this campaign that Hawley first made another important contact to add to those who he already enjoyed. This time it would be a fellow soldier. In 1743 William Augustus, Duke of Cumberland (1721-1765), the King's third and youngest son took part in the campaign as a major general. Cumberland had been initially placed in the Royal Navy but had adopted soldiering as a career. He had acquitted himself well on the battlefield of Dettingen, though had been wounded, and his service had been noted and admired by contemporaries. His support over the years was to be of immense value to Hawley. He and Hawley were decades apart in age but had similar interests; women, horses, and gambling as well as a desire to professionalise the army.

Wade, now a field marshal, was appointed to command the army in 1744. Hawley wrote to him imploring leave of a fortnight to return to England to transact some business, asking that the King temporarily appoint another in his stead. This was because he 'not being able to bear the expense nor to live upon the same foot with others on an inferior ranke' as he had no additional income besides his pay. Yet the King refused him leave and said nothing about his second complaint.[26]

On 1 May the army took to the field and camped by Brussels. In July, Hawley sent a memorandum to Wade complaining about his lack of additional income. He wanted to sell his commission as a colonel, setting down 'the hardship I lye under', having his father and two brothers being killed in war and then his sister risking the loss the pension allocated to her mother. Hawley gave her the £200 he received as an aide to the King, but this was lost when he went abroad on active service, and so he had to find her money from his own resources, 'The little I had saved which was about five hundred pounds is all gone'. He was loath to be in debt as he was not

---

23  RA, HT, 7411-24-101, p.20.
24  *London Gazette*, 8269, 22-25 Oct. 1743; 8271, 29 Oct- 1 Nov. 1743.
25  RA, HT, 7411-24-101, p.20.
26  RA, HT, 7411-24-101, p.20.

William Augustus, Duke of Cumberland. (From Evan Charteris' *William Augustus, Duke of Cumberland: His Early Life and Times, 1721-1748*)

rich, and unlike fourteen officers junior to him he had no other employments. To sell his colonelcy was crucial to save 'a sister from starving'.[27]

Wade recommended his petition, which was sent to Carteret. The latter laid it before the King, who declared he 'had a very good opinion of his service but that he did not approve of his proposal aboute the troope'. Yet all the King could offer was to have Carteret make assurances, thus, 'that gentlemen may however be assured that the King is very well pleased with his services, and in a gracious Disposition towards him'.[28] So Hawley had to serve throughout 'an idle inactive campagne'. At its anti-climactic conclusion, he remained a third winter in Ghent, when all the other senior officer except for him and Ligonier, went home.[29]

In Ligonier's absence, Hawley was in temporary command, but had the task of routine military administration to deal with. He corresponded with his superior when necessary and this is the only evidence of his activity at this time. On 15 November he told Ligonier that he had received his letter and was making the Welsh Fusiliers ready for service. He passed on the intelligence he had learnt

27  TNA, SP87/14, f.251r.
28  TNA, SP87/14, f.252r.
29  RA, HT, 7411-24-101, p.20.

about the enemy; the French had broken up their camp and were wintering 27,000 men in and near Dunkirk. He also thought that there was no winter campaign being planned by the French.³⁰ In January he passed on concerns that the French might be targeting Ostend or Bruges, but that both he and a British engineer there discounted this possibility.³¹

In January 1745, Ligonier was ordered to the Hague to meet Philip Dormer, fourth Earl of Chesterfield (1694-1773), and so command was temporarily Hawley's. In February he corresponded with Lord Harrington, one of the principal Secretaries of State, who had replaced Carteret at the end of the previous year. On 6 February he reported that in Ligonier's absence, he was 'directed to acquaint your lordship from time to time with any thinge that may occur in these parts during his absence'. He reported French troop movements, such as the marches of the French Household Cavalry, the French gathering ladders, and elsewhere, herds of cattle for feeding the army, and the uncertainty of where the Marshal de Saxe was intending to campaign. Hawley was concerned that 'your lordship will thinke this too trifling to trouble you with'.³²

Of more concern was that recruits were being taken from Scotland to France to serve in the French army's Régiment Royal Ecossois. Apparently 101 arrived at Dunkirk, and that there were another 150 new recruits who had deserted from the British Army, 'most of them Scotche'. This Hawley had learnt from a deserter. At least the prospective French attack on St. Guilian had been countermanded due to the frost. Meanwhile two Dutch battalions marched to Mons and two more went from there to reinforce those at Tournai.³³ There was very little to report a week later, though it was now known that de Saxe's French army was at Lille and the French were repairing their artillery transport, as were the British. There was a rumour that Philip V of Spain was dead and that desertions in the French army were more than usual.³⁴

In April, Cumberland was made Captain General of the British Army in Europe. He came to Brussels with Ligonier and the garrisons were to march out and rendezvous at Anderlecht. Campbell and Hawley were the first to march with the garrison of Ghent. Hawley also brought up the troops at Bruges and when Cumberland saw both garrisons march into camp he 'was pleased to thank him [Hawley] publicly for the good order he found them in'.³⁵

30  TNA, SP87/15, f.220r.
31  TNA, SP87/16, f.30r.
32  TNA, SP87/16, f.53r.
33  TNA, SP87/16, f.53r.
34  TNA, SP87/16, f.59r.
35  RA, HT, 7411-24-101, pp.19-20.

Some of Hawley's dark reputation originates from this period. Much of it comes from the pen of Horace Walpole (1717-1797), of Arlington Street, London. Son of Sir Robert, chief minister from 1721-1742, Walpole was well travelled, cultured, and intellectual: the anti-thesis of Hawley. He was also a great correspondent and one of his principals was Sir Horace Mann, a British diplomat of Florence. Over the decades Walpole passed on a great deal of gossip to Mann about figures in British society and his writings have been in print for almost two centuries. They have provided a plentiful crop of material for historians ever since, but their accuracy is uncertain.

On the eve of a major battle, on 17 January 1746, Walpole wrote to Mann about Hawley, the second time only that he was to be mentioned in his correspondence, and the first of his reminiscences is invariably quoted by historians writing about the Jacobite campaign of 1745-1746, though these refer to incidents prior to that when Hawley was serving on the Continent. The first was thus:

> He is called Lord Chief Justice; frequent and sudden executions are his passion. Last winter [December 1744?] he had intelligence of a spy come from the French army: the first notice our army had of his arrival, was by seeing him dangle on a gallows in his muff and boots. One of the surgeons of the army begged the body of a soldier who was hanged for desertion, to dissect, "Well", said Hawley, "but then you shall give me the skeleton to hang up in the guard-room".[36]

This may be a reference to the fact that in April 1745 Hawley presided over a court martial at Ghent in which five men were tried as being spies for the French; they were found guilty and duly executed.[37] This was conventional military practice, but whether Hawley asked for a skeleton of one of the offenders is uncorroborated.

Another anecdote referred to earlier in 1744:

> when he arrived at Ghent, the magistrates, according to custom, sent a gentleman, with the offer of a sum of money to engage his favour. He told the gentleman, in great wrath, that the King his master paid him, and that he should go tell the magistrates so; at the same time dragging him to the head of the stairs and kicking him down. He then went to the town-hall; on their refusing him entrance, he burst open the door with his foot, and seated himself abruptly: told them that he had been

---

36  W.S. Lewis (ed.), *Correspondence of Horace Walpole* (New Haven: Yale University Press, 1944), Vol.19, p.201.
37  Lewis (ed.), *Walpole*, Vol.19, p.201.

affronted, was persuaded they had no hand in it, and demanded to have the gentleman given up to him, who never dared to appear in the town while he stayed in it.³⁸

This story surely rebounds in part to Hawley's credit. He had clearly been offered a bribe in order to show his favour to the Ghent corporation. Rightly, but perhaps eccentrically in an age where corruption was the norm, he indignantly refused. The elder William Pitt (1708-1778) at this time also gained a reputation for incorruptibility by refusing to feather his nest whilst Paymaster General to the Forces, a post where significant wealth could be made by its holder. Hawley acted honourably and honestly, though his temper was aroused, too and his behaviour was seen by Walpole as lacking all manners.

Walpole's third anecdote is also not entirely unfavourable to Hawley, though was meant as anything but. He related:

> When the Prince of Hesse, our son in law [married to Princess Mary, daughter of George II], arrived at Brussels, and found Hawley did not wait on him, the Prince sent to know if he expected the first visit? – he replied, "He always expected that inferior officers should wait on their commanders; and not only that, but he gave his Highness but half an hour to consider of it".³⁹

As to Walpole's furore over etiquette, by this time, Hawley was a lieutenant general and the Prince was not of this exalted military rank. Hawley clearly had no time for the social niceties of polite society that venerated royalty of whichever country and whatever its magnitude. He saw this in purely military matters.

However, Walpole was not necessarily accurate; his anecdotes are, after all, uncorroborated.

In more detail, there were three major court martials which Hawley was involved with at this time, when Ligonier was absent, which cast a more substantiated light on his approach to discipline. The first concerned Private Thomas Squire of Howard's Regiment, who had become drunk, quarrelled with Sergeant Sheppard's wife and then struck the said sergeant. Hitting a senior soldier was a capital offence. Squire had had 11 years' good conduct and a petition for mercy was sent to Hawley as acting commander. The man was pardoned.⁴⁰

---

38  Lewis (ed.), *Walpole*, Vol.19, p.202.
39  Lewis (ed.), *Walpole*, Vol.19, p.202.
40  RA, HT, 7411-24-128, 233.

The second was in Ghent on 2 February 1745 by Hawley's orders, with Lieutenant Colonel Robert Rich of Barrell's Regiment presiding. Five privates from Howard's Regiment; Thomas Anderson, Edward Fletcher, Henry Fox, Daniel Hyndman and John Offerton were accused of 'getting drunk, stripping a woman in the Barracks, giving insolent language and striking sergeant Manton of the said regiment, drawing their swords and resisting the Guard, when ordered prisoners, and for taking their arms and Declaring they would kill either sergeant, corporal or private man who would offer to enter their room'. These were serious charges indeed, and witnesses were brought forward to give their evidence against them. However, their company commander, Captain Lake, stressed the men's previous good behaviour. The verdict was that Fox, Hyndman and Offerton were sentenced to 600 lashes each and Fletcher and Anderson were acquitted.[41]

The third took place in the next month. One Edward Maguire had been arrested by the provosts and, on Hawley's orders, statements were taken against him before the Judge Advocate by British soldiers from Bragg's Regiment who had deserted to the French but who had returned to their own ranks. Maguire had been seen among the French army at St. Omer in the uniform of an officer of Lord John Drummond's Royal Ecossois. Private Joseph Broomhead claimed, 'he heard it said and he believes that the prisoner Maguire was one of those persons, who are sent out to pick up men in the English garrisons, and to persuade them to desert to the said regiment'. James Evans saw and heard French officers in a hostelry say 'Here is Maguire, come back again, with some more Recruits'.[42] These statements were read out in court on 11 March before Hawley and 12 other officers. Apparently, 'The question put by Lieutenant General Hawley to the following officers present, whether the prisoner Edward Maguire in their opinion was a spy and seducer of our men, yes or no?' The verdict was unanimous against Maguire. Therefore, Hawley wrote 'According to the laws and customs of war, I order the provost to hang the prisoner Edward Maguire at the usual place of execution on the Kauter'.[43] Hawley was not unduly harsh and in any case, other senior officers did not veer on the side of leniency, with Ligonier writing on 2 February 1745, 'I am pretty much determin'd in my mind never to pardon a deserter, their crime is generally a complication of treason, perjury and Robery…I never was president in my days that I did not speak it in that light'.[44]

In the meantime, Hawley and Lord Harrington were in discussion on various military matters. Hawley was taking steps to deal with agents recruiting Scottish

---

41   RA, HT, 7411-24-108, 21.
42   RA, HT, 7411-24-128, 234-236.
43   RA, HT, 7411-24-128, 234-236.
44   RA, HT, 7411-24-108, 7.

soldiers for service in the French army, and Harrington approved, telling him to keep Lord Tweeddale, Secretary of State for Scotland, informed. Hawley inquired about how he should deal with deserters, and of all people, coiners. His other worry was that there might be a coup de main against Nieuwpoort, but Harrington could only state that he trusted that Hawley would co-operate with the Dutch and Austrians to prevent this.[45] Yonge, the secretary at war, told Hawley that he would check with the Attorney General as to the clippers of ducats but that he should detain the men in the meantime. The issue was finally resolved on 29 March when Yonge told him that they could be punished under the 46th article of war but that the King would sign a new articles ar to be inserted to cover the offence in future. Hawley suspected an unnamed person in England as being behind these offences.[46]

The army was camped at Anderlecht by 29 April and on 3 May went to Hal. It was about to fight the French in what would be the Battle of Fontenoy. As ever, Hawley had the command of the second line of cavalry on the right wing. In early May the allied army marched to relief of the fortress of Tournai, held by 7,000 Dutch infantry, under threat from de Saxe's superior French forces. On 10 May Campbell took 12 squadrons of cavalry and all the grenadiers to take up posts at the village of Vezon.[47] On 11 May the army woke at daybreak and reached Vezon at 5:30 a.m. They began to be bombarded by the French guns. At 6.30 a.m. Campbell brought up his cavalry, forming up beyond the village to the left in open ground behind the infantry. They were then fired upon by a concealed battery from the Bois de Barry. Campbell was hit and removed from the field; possibly as with Hawley and Evans at Sheriffmuir in 1715, he was singled out by having a different colour horse (grey) to Hawley's regiment (black) to which he was nearest.[48]

With this casualty, Hawley became commander of the entire right wing, made up of 47 squadrons and three battalions of infantry, the latter being on the right of the former to cover them. They formed two lines beyond the village, but were under bombardment from the French guns. Attacks by Brigadier Ingoldsby and the Dutch on the French held points were ineffectual. Elsewhere, though, the French infantry, including the Guards, were pushed back by superior British infantry volley fire, 'everything seemed to give way on their fire'. However, Hawley noticed that the Dutch cavalry fled and positioned his British and Hanoverian cavalry to the right of where the British infantry had advanced upon, 'expecting, as it soon happened, that our Foot would not hold it long and must come back'.[49]

45   TNA, SP87/16, f.70r.
46   TNA, WO4/40, pp.242, 272.
47   RA, HT, 7411-24-101, p.20.
48   RA, HT, 7411-24-101, p.20.
49   RA, HT, 7411-24-101, pp.21-22.

The cavalry could do very little because the infantry was ahead of them and took up all the space between the woods on the right and left.

Sure enough, numbers told and Cumberland, who had been leading the infantry assault, rode over to Hawley and told him that Ligonier was to order the retreat 'for they could do no more and the Dutch were gone'. He said, 'Surely the enemy are going to eat us'. As the infantry fell back, Hawley told his commander, 'Sir, you see I have secured theyr flank for theyr retreat but I must go and make the retreat after the Foot with the first line of Horse'. The French did not pursue, except that the artillery continued to fire at long range, and Hawley began to retreat with the cavalry on the flank of the infantry. When he came to the churchyard of Vezon, held by two battalions of infantry, he added two of those battalions he had had to secure the cavalry's flank.[50]

The retreat was proceeding well, but given that Hawley had transferred two of his flanking battalions form the wood, the French were able to take the position and began to pour fire on the flank and rear of the British cavalry. Hawley was shot in the thigh and suffered a contusion. His cavalry, on receiving such a fire began to trot in order to push through the hedges and to safety. They could not be stopped and Hawley was driven through a thick hedge and into a hollow way. Arriving by that way to the churchyard, he found Cumberland and told him what had happened. Cumberland told Hawley to ride through the village and try to stop the near rout of the cavalry by getting to the rising open ground there. Hawley was able to do so and had the cavalry form up in case of a French pursuit. Cumberland joined him until most of the wounded could be taken away by waggons. That night Hawley commanded the rear guard with 13 squadrons as they marched towards Ath.[51]

This was a significant, though costly, victory for the French, as they now could proceed with the siege of Tournai as their enemies were in retreat, and indeed with no further hope of relief the garrison capitulated soon afterwards.

Two days later, Campbell died and Cumberland recommended Hawley to the King for the now-vacant governorship of Edinburgh Castle, which was a useful sinecure. However, Hawley was passed over and it went to Lord Mark Kerr, lower in seniority to Hawley. He had to be content to lead the right wing of the cavalry for the remainder of the campaign. By degrees the army had to retire behind the canal at Brussels to secure that city and Brabant as the French mopped up further towns, cities, and fortresses, ending the campaign masters of the Austrian Netherlands. Hawley noted 'the rest of the campagne was but idle'.[52]

---

50   RA, HT, 7411-24-101, p.22.
51   RA, HT, 7411-24-101, p.22.
52   RA, HT, 7411-24-101, p.22.

In the summer of 1745, following the setbacks in the campaign after Fontenoy, there were major developments that would lead to the transfer of the majority of the British troops currently on the Continent, back to Britain. These included Cumberland and eventually Hawley. Yet initially the danger was not seen as being of particular importance.

Since 1719 there had not been any serious attempt by the Jacobite cause to regain the British throne. It was true that there was a French invasion scheme of February 1744 in which Charles Edward Stuart (1720-1788), eldest son of James Francis Stuart, was to have sailed. Storms in the English Channel led to the invasion attempt being postponed indefinitely, but Charles was undeterred. Resident in Paris for the next year and more, he worked to make another attempt to restore his father to this thrones that he never had had.

Taking two ships, arms, money, and volunteers from the French army, Charles made the voyage to Scotland in July. Yet en route one of his vessels was involved in a firefight with a Royal Navy ship and was forced to turn back. On 23 July Charles arrived at Eriskay and was on the mainland of Scotland two days later. Initial responses in Scotland to his arrival were unenthusiastic, but rumours of his arrival were to cause concern in Edinburgh and London.

News on the Continent of this danger was first articulated by Cumberland on 31 July, writing that 'I am extremely sorry to find that the King has certain & infallible intelligence that the Court of France has actually form'd a resolution to attempt an invasion of His Majesty's British Dominions'. Yet he did not believe it, adding 'But there seems to me to be great reason to doubt whether that is the real intention of France, because by what we can perceive, & the little intelligence we have, the French seem to be rather filing their troops towards the Rhine than making a detachment for Dunkirk'. However, 'his Majesty may be assured that the first consideration with me here will be the defence of England…in case the design should prove to be real, those two Battallions as well as the two others who were there before, may be immediately sent back upon the first occasion'.[53]

Additional fears resurfaced on 30 August, Cumberland writing that he was 'surprised to see this Romantick Expedition revived again, & that it has taken place so far as the landing any Troops in Great Britain. But I don't doubt but Sir Jn Cope will be able to put a stop immediately to this affair'.[54] By now there was definite news that Charles had arrived in Scotland and was busily raising the Highlands to retake the throne. Cope was commander in Scotland and was drawing together his forces at Stirling to confront what was then but a small insurrection.

---

53   RA, CP3/309.
54   RA, CP4/201.

In September, at Newcastle's insistence, Cumberland had ten battalions of infantry under Ligonier's command readied to return to England. As he wrote, 'I assure you that if England wants them I am intirely of opinion that this country & even the whole alliance ought not to be considered comparatively with our own Country, but the Detaching from hence at so critical a juncture may be so fatall that I have sent to the King for immediate orders'.[55] Meanwhile, the situation in Scotland had altered. Cope had been unable to bring the Jacobites to battle on favourable terms and had had to march northwards. The Jacobite army marched towards the Lowlands and menace Edinburgh. Yet Cumberland was unperturbed, writing on 20 September, 'I am rather rejoyced than frightened at the Pretenders Son being got between Sir John Cope and Edinburgh since I see no retreat left them, & I hope that Great Britain is not to be conquered by three thousand rable gather'd together in the Mountains but should they dare to advance I will answer man for man for the ten Battalions Sir John Ligonier will bring you'.[56]

He later wrote:

> Sir Jn Ligonier since with the ten Battallions under his Command will be embark'd as today at Williamstadt, so that in all likelyhood before this Letter arrives, they will be in the mouth of the River...
>
> I don't know whether his Majesty may not think it necessary for recruiting the three last Battallions which came over, to give them two additional Companys as the other Battalions in Flanders have & should the King think fit, I hope his Majesty will have the goodness to think of the Captain Lieut of those three battalions who are here in service.[57]

Disaster befell the King's troops: on 21 September, Cope was routed at Prestonpans; almost all his infantry being killed or captured; only a handful of them escaping along with the bulk of the cavalry. Scotland was lost to the Jacobite cause except for a few isolated garrisons which were unable to threaten them. The Jacobite army increased in strength from under 3,000 men to double that. They received guns, supplies, gunners, and diplomatic accreditation from France. By the end of October, they were able to threaten to march into England. More and more British troops, including Cumberland, arrived in England. The danger was seen not just as being from Scotland but from France, too, and the latter was seen as the worse of the two.

---

55   BL. Add. Mss, 32705, f.113r.
56   BL. Add.Mss., 32705, f.155.
57   RA, CP5/151.

There was but one more task for Hawley in the campaign abroad in early October. Cumberland wrote to Lord Harrington:

> The effect of the little skirmish I mentioned in my last between the Hussars & the French, was such that Count d'Estrees left his camp with precipitation that night, & has given us an opportunity of retiring the English out of Mons, which has so well succeeded, that they arrive as this day into Camp. Genl Halley's Corps has been since reinforced by four Austrian Battalions, & four Companys of Grenadiers, & the Highlanders & he has had orders to march towards Mons with his whole Corps in order to throw his infantry into that place, & St. Guillain, should the Enemy attempt anything against it or else to harass & incommode them during the siege of Ath, which I fear has held out as ill as all the places have done in this Country. I having intelligence that it is already given up, tho I cannot affirm it.[58]

The allied garrison in Mons had been endangered by French troops at Arguennes with 28 squadrons and 1,800 infantry. Hawley was selected to lead the force to do so. He was given 30 squadrons and 100 hussars, five battalions of infantry, and 600 grenadiers and marched to Hal. The garrison had orders to either join Hawley half way at Soignes or to march another way to Brussels. They chose the latter.[59] Hawley sent 200 dragoons and 100 grenadiers to reconnoitre from Hal towards Arguennes. They met with 400 French cavalry and infantry coming towards Hal on the same errand. In the fighting the French were defeated and lost their entire force except for 20 men, with 63 prisoners and the colonel dead. Next day the French, under d'Estrées, retired to Lessines. The garrison had been saved, and then Hawley was ordered to try and relieve the siege of Ath if at all possible, or failing that, to distress the French supply lines. Hawley marched to Soignes and then to Mons but once there found that Ath had already fallen. As ordered, he left four Austrian battalions in Mons and returned to the main camp. By a forced march through the night it took him but one day.[60]

Writing on 11 October, Cumberland expressed his pleasure that the job had been well done:

> General Hawley is returned as far as Genap in his way hither, with his whole detachment except four Austrian Battallions which he has thrown

---

58  RA, CP5/200.
59  RA, HT, 7411-24-101, pp.22-23.
60  RA, HT, 7411-24-101, p.23.

into Mons. By their motions the Enemy have made since the surrender of Ath, it looks as they had some design on Mons or St. Guilaim, tho I cannot imagine they will attempt either at this season of the year, if the town is well provided & strongly garrisoned, tho I fear St. Guillain is not in so good order.[61]

Once the French began to go into winter quarters, Hawley was ordered to return to Antwerp, to stay there that winter along with 18 British battalions and 12 squadrons there and another six at Liege. However, the progress of the Jacobite army in Britain led to all the infantry being sent back to Britain, along with three regiments of dragoons, including his own, and one of horse. Once they were gone, his command was reduced to 12 squadrons of British cavalry at Antwerp and six battalions of Hessians and a further six British squadrons, these to be based at Liege.[62]

In November, Hawley was in Antwerp and was dealing with the issues of his officers. Cornet Creighton had tried to desert whilst on parole and his fellow officers refused to serve with him. Hawley referred to Creighton as 'a scoundrel and a declared coward'. The solution was that Creighton should sell his commission to another and Hawley desired that Richard Shedd, his eldest second cornet, purchase it. According to Hawley, Shedd was 'as gallant a man and as good ane officer as anyone else in the army'. However, there was no obvious candidate to replace Shedd as second cornet. Another problem was that Captain Godfrey had been seconded to Richmond as an aide and so there was a vacancy created for a brigade major. As commander in chief, Cumberland was asked about these issues.[63]

The campaign was another pressing issue. Hawley wrote, 'I thank God and the Duke I am only a subaltern here' and believed that the town of Antwerp was 'not tenable 12 hours'. The citadel might hold out for four days, but that was all. He was despondent in the event of a French attack, 'I believe we shall be the last devoured'. He also had a large amount of camp equipment but had no idea as to what to do with it and was very uncertain about the immediate future, 'wither we go or stay the state of incertitude is anxious to all'.[64] However, Hawley would not be in Flanders for much longer and was, unknowingly, about to be thrust into the limelight.

61   RA, CP5/242.
62   RA, HT, 7411-24-101, p.23.
63   RA, CP7/24, 35.
64   RA, CP7/24, 35.

5

# The Jacobite Campaign: the First Phase, 1745-1746

Hawley was one of the last of the British soldiers to be recalled to England during the Jacobite campaign of 1745. His absence had been sorely missed by Lieutenant Septimus Robinson, an aide to the 72-year-old Field Marshal Wade who was in command of a sizeable army at Newcastle. By late November, the strategic position in Britain had altered since the great Jacobite victory at Prestonpans on 21 September. The Jacobite army, nearly 6,000 strong, advanced south from Edinburgh and crossed into England on 8 November, taking Carlisle a week later. It then progressed southwards towards Lancashire after Wade's attempt to intercept it at Carlisle had failed with the army marching too late from Newcastle and then being forced to stop and retire at Hexham due to bad weather, poor supplies, and the news that the Jacobite Army had already left Carlisle. Robinson wrote thus in a letter to Colonel Joseph Yorke on 24 November, 'I began now to think that Hawley would be invaluable in our army'.[1]

A second field army was being formed in the Midlands, initially to be led by Ligonier but ill health led to his replacement by Cumberland. By 24 November, there was the possibility that Hawley would join the army under Cumberland at Lichfield. The Duke of Richmond, as a lieutenant general of cavalry, who was with them, was pleased, writing of his fellow huntsman, 'For Gods sake don't thinke of sending Hawley from us, indeed he is equal to any body, & will speake his mind'.[2] Both Robinson and Richmond had a high opinion of Hawley as a soldier and looked forward to his presence among the high counsels of the army.

On 5 December, NS, Hawley received an order from Cumberland, 'come away with all haste and take control of the 17 regiments ordered here', as Ligonier was too unwell to do so. On 9 December he took a boat from Antwerp to Helvoetsluys

---

1    Philip C. Yorke (ed.), *The Life and Correspondence of Lord Chancellor Hardwicke* (Cambridge: Cambridge University Press, 1913), Vol.I, p.468.
2    McCann (ed.), *Correspondence*, p.188.

and then to London. On the next day he had an audience with the King, who told him to join Cumberland at Stone, and left that afternoon.³

On the same day, 29 November OS, Hawley met Newcastle in London and on the next day travelled towards Lichfield. Newcastle sent a letter with him for Cumberland, showing the degree of trust imposed on Hawley.⁴ By now the Jacobites were at Manchester. Cumberland hoped to intercept the Jacobite army as it marched through the Midlands and defeat it in battle. However, Lord George Murray (1694-1760), one of the Jacobite lieutenant generals, led a feint towards Stone on 3 December, whilst the main force advanced towards Derby where it arrived on 4 December. This put them in marching distance of London, but the Jacobite officers, lacking evidence of support from France or England, advocated retreat though Charles was adamant for an advance on the capital. The former won and on 6 December the army fell back on Scotland. Cumberland was not apprised of this immediately, but by 8 December had a flying column of infantry and cavalry pursue them.

It is not known when Hawley joined the army, but presumably by 1-2 December. There is no note of his words or deeds for the first week of joining them. Yet Hawley and Bland with the 1,000 infantry on horseback met Richmond with his cavalry at Birmingham on 8 December.⁵ However, they were unable to intercept the Jacobites because the latter had a head start and because the British force was slowed down by the concerns of the government in London about a possible French invasion on the south coast, thus necessitating that they halt in case they had to march south. Despite a skirmish at Clifton in Cumberland on 18 December, the Jacobite army was able to retreat almost intact to Scotland, leaving a garrison in Carlisle.

Of the two main British field armies, Cumberland had the smaller of the two, given that much of his command had been diverted to southern England. At Newcastle was Wade's army. Yet the elderly Wade was unwell and his command had been undynamic to say the least. Wade and others made several references to his age and ill health in November 1745 and he eventually told Newcastle, 'I hope His Majesty will please to appoint a General more active and capable than myself in undergoing so great a fatigue both of body and mind, which my age and constitution cannot support'.⁶ Newcastle wrote on 15 December, 'Marshal Wade himself declined going to Scotland, on account of his age and for other Reasons. I really think upon the whole, a very honest, and a very able man, and I do not know where we shall be able to replace him'.⁷

---

3   RA, HT, 7411-24-109, p.23.
4   McCann (ed.), *Correspondence*, p.191.
5   TNA, SP36/76, f286r-288r.
6   TNA, SP36/76, f.167r.
7   Chatsworth House Mss, 182.34.

However, Cumberland had lost confidence in the old man, writing to Newcastle on 4 December, 'experience everyday shows us his insufficiency and it is of infinite consequence that someone more able is sent there'.[8] Another senior general was needed in his stead. There had been three lieutenant generals in Wade's command; his deputy had been Lord Tyrawley; the others were Roger Handasyde, in command of the troops in Edinburgh, and Thomas Wentworth. All three, however, were younger than Hawley and more importantly had commissions dating back to only the 1700s. Handasyde was unwell, writing on 10 January, 'By violent colds the Gout has seized me in my stomach'. Tyrawley was despatched to London and Wentworth was put in charge of the garrisons in the north of England.[9]

Hawley had several recommendations. First, he was the longest-serving army officer who was fit and well, for the older Ligonier was in poor health. Secondly, he had served against the Jacobites in 1715, unlike any other senior officer. Cumberland had a high opinion of his service on the Continent, where, as noted, he had done well in the autumn. Finally, he was well known to both Newcastle and Pelham as the state's senior politicians (Secretary of State and First Lord of the Treasury, respectively) and he may also have been in good stead with the King who knew him personally from the Dettingen campaign. Hawley seemed, therefore, the logical choice to replace Wade, and, in Cumberland's absence, to become commander in Scotland. The only fly in the ointment was, as Hawley had noted in 1741 when turning down the Cartagena assignment, that he had never commanded an army in battle, though since 1741 he had had a larger command than he had up to that year.

On 20 December, Newcastle wrote an important letter to Hawley, 'I have the pleasure to acquaint you that His Majesty has been pleased to give you the command of the army, which is to be sent to Scotland'. He added, 'I must heartily congratulate you upon this great mark of His Majesty's Favour and approbation which your Abilities and Zeal for the King's service have procured you'. More prosaically he told Hawley that Cumberland and Wade would arrange which troops he would have under his command, and that Huske, his fellow huntsman and now a major general, would be his second in command due to 'his long experience and particular knowledge of Scotland'.[10] Newcastle thought that this applied to Hawley, too, 'they having both been in that country and they perfectly informed of the situation of it'.[11]

His actual orders read as follows:

---

8    BL. Add.Mss. 32705, f.403r.
9    TNA, SP36/80, f.221r.
10   TNA, SP36/77, f331r-332v.
11   TNA, SP36/77, f.350v.

you are to employ the said forces, in such manner, as you shall thinke the most proper for reducing the Rebels, and for putting a speedy end to the rebellion…cause the most exact military discipline to be had and observed amongst our Forces and in an army, to take care that the officers do duly attend their posts…We do promise you our Royal Protection, and that we are indemnify you as to all and every action on acting what you shall do in persecution of this trust we repose in you.[12]

Hawley received the letter three days later. At that time, he was near Carlisle, doubtlessly assisting Cumberland and the troops who were besieging Carlisle Castle, awaiting the heavy artillery from Whitehaven. Hawley was content, writing to Newcastle on the following day, 'His Majesty was pleased to give me I take it as a particular mark of His Majesty's favour and shall do all I can to deserve the good opinion of His Majesty' and that he was 'pleased to express of my poor ability. My Zeal I can answer for'.[13] He received his official appointment, which was the same as Wade had received in October, on 27 December.[14]

However, he did have one practical concern; that of the necessity of having a greater number of staff officers than he possessed at present, as he only had one aide and a secretary. This would mean that he would require an additional allowance of money to provide for more staff. Hawley explained that he was not a rich man, but nor was he avaricious. He told Newcastle, 'I must live in a more expensive manner' but 'I have no money for I am in debt. I want none for I have no heirs. I only desire to live as others of my rank and to serve His Majesty with pleasure'.[15] Newcastle replied promptly on 28 December, thanking Hawley for his 'zeal for this service, and your Readiness to undertake this important command', referring to his 'experience and abilities'. He promised he would settle Hawley's expenses incumbent on his new role and added 'I sincerely congratulate you upon this great mark of His Majesty's Favour'.[16] Yet as we shall see, the appointment was to prove an arduous one.

Newcastle, in his correspondence with both Wade and Cumberland, impressed on each that they assist Hawley as he was now the principal opponent of the Jacobite army; presumably he hoped Wade could provide Hawley with intelligence and advice. They needed to 'order the junction of the troops', 'that as strong an army as possible, should be made'. The King's intention was that it was of the 'utmost importance that a speedy end should be put to it', given the damage the rebellion

12   TNA, SP54/26, f.68r.
13   TNA, SP36/78, f.78r.
14   TNA, SP36/78/334r.
15   TNA, SP36/78, 79v.
16   TNA, SP36/78, f211r.

posed to both the public finance and peace.[17] A contemporary historian was unimpressed. Andrew Henderson, an Edinburgh schoolmaster and Hanoverian loyalist, noted in 1748 that Hawley, though 'an old experienc'd Officer' was 'but indifferently beloved by the private men. He had been a Lieutenant Colonel in Evans' dragoons at the battle of Sheriffmuir, a circumstance which promoted this choice more than the rigour and severity of which he was but too remarkable'.[18] Yet this may have been with the benefit of hindsight because the contemporaries that we know of thought differently. Richmond stated that Huske would be second in command and that the two men got on well together. Apparently, 'every body here is extremely pleased with their being sent to Scotland'.[19] Walpole, as noted, was no admirer of Hawley, yet he wrote approvingly, to Mann on 3 January 1746, 'There is a military magistrate of some fierceness sent into Scotland…He will not sow the seeds of future disloyalty, by too easily pardoning the present'.[20]

Walpole's approval of Hawley was undoubtedly because he was eager to see the Jacobites punished in no uncertain way. He had prefaced his above remarks about Hawley with the hope that Cumberland 'should not be [sent in charge of the army to Scotland] with that sword of mercy, with which the present family have governed these people', but:

> All the world agrees in the fitness of severity to highwaymen, for the sake of the innocent who suffer – then can rigour be ill-placed against banditti, who have terrified, pillaged, and injured the poor people in Cumberland, Lancashire, Derbyshire, and the counties through which this rebellion has stalked! [21]

For Walpole, as with many others in the political elite of Hanoverian Britain, the Jacobites were not honourable enemies of war, as were the French, but criminals who should expect no mercy. His comments were unfair, for the Jacobite army on their march through England had not looted or stolen, but merely taken money in the hands of tax collectors; though some thefts had occurred on the retreat northwards, these had not been extreme.

Not all loyalists were impressed with Hawley's appointment, as John Forbes wrote to Duncan Forbes on 9 January: 'No mortal disputes Mr Hawley's genius for the management of a squadron, or prosecuting with vigour any mortal to the

---

17 TNA, SP36/77, f349r, 78, f226r.
18 Andrew Henderson, *Life of William Augustus, Duke of Cumberland* (London: J. Ridley, 1766) pp.214-215.
19 McCann (ed.), *Correspondence*, p.199.
20 Lewis (ed.), *Walpole*, Vol.19, p.193.
21 Lewis (ed.), *Walpole*, Vol.19, p.193.

Charles Edward Stuart. (From R. Fitzroy Bell (ed.), *Memorials of John Murray of Broughton, 1740-1747*)

gallows although at the same time, they wish he had the lenity to make converts, or the absolute force to make all fly before him'. Forbes thought that the infantry were too under-strength to deal with the Jacobites and the cavalry had a reputation for flight.[22]

On hearing news from the Messenger Dick about Hawley's replacing Wade on 24 December, Cumberland informed Wade of the need to form an army for Scotland and to discuss this with Hawley. Hawley left Blackhall on 25 December – no peaceful Christmas Day for him.[23] George II made the appointment official on 28 December, appointing Hawley as commander in chief in Scotland.[24]

Hawley's command was currently made up of the following:

---

22  Duncan Forbes, *Culloden Papers* (London: T. Cadell and W. Davies, 1815), p.468.
23  RA, CP8/110.
24  *London Gazette*, 8496, 28 Dec. 1745.

Subordinate commander: Major General Huske.
Infantry
1st Brigade: Brigadier Mordaunt
    Wolfe's Regiment
    Munro's Regiment
    Blakeney's Regiment
    St. Clair's Regiment
2nd Brigade: Brigadier Cholmondeley
    Howard's Regiment
    Cholmondeley's Regiment
    Pulteney's Regiment
3rd Brigade: Brigadier Fleming
    Battereau's Regiment
    Fleming's Regiment
    Barrell's Regiment
Cavalry
    Cobham's Dragoons (arrived just before Falkirk and took part in the battle)
    Hamilton's Dragoons
    Ligonier's Dragoons
Volunteers
    William Thornton's infantry [25]

In addition, in and around Stirling were two battalions of infantry (Price's and Ligonier's) that had been sent to Edinburgh by Wade in November.

On paper this would seem to be a strong force, with veteran infantry who had seen recent service on the Continent, but its experience under Wade had been tough, both physically and psychologically. They had marched from Newcastle to Hexham in an attempt to relieve Carlisle, in appalling weather conditions. However, they turned back, due to hearing news that the city and castle had fallen to the Jacobite army. They then returned to Newcastle, having achieved nothing except for many men to become exhausted and ill. By the end of the month the army marched southwards through Yorkshire in another attempt to confront the Jacobite army. Yet the slow-moving army did not reach beyond the county before news arrived that the Jacobites were retreating from Derby. Urged by Cumberland to intercept the retreating Jacobites, Wade was unable to do so and so the decision was taken yet again to march back to Newcastle. Many were in no fit condition to

---

25  *The Newcastle Gazette*, 76, 26 Nov. 1745; TNA, SP36/70, f.215; Sheffield Archives, WWM1/357.

march let alone fight and even those which could would hardly be in high spirits. Apparently, 753 infantrymen had been hospitalised.[26] This was not an army ready and fit to fight and win that Hawley was inheriting. Sir Everard Fawkener (1694-1758), Cumberland's military secretary, observed in the following year, 'their fruitless marches under Marshal Wade in the dead of winter and always encamped, had quite worn them down'.[27]

Cumberland told Newcastle on 1 January, just after the Jacobite garrison had surrendered at Carlisle, that he was doing his best for 'His Majesty's intentions of making the Army in Scotland under General Hawley as strong as possible'. Yet he knew that only some of the cavalry regiments should be sent there, because otherwise 'should he send more Cavalry there than that already ordered, they must necessarily starve'. Both Wade and Hawley 'both write me word...it will be absolutely impossible for want of forage'. Yet there would be cavalry in the north of England should they be needed.[28] Lack of forage had limited the army's use of cavalry in 1689, too.

By 25 December in Edinburgh there were the dragoon regiments of Ligonier and Hamilton and the infantry battalions of Price and Ligonier.[29] Hawley arrived at Newcastle on the Friday morning of 27 December. He found that the march of the troops from there to Edinburgh had been rescinded. So, on the following day, he began to have them marching north again.[30] From 28-31 December, the eight battalions of British infantry were sent from Newcastle to Edinburgh, under the command of Huske and Brigadier James Cholmondeley. Huske was to follow in two or three days. The first division of these (Fleming's and Blakeney's) reached the Scottish capital on 1-2 January; the second (Battereau's and St. Clair's) on the 4th and the third (Wolfe's and Cholmondeley's) on the 7th; Howard's and Munro's on the next day and Barrell's and Pulteney's on the 10 January. Sempill's and Campbell's Regiments were expected at Newcastle on 6 January and would then join the forces at Edinburgh. However, it was not until 10 January that there were 12 battalions of infantry in Edinburgh.[31] Cobham's Dragoons were quartered at Dunse on the 13th.[32]

Hawley was not entirely happy with some of the men under his command. Sempill's and Campbell's were mostly Scottish 'whom I had rather have been

---

26  TNA, SP36/76, f.166r.
27  HMC 14th Report, IX, p.145.
28  TNA, SP36/80, ff3r-4r.
29  John Marchant, *History of the Present Rebellion* (London: R. Walker, 1746), p.104.
30  RA, CP8/168.
31  Marchant, *History*, p.275, 279; Francis Douglas, *History of the Rebellion in 1745 and 1746* (Aberdeen, 1755), p.108.
32  RA, CP9/43.

without' (about 80 percent of the rank and file of thee battalions were Scottish). As to his cavalry, Ligonier's and Hamilton's were 'the Remains of the two Irish regiments here, which I can't much depend upon', as at the Battle of Prestonpans they had refused to charge the enemy and fled, but he looked forward to being reinforced by Cobham's Dragoons.[33]

Hawley also learnt that the Dutch and Swiss troops, once part of Wade's command, were obliged to return to the continent because under their terms of deployment they were forbidden to fight against the French (several hundred French troops having arrived in Scotland in November). Walpole related another tale of Hawley's blunt and brisk character which relates to this period. He told Mann:

> I believe I told you of Lord John Drummond sending a drum to Wade to propose a cartel. Wade returned a civil answer, with had the King's and Council's approbation. When the drummer arrived with it at Edinburgh, Hawley opened it and threw it in the fire, would not let the drummer go back, but made him write to Lord J. Drummond, "That rebels were not to be treated with".[34]

The Dutch troops were to be replaced by a corps of about 5,000 Hessian infantry and a handful of hussars. Hawley was told that these forces would arrive at Leith soon. He did not expect them for some weeks and when they did arrive he thought that there would be insufficient supplies for them.[35]

The main Jacobite army had retreated across the Esk into Scotland on 20 December, but their plans were unknown. Some believed that they might try to besiege Stirling Castle, 'but I doubt this' wrote Hawley.[36] The main difficulty for the army was the lack of money and thus supplies. Hawley pointed out this to Newcastle:

> But the worst article I have to acquaint your Grace with, is that I am still wind bound for want of money & the Troops are only paid some on account to the 29th of January, out of which they must pay all their carriages and furnish the Men with shoes &c so that they will want soon. Besides, money to be advanced to the contractors of forage & cattle when they are found…these must be by the nearest calculation I can make,

33  RA, CP8/168.
34  Lewis, *Walpole*, Vol.19, p.202.
35  RA, CP8/168.
36  RA, CP8/168.

400,000 Rations of Forage & that still supplyed, for Scotland is not like other countries.[37]

However, 'As to Bread & Biscuit, I hope in 10 Days we shall be pretty well'. This was Hawley's first letter to Newcastle and he ended 'I hope your Grace will pardon my rough military style', but he assured him of victory, 'depend on me for doing all that's possible for His Majesty's Service'.

There was no magazine of provisions and forage ready in Scotland and the men would need 4,000 Rations per day. Huske was sent to Berwick to negotiate with a contractor for live cattle. Furthermore, there was no money in the military chest that Wade had been supplied with. There was an agent by the name of Abbott but Hawley deemed him 'an odd fellow' and refused to deal with him.[38] He added, 'Marshal Wade won't let me have his map'.[39]

On 11 January, Newcastle finally replied to Hawley's concerns about money and supply, beginning by stating that he had shown the King his letter and he was 'extremely pleased with your activity and zeal for his service'. Mr Sawyer had been sent northwards with £15,000 and the paymaster was to provide another £10,000. Newcastle also promised to let Cumberland and the Duke of Montague, as Master of the Ordnance, to help solve the difficulties with artillery.[40]

On Monday 6 January, Hawley arrived in Edinburgh. On the way there, he was met at Prestonpans by the regiments of Ligonier's and Hamilton's Dragoons. The former had been his regiment from 1730-1740, 'but he upbraided them with their Cowardice, and desired them to put up their swords at that time, and see to use them better in the Hour of Action'.[41] According to the Jacobite John Murray of Broughton, when Hawley arrived at the city, 'they were quartered in the gentlemens houses within the City by Sixes and Sevens at free quarters, and every inhabitant obliged to furnish sheets and blankets for their use, few if any of which were ever returned' and contrasted this with the quartering of the Jacobites in non-domestic properties.[42]

Cumberland was pleased with Hawley's actions, writing from London on 11 January 1746:

---

37   RA, CP8/168.
38   TNA, SP36/78, f.244r.
39   TNA, SP36/78, 247r.
40   TNA, SP36/80, f249r-251v.
41   Henderson, *History*, p.88.
42   Robert Bell (ed.), 'Memorials of John Murray of Broughton, 1740-1747', SHS, 1st series, 17, (1897), p.211n.

Lieut Genl Hawley,

I was very glad to see by your Letter to the Duke of Newcastle that you was got safe to Edinburg & that you proposed marching on to Stirling as soon as all your Foot should become up, you & I being of the same opinion with regard to that despicable Enemy you have to deal with. I am fully convinced that far from besieging Stirling, they will retire to Perth upon the first appearance of the Kings Troops, but how you will be able to come at them there til the Season of the year shall be more favourable, I am not aware.

People here have a scheme for landing a Number of Battalions at Aberdeen to be behind the Rebels at Perth, & to prevent there having any provision there, the want of which must oblige them to abandon the place to you. If this is feasable I shall be glad to have your opinion upon it, as People's sentiments here are divided & as others say that wth a small force we might possess ourselves of Montrose, & so cut the Rebels off from their communication with France, which would be one of the effective & speedy ways of destroying them. On this head I shall write to Admiral Bing, to have his account of the condition of that place & of what strength the Rebels may have made it.

Major Genl Bland is ordered with a Corps of Cavalry, to remain on the Esk, for fear the Rebels should give you the slip, & return into England, which fear groundless as it is, many people here are not without. Inclosed you shall have a Copy of my Letter to General Bland that you may know what his orders are.[43]

On 15 January Hawley dined with Rear Admiral John Byng (1704-1757) and Andrew Fletcher (1692-1766), the Lord Chief Justice, Scotland's most important civil and judicial officer, and they had discussed Cumberland's suggestion of landing men at Aberdeen. They rejected them on several grounds; Hawley stating that wind and weather would prove problematic, but also because 'we have other irons in the fire'. This was because the army was moving to relieve Stirling Castle, 'driving the rascally scum out of Stirling to relieve Blakeney…they will go off or they are mad' so could not divert troops on another expedition.[44] Hawley clearly held the Jacobite army in contempt, as did many in the Hanoverian political and military elite, despite the defeat at Prestonpans. It probably led him to underestimate their fighting qualities.

43   RA, CP9/66
44   RA, CP9/81.

Yet Hawley's attentions were focussed on his own forces. Supply issues had yet to be resolved, 'We are still in the utmost Distress for Money...There is not a penny to be got hear'. The tax collector had none. London Bills were not accepted. Wade had insisted to Hawley that the two Banks in Edinburgh would provide up to £70,000 if required. This meant that 'there is as yet no sort of magazine yet begun to be made'.[45]

Discipline was another concern. Hawley wrote on his arrival in the Scottish capital, 'I have no power to order courts martial. Marshal Wade's would not do, being only to himself. I thought to have found one here...There are 50 prisoners to be tried for desertion, Treason, rebellion &c.' Apparently Major General Joseph Guest (1660-1749) at Edinburgh Castle had such an order, but had lost it, then claimed Cope took it with him and Hawley thought 'Guest has quite lost his memory'.[46] The number of prisoners there was because a French ship, the *Louis XV*, carrying troops to Scotland had been seized by the Royal Navy on 28 November, and its prisoners from the Irish Picquets were initially housed in Edinburgh; those who were French were sent to Berwick but those 16 Britons in the French army remained at the Scottish capital.[47]

Because of these prisoners, and also, perhaps, in the anticipation of beating the Jacobite army, Hawley had gibbets erected in the Grassmarket, anticipating the execution of prisoners. He had also assembled a number of hangmen to do the business. Apparently, this gallows remained there until September 1746 when it was sawed through by person or persons unknown.[48] On 11 January, Newcastle told Hawley that the War Office had sent him power to hold courts martial.[49]

Whilst in Edinburgh, John Home (1724-1807), a lieutenant in the Edinburgh Volunteers, met Hawley and asked if the volunteer unit could accompany the army when it marched out against the Jacobites. Initially Hawley granted the request. On the next day, however, a message was sent to Home asking that he call at the Abbey on the next morning. Home did so, and Hawley told him that he wanted the men to undertake another duty 'which he thought very essential'. This turned out to be to rescue prisoners held at Glamis Castle. Home asked him if action was anticipated therein and was told that there was a possibility, but it could not be guaranteed. Home asked Hawley if he could consult his fellow officers, which he did and on his return then said that the volunteers had been formed 'with a view to serve in the field' so could not undertake anything else

---

45   RA, CP9/43.
46   RA, CP9/43.
47   A.G. Arnot and B.S. Seton (eds.), 'Prisoners of the '45', I, SHS, 3rd series, 13 (1928-1929), pp.236-237.
48   Charteris, *Short Account*, pp.379-380.
49   TNA, SP36/80, f250r.

and they hoped that Hawley would allow them to march with the army. Hawley agreed that they might do so.[50]

Hawley also met Walter Grossett, a customs officer, who procured transports to take troops up the river to Leith to attack the Jacobites there. A boat that had been taken later had to be burnt and Grossett arranged that.[51] He also took a letter from Hawley to Major General William Blakeney (1672-1761), lieutenant governor in command of the garrison at Stirling Castle on 10 January. Hawley had written:

> I had a verball message from you by a man this morning, desiring reliefe. I am getting the foot, who are come up, repaired as soone as possible, for with the nine days marche, after all things kothers they are good deale harassed butt in good spirits.
>
> 'I shall move towards you, if possible on Sunday, in the mean time let me know by the bearer or some other way, how long you can hold out, no more now, but I am sincerely yrs.[52]

Meanwhile, Hawley was doing what he could to proceed with the campaign. He also stated that 'I have other secret expeditions in hand all concerted', and this may be a reference to Huske's expedition at Linlithgow.[53] He was also in correspondence with Major General John Campbell, who had written to Hawley for instructions on 10 January. Hawley replied at once, instructing him to move his forces towards Linlithgow, though to 'march with great caution' and if a stronger force of Jacobites threatened him, he was to 'retire towards Glasgow' and that he should keep advance guards to provide intelligence.[54]

Apart from money issues, there was also the question of reliable intelligence. That from Fletcher and other Scots was 'so unmilitary'. It was not so much in short supply, but 'The accounts varies so much every hour, and afterwards proves so often false that I can depend on nothing'. However, he did think it worth noting that he had heard that the Jacobite Earl of Kilmarnock (1705-1746) was fortifying his house at Callendar, near Falkirk, in order to cover the siege of Stirling and that the Jacobite army had been making boats in order to move cannon down the river from Alloa to Stirling.[55] Attempts were made to harry these movements, but without success and the guns arrived near Stirling.

---

50   John Home, *The History of the Rebellion of 1745* (London: Cadell jun. and W. Davies, 1802) pp.164-165.
51   Walter Blaikie (ed.), 'Origins of the Forty Five', SHS, 2nd series, 2 (1916), pp.353, 358.
52   Blaikie, 'Origins', pp.358, 393.
53   RA, CP9/81.
54   NLS, MS3734, 76, 81.
55   RA, CP9/43.

The army was thus being readied to march. Hawley wrote 'I am getting the Foot into Repair, as fast as they come up, in order to go to them. I will not go to have the King's Troops affronted'. On the whole he was confident of success, writing, 'hope to give your Grace a good account of them, if they stay which I neither believe nor expect', telling Campbell that he had heard the rebels were 'distressed' and hoped to leave Edinburgh on 15 January. In this he was in the same vein as Cumberland, who looked forward to battle but did not think the Jacobites would stand. Yet Hawley was concerned about his artillery, 'as to artillery; there is not a Gun here can move for want of Gunners'. There was one gunner at Berwick; Major John Belford was still at Carlisle. There were few horses to pull the guns, other than those at Newcastle, and the train there could not move without Belford. There was an 18-year-old gunner at Edinburgh but that was apparently all.[56] Wade had been unhelpful, stating that the gunners at Newcastle could not join Hawley's command until those he had detached to Carlisle returned.[57] On 15 January he told Cumberland, 'I can only promise your Royal Highness I'll do all I can, the men tho' naked are in good spirits'.[58]

It was not only Hawley and Cumberland who looked forward to either battle or pursuit of the enemy. On 15 January, Huske wrote that the Jacobites were 'in a very great pannick and march in the utmost confusion by all accounts'. He believed that they would abandon the siege of Stirling as soon as Hawley began advancing towards them. Huske was concerned about the castle there, 'They certainly will try their best efforts to take the castle of Stirling if possible, the loss of which may be of very ill consequence'.[59]

56   RA, CP9/43, NLS, MS.3734, 87.
57   TNA, SP36/80, f.62v.
58   TNA, SP36/80, f.81.
59   TNA, SP36/80, f.82.

# 6

# The Battle of Falkirk

Hawley had never led an army into battle before. Many generals never did; among Hawley's contemporaries neither did Wade, Bland, Huske, or Honywood. At Almansa and Sheriffmuir he had been a relatively junior officer, at Dettingen and at Fontenoy he had led the cavalry in the army's second rank, and he had had a lesser independent command in the Low Countries in the autumn of 1745. This was his fifth battle. He had faced the Jacobites 30 years previously, but, again, in a subordinate role. Therefore, he had a new challenge on his hands, but given his contempt of the enemy, despite the Jacobite victory at Prestonpans, and the lack of confidence he felt in his cavalry, he felt sure enough. After all, the Jacobites had retreated from the military challenge in England. On the other hand, they possessed the largest and best equipped Jacobite army in the campaign to date, with regular French troops as well as Scottish, reinforced with men who had not marched into England in 1745.

This was the biggest battle of the Jacobite campaigns in terms of men involved. Yet it is one of the least studied, perhaps because it ended indecisively. That having said, it has been the subject of a fair-minded local study, though somewhat unmilitary account, published on its 250th anniversary.[1] In some ways the reason why it was fought was a very common one in 18th century warfare; the relief of a strongpoint. On the day of the battle, Walpole wrote to Mann with anticipation, 'what a despicable affair is a rebellion upon the defensive! General Hawley is marched from Edinburgh, to put it quite out…[he] will give a mortal blow to the pride of the Scotch nobility…He is very brave and able; with no small bias to be brutal'.[2] Others of the elite shared Walpole's views, too, with Newcastle writing to Chesterfield, now Lord Lieutenant of Ireland, on 6 January, 'I hope General

---

1    Bailey, *Falkirk or Paradise!*
2    Lewis (ed.), *Walpole*, Vol.19, p.201.

Hawley will not only be able to prevent their return [into England], but entirely to reduce and beat them'. His correspondent's letter of five days later included the wish, 'if Hawley acts with spirit, as I verily believe he will do, you will see the trouble in Scotland ended in two months time at the furtherest'.³

James Henshawe took comfort in the army's size, allegedly 'about 15,000 men, so that our apprehensions are pretty much abated'. Likewise, Thomas Grimston of Beverley wrote 'I hope in a short time the rebellious rascals will receive their due punishment, for we are told that Hawley and Huske are within twelve miles of them. If they dare stay their coming up, I don't doubt a good account of them'.⁴

On 15 January the Jacobite army was drawn up on a plain or moor which was a mile to the east of Bannockburn. Cavalry were sent off to Falkirk to reconnoitre and found a large body of British dragoons near the town, but no infantry were seen there. The Jacobite army returned to its quarters, 'in the scattered huts around Bannockburn' but leaving some of the cavalry to patrol that night as near to Falkirk as possible. According to James MacDonald, a Jacobite cavalry officer, the cavalry was 'composed chiefly of gentlemen without discipline or experience, whose horses, worn out and ill cared for, were in a very bad state', so that he thought the army's protection in case of attack was minimal.⁵

Next day the patrols reported that British infantry had arrived at Falkirk from Linlithgow, consisting of eight battalions, Hamilton's and Ligonier's Dragoons, and the Glasgow Militia, all under Huske. They were in a camp just to the north of the town. The cavalry had advanced as far as the bridge of Carron. Meanwhile the Jacobite army drew up again on the same plain as they had on the previous day. By 3:00 p.m. they had seen no sight of the enemy and so returned to their scattered – and thus vulnerable – camps. Had Hawley's army attacked them in that condition, although he could not have done so as not all the army was together, Elcho estimated that only 3,000 men could be brought together to resist them. Additional troops joined the Jacobite army in the shape of Lord Lewis Gordon's 800 men, Sir James Kinloch's 600, and Lord John Drummond's 350-strong Royal Ecossois. Morale was high.⁶

---

3   Richard Lodge (ed.), *Private Correspondence of Chesterfield and Newcastle, 1744-1746* (London: Royal Historical Society, 1930), pp.94, 100.
4   Anon, *Report on the Manuscripts of Lady Du Cane* (London: Historic Manuscripts Commission, 1905), pp.84, 89.
5   Elcho, *Short Account*, p.370-371; Alastair and Henrietta Tayler (eds.), *1745 and after* (London: Thomas Nelson & Sons, 1938) p.115n.
6   Elcho, *Short Account*, p.371.

That evening a council of war was held and a unanimous decision was taken to attack on the next day.[7] Later that day the remainder of the British army arrived at Falkirk. Hawley stayed at Callendar House from 8:00 p.m., turfing some Glasgow Militia officers out of their rooms to do so. The artillery arrived at 7:00 p.m. The Argyllshire Militia and Cobham's Dragoons arrived from Edinburgh at 8:00 a.m. on 17 January. The Earl of Hopton gave the infantry battalions twelve guineas each and the same to the first two of the dragoon regiments in order that they might buy beef for themselves. The plan was to attack on 18 January.[8]

Callendar House, near Falkirk. (Author photograph)

Meanwhile, the British camp was in a strong position, 100 paces to the west of the town. In front of the camp was a deep hollow, with a morass to the right flank and on the left an enclosure with large wet ditches. Cholmondeley wrote that it was 'very strong'. The tents were lined up in two ranks. The evening of the 16th was frosty.[9]

---

7   James Maxwell, *Narrative of the Expedition in Scotland of Prince Charles Stuart* (Edinburgh: T. Constable, 1841), p.98.
8   Forbes, *Culloden Papers*, p.270; Douglas, *History*, pp.113, 116; Anon, *Report on the Manuscripts of the Earl of Eglinton* (London: Historic Manuscripts Commission, 1885), p.440.
9   Anon, *Eglinton*, p.440.

Hawley was looking forward to battle and victory. He had a poor opinion of his enemy, writing on 11 January, 'I do and always shall despise these rascals'. Cumberland agreed with him, believing 'that despicable enemy' would flee before them. So Hawley was eager to fight; on 15 January he had written, 'I am resolved to strike while the iron is hot'. Another reason for his eagerness was that he was concerned that Stirling Castle might fall to the Jacobite siege, 'The rebels are busy at Stirling, but I hope they'll find it a tough nut, tho' I fear we can't be time to save it'.[10]

Meanwhile on 17 January the siege of Stirling Castle began, the Jacobite besiegers being under the command of the Duke of Perth with 1,400 men.[11] These were made up of the Perth's own regiment, 700 strong; John Roy Stewart's Regiment, 400 strong; Glenbucket's 300 men, and the fusilier companies of the Royal Ecossois. There were also two 18-pounder guns and some 12 and 16-pounders.[12] They remained on guard there on the day of the battle.

According to MacDonald, it was three in the morning when one Brown 'came to rouse the Prince telling him that the enemy were beating to quarters. It was then feared that we might be surprised and we sent all around to collect the troops, which were not assembled until about 10 o'clock', though there is no evidence that they were under any threat whatsoever.[13] Early that morning, Lord George Murray gave a scroll detailing the line of battle to Charles. It showed that the French and Irish regulars should be split between each flank of the second line in case the army was attacked in the flank by the dragoons. Murray asked Charles that he appoint officers to command and suggested their location. However, no such appointments were made; nor were the French troops so deployed.[14]

For the third time in as many days, the Jacobite army formed up. James Johnstone, a Jacobite officer, thought that everyone believed that the review was merely to choose a battlefield and find out what the ground was like there as they believed that they would be attacked there imminently.[15] Again the cavalry was despatched to ascertain Hawley's movements. Once more there was nothing to report. A council of war was held, where Murray explained that whereas the Jacobite army was divided, and thereby vulnerable, their enemies were united. He added, 'by holding above the Torwood, we would gain the hill of Falkirk as soon as them, as it was a thing they did not expect. I knew the ground well, and thought there was no

---

10 TNA, SP54/27/18a, RA, CP9/66, 81, 134.
11 Elcho, *Short Account*, p.372.
12 TNA, SP54/27/32D.
13 Tayler and Tayler (eds.), *1745*, p.115n.
14 Robert Forbes, *Jacobite Memoirs of the Rebellion of 1745* (Edinburgh: William and Robert Chambers, 1834), p.91.
15 James Johnstone, *A Memoir of the Forty Five* (London: Folio Society, 1958), pp.85-86.

difficulty of taking it before they could'. Colonel John William O'Sullivan (1700-c. 1760), Jacobite quartermaster, added that additional reasons were that because the enemy was not stirring from their camp, it would be 'fatiguing his men to keep them under armes every day'. Charles approved the plan and so the decision was taken to take the offensive.[16] O'Sullivan wrote that 'every one was of yt opinion, & it is very happy they were, for the enemy was to march yt night and attack us in our quarters'.[17]

Drummond would take the main road to Falkirk as far as Torwood with his own regiment, the Irish troops and the cavalry, though, as events transpired, he merely went with the grenadier company and a single picquet of the Royal Ecossois, and the Irish. Murray would lead the two columns of infantry on the south side of Dunipace and began to ascend the hill there.[18] This was so that the main force would be hidden from the enemy's sight by the trees of Torwood. Following behind the main column were the train of artillery (except for the heavy siege guns), with Farquharson's men escorting them. It was noon when the army began to move.[19] This was because, as Murray noted, 'how difficult it was to bring our men together from so many cantonments for several miles round'.[20]

Morale seemed high among the Jacobite army as they marched to possible battle. John Daniel, an English Jacobite, wrote, 'the soldiers shewed the greatest alacrity; the foot marching with such celerity as kept the horse on a full trot'.[21] Maxwell wrote that 'they were all in fine spirits, and confident of victory'.[22] Charles did his best to keep up the men's morale, 'was occupied of encourgaeing the men, & forming them, as they us'd to come out of those bad steps, to get them to march in order & presse them on, yt there should be no interval nor time lost'.[23] In fact, according to one soldier, the men had been so disappointed in not being allowed to march on the previous two days that they would have advanced towards the enemy with or without orders on the 17th anyway.[24]

Half an hour after the march began, O'Sullivan rode up to Murray and told him he had been talking to Charles. The two had decided that it was unadvisable to cross the river until nightfall, when it could be done without being seen, for to do so before then would be dangerous in the face of the enemy. Murray was surprised and

16  Forbes, *Jacobite Memoirs*, p.80; Tayler and Tayler (eds.), *1745*, p.116.
17  Tayler and Tayler (eds.), *1745*, p.116.
18  Elcho, *Short Account*, p.372.
19  Maxwell, *Narrative*, p.99.
20  Forbes, *Jacobite Memoirs*, p.80.
21  Blaikie, 'Origins', p.194.
22  Maxwell, *Narrative*, p.99.
23  Tayler and Tayler (eds.), *1745*, p.116.
24  Henry Paton (ed.), 'Lyon in Mourning', Vol.II, SHS, 1st series, pp.196-7.

pointed out that it was only a quarter of an hour before they would have to make the crossing and that was two miles distant from the British army's camp. Murray did not halt and O'Sullivan returned to see Charles. He added that if they stopped, the British would gain the high ground they desired and if the Jacobites did not move forward before nightfall they would have to take shelter in the houses and villages nearby and so not be brought together until noon of the next day.[25]

Charles was riding between the two Jacobite columns. He, O'Sullivan, Brigadier Walter Stapleton, in command of the Irish troops, and others soon rode up to Murray. The latter expanded on his reasoning why halting the march would be folly. It would mean that the men would have to 'lie in the open fields all night' and in the cold January weather this would lead to men leaving to find food and shelter elsewhere. They must either march forwards or return to their quarters. Stapleton agreed, 'To be sure if the enemy were not near enough to dispute our passing, there could be no other objection'. Murray surmised that their enemy were still at dinner and that the Jacobites should march forward with all haste so as to secure the high ground and that would give them the initiative. Charles and Stapleton agreed with him and, as they had been riding forward all this time, the crossing was near at hand. It was then that they first saw their enemy.[26]

The British army had been unaware of their peril, as Daniel noted, 'thinking it not worth their while to take the necessary precaution of having spies out, as other prudent generals would have done, notwithstanding the contempt they might have for us. We now roused them out of their lethargy'.[27] According to a Glasgow gentleman, Hawley did not think the Jacobites would attack them, 'such was the General's intelligence or his contempt for the enemy'.[28] They were not completely caught napping for there were sentries placed a mile distant from the camp.[29] Given the role of the cavalry is to provide the army with eyes and ears with regard to the movement of the enemy, it is not certain why Hawley did not make use of his dragoons to do so; possibly he lacked confidence in them as noted earlier.

So far, the day's weather had been fine but it now turned for the worse. According to Daniel, 'all the elements in confusion, so that the heavens seemed to fulminate their anger down upon us, by the impctuous storm of hail, wind and rain, that fell just at the time of the engagement'.[30] It beat down on the faces of Hawley's men.[31]

---

25  Forbes, *Jacobite Memoirs*, pp.80-1, 92.
26  Forbes, *Jacobite Memoirs*, pp.81-82.
27  Blaikie, 'Origins', p.194.
28  Anon, *A Letter from a Gentleman who was an eye witness of the late Battle of Falkirk* (Glasgow: Unknown Publisher, 1746), p.3.
29  Henderson, *History of the Rebellion*, p.91.
30  Blaikie, 'Origins', p.194.
31  Douglas, *History*, p.115.

There is a widely disseminated tale which militates against Hawley at this time. Andrew Henderson, Cumberland's first biographer, uses every attempt to denigrate Hawley, and his comments have been followed by others. He wrote that at this point, Hawley 'fell unto one of these mistakes which since the days of Sampson have been accounted fatal to a commanding officer'. This was that on arrival at Falkirk he received a message from the Countess of Kilmarnock whose husband was an officer in the Jacobite army. Henderson adds, 'An invitation from a Lady so remarkable for wit and gaiety, could not be refused'. He went to her home at Callendar House and was 'entertained with great politeness and decorum' and on the 17th 'she made a posset for him with her own hands, to fortify him against the damp and cold' so that he remained at the house until between 12 and 1, despite frequent expresses to him telling that the Jacobites were arriving.[32] The truth was rather different, as we shall see.

Hawley had gone to the camp at 5:00 a.m. and again at ten went to the hilly ground nearby to the left of the camp but neither he nor Corse, a Glasgow Militia officer, could see the enemy.[33] Brigadier Cholmondeley later wrote, 'I saw them very plain with a glass' at 11 that morning. Yet, there were several hills between them and the Jacobite army, so he was uncertain where they were marching to. The men were turned out.[34] Hawley recalled that this was 'when the men were all boyling their kettles' and were stood to arms within minutes of the call. However, he then claimed that the next news was that the Jacobites had halted their march and were merely changing their grounds, as demonstarted by the evidence of camp fires being lit. So he ordered the troops 'to lodge their arms and go on with their kettles'.[35]

It was only when Drummond's force was on the hill at Torwood that there was movement again seen on the part of the British army. They seemed to believe that all the Jacobite army was with Drummond and it was only later that the majority were seen.[36] It was 1:00 p.m. that repeated reports came of the Jacobite march towards them and these then had to be confirmed. The Jacobite army was then three miles away.[37] In the interim, the troops were permitted to eat their dinners, which they just completed before the crisis developed.[38]

Just before 1:00 p.m., two officers from Howard's Regiment, one by the name of Teesdale, climbed a tree near the camp and fixed a telescope. With it they saw

---

32 Henderson, *Cumberland*, pp.216-217.
33 Forbes, *Culloden Papers*, p.271.
34 Anon, *Eglinton*, p.440.
35 RA, 7411-101-11, p.24.
36 Elcho, *Short Account*, p.373.
37 Douglas, *History*, p.114, 116.
38 Henderson, *History*, p.91.

the main bodies of the Jacobite army, not just the cavalry. They immediately told Lieutenant Colonel Howard and he went to Callendar House, to tell Hawley of the news. Hawley gave orders for the men to put on their equipment but not at this point to stand to under arms. During the next hour, horsemen rode about to gain more intelligence and they came back quickly with the news that the Jacobite army was on the march to the south of Torwood, about to cross the river at Dunipace, three miles from Falkirk. It was clear that the Jacobite army was marching to Falkirk Muir, which was to the left of the army's camp.[39]

This news became widely known throughout the army and because Hawley was still at Callendar House, alarm began to rise among the officers who wondered where he was, what should be done and what their orders were. Senior officers had the infantry battalions formed up in front of the camp.[40] According to Corse, 'I was surpriz'd to see in how little time ye regular troops were form'd (I think in less than half an hour').[41] Once the men were stood to, they were marched in two columns for a half mile from the camp, but as Cholmondeley wrote, 'but as we had hollow roads, and very uneven Ground, to pass, we were in great confusion'. They formed up for battle again, 'in my opinion a very good situation'. They then had to form up for a second time, to the left of the first position. When Hawley arrived, he had the cavalry march to seize the high ground and for the infantry to follow. The former soon outpaced the latter and a noticeable gap grew between them.[42] Corse noted that the infantry were 'running & quite out of breath with the Fatigue'.[43]

There were also numerous spectators of the battle, as a Glasgow gentleman who was there later wrote, 'The whole country had broke loose after the army, to be witnesses of a certain Victory, and many to get a pluck at the Highlanders for what they had suffered. A finer little Army of its numbers could not be seen'. The same observer was most complimentary about Hawley, writing, 'The General came down with the Reputation of a good soldier, and much liked by the Army'.[44]

It was now about 2:00p.m. The armies met on Falkirk Muir, about a mile to the south west of the town, but fighting did not begin until about 3:30 p.m.[45] Murray later wrote that the Jacobites had all the advantages that they could wish for. These were that they were close to their opponents before the assault; that they were descending a hill to do so; that the wind was at their backs and at their enemies' faces; that they had boggy ground on their left to prevent the cavalry outflanking

---

39　Home, *History*, pp.166-167.
40　Home, *History*, p.167.
41　Forbes, *Culloden Papers*, p.271.
42　Forbes, *Culloden Papers*, p.271; Anon, *Eglinton*, p.440.
43　Forbes, *Culloden Papers*, p.271.
44　Anon, *A Letter from a Gentleman*, p3.
45　Anon, *A Short Account of the Battle of* Falkirk (Bannockburn: Unknown Publisher, 1746).

them; and that due to poor roads and steep hills the artillery could not be brought to bear against them. To summarize, 'in a word the Highland army had all the advantages that nature and art could give them'.[46]

O'Sullivan claimed that Charles told him to arrange the front line according to the order of battle as planned. He arrived at the right and saw the ground that Murray had occupied was 'full of old stone walls, & had one of them just at the heels of his last rank'. O'Sullivan said that such a position was dangerous and that he should advance the men to a better position, which Murray consented to. O'Sullivan was also concerned about the vulnerability of the right flank and suggested that the Atholl Brigade be placed there, advancing in column, so they could face any way which was necessary. Murray refused this suggestion. O'Sullivan then went down the front line, telling all the colonels and majors that 'the second & third rank shou'd fire only, & yt as near the enemy as possible'.[47]

The Jacobite army was forming up as follows, with the clan units in the front line, the Lowland ones in the second, and the cavalry and French in the third.

> First Line (left, commander Lord Drummond, to right, commander Murray.)
>
>> Lochiel's, including McKinnons and MacGregors, 800-900.
>> Stewart of Appin's, 300, led by the clan chief.
>> Fraser's, 300-500 led by the Master of Lovat.
>> Mackintosh's, 200.
>> Farquharson's, 200.
>> Cromartie's, 200.
>> MacPherson's, 300-400 led by Cluny Macpherson.
>> MacDonald of Clanranald's, 400, led by Clanranald.
>> MacDonald of Glengarry's, 800-900, divided into two battalions, led by Lochgarry, the chief's son.
>> MacDonald of Keppoch's, 400-600, led by Keppoch.
>
> Second Line
>
>> Lewis Gordon's, 400-900, led by Lord Lewis.
>> Lord Ogilvy's, 700-1,000, divided into two battalions.
>> Atholl Brigade, 600-1,000 led by Lord Nairne.

---

46   Forbes, *Jacobite Memoirs*, p.83.
47   Tayler and Tayler (eds.), *1745*, p.117.

Third Line

> Pitsligo's Horse, 100-120.
> Perthshire Horse, 40-140.
> Kilmarnock's Horse, 40-150.
> Irish and French, 300-450 led by Brigadier Stapleton.
> Hussars, 40.
> Balmerino's Lifeguards, 40-60.
> Elcho's Lifeguards, 80-120.
> Unregimented gentlemen with Charles, 100.

Artillery

> Two Swedish guns; four-6 pounders; two French guns, 18-pounders (none was ever brought into action).

According to Elcho there were 6,000 infantry and 360 cavalry. There was no artillery.[48] Maxwell claimed the army was 7000 strong.[49] Another Jacobite put them at 6,100 infantry and 580 cavalry.[50] The figures cited above for the individual units suggest 5,900-7,350 infantry and 360-630 cavalry. The Jacobite army thus numbered between 6,000 and 8,000 men, the largest it ever had except for at the Battle of Sheriffmuir. The bulk of the infantry were in the front line. This meant that there were large gaps between the units in the second line, especially between the centre and the wings.[51]

Hawley's army was deployed as follows:

In Front of the First Line Colonel Francis Ligonier in command.

> Ligonier's Dragoons, 253 (two squadrons).
> Hamilton's Dragoons, 266 (two squadrons).
> Cobham's Dragoons, 253 (three squadrons; assumed strength based on later figures).

---

48  Elcho, *Short Account*, p.373; TNA, SP54/27/32C.
49  Maxwell, *Narrative*, p.99.
50  James Atholl, *Chronicles of the Atholl and Tullibardine Families* (Edinburgh: published privately, 1908), Vol.III, p.145.
51  Maxwell, *Narrative*, p.100.

First Line (left (commanded by Hawley) to right (commanded by Huske)

> Glasgow Militia, 572 (10 companies).
> Wolfe's, 522.
> Cholmondeley's, 540.
> Pulteney's, 504.
> St. Clair's, 532 .
> Price's, 255.
> Ligonier's, 318.

Second Line

> Blakeney's, 460.
> Munro's, 525.
> Fleming's, 426.
> Barrell's, 378.
> Battereau's, 474.

Third Line

> Argyll Militia, led by Lieutenant Colonel Campbell, 765 (13 companies).
> Howard's, 554.

For the regular infantry, adding 16 percent based on figures for Culloden for officers, sergeants, and drummers gives an additional 880, so total of 6,368

> Reserve

> Paisley Volunteers (174 men, divided into three companies), three companies of Loudoun's, (185 men), Captain Thornton's Yorkshire company of volunteers (64 men), Edinburgh volunteer company, unknown strength.
> Total strength: At least 8,854.

Artillery

> 10 guns, including 4-pounders and 1½-pounders.
> Captain Cunningham and 28 men, including 12 civilian drivers.[52]

---

52   TNA, SP54/27/32C, 38B.

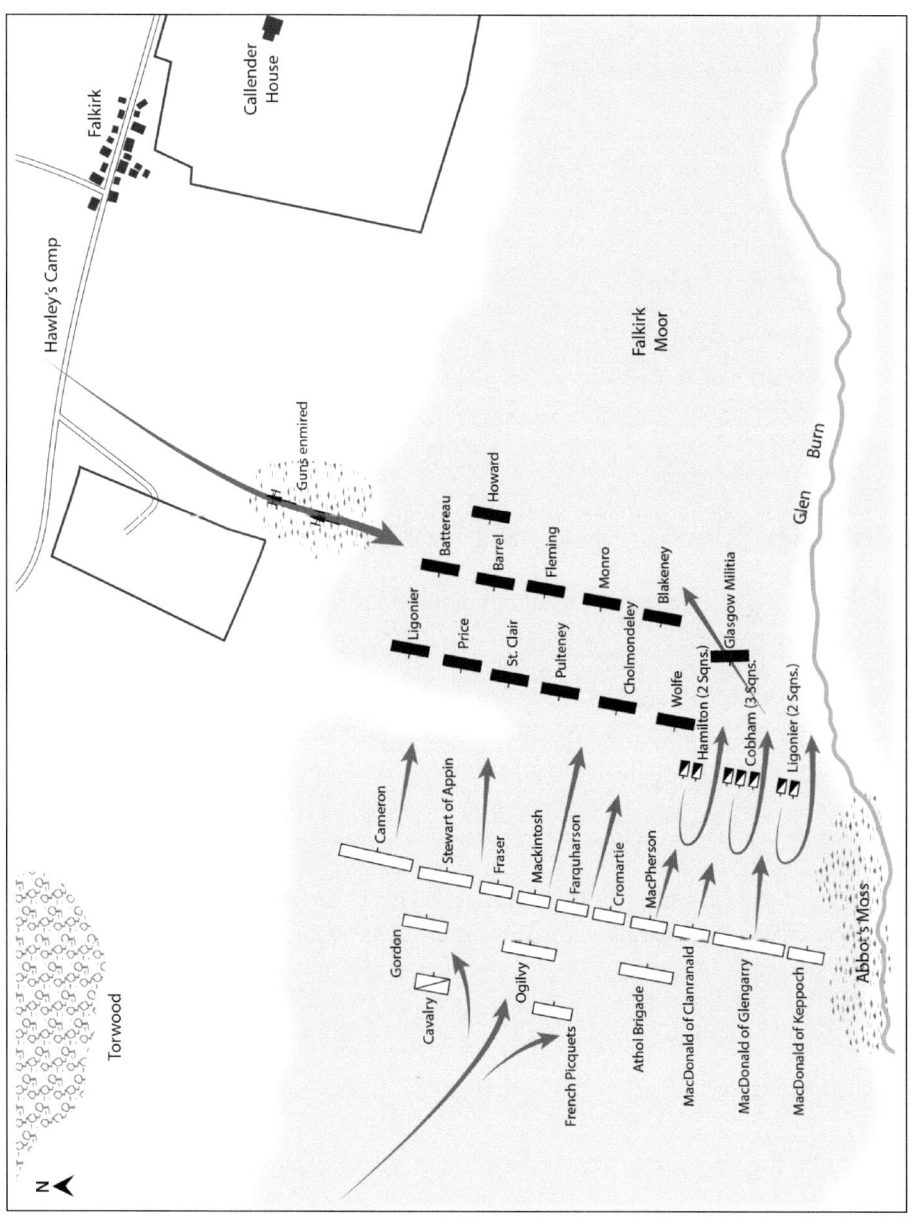

The Battle of Falkirk, 17 January 1746.

Hawley had more men, especially in cavalry, and more guns than the Jacobites, although nearly 2,000 of his men were militia and volunteers.

As with Cope at Prestonpans, Hawley had difficulties with the artillery. On 13 January he told Newcastle, 'no diligence shall be wanting in me, but my lord, no body can worke without tooles, and as to that point, my situation is as bad as ever any body was'.[53] He wrote 'We are in the greatest want of Guns…We want nothing but Gunns to go to Stirling and drive them from there'. But he was also disappointed in the senior artillery officer that he was provided with, 'Major Belford dos not come at all & this Cunningham is so ignorant & such a beast, he is no use'.[54] Belford was allegedly unwell, 'the sickness I suspect to be only a young wife he wants to be with, I know him'.[55] Captain Archibald Cunningham was despised by Hawley, 'ane old trooper of the Duke of Argilles…who is such a sot and so ignorant that as I live he and I shant agree long'.[56] Finding the crews to man his guns was another headache. Grossett was ordered by Fletcher and Hawley to go to Bo'ness to find some men. He went there and recruited 'nine or ten sailors for that purpose who had been Gunners on Board Men of war' at the cost of £16 8s to be advanced to their families.[57] Hawley later wrote, 'the train is more for show than for use'.[58] Nor was he impressed with the cavalry, writing 'the debris of two Irishe regiments of dragoons, very weak and all the rest intimidated and cowed since the battle of Prestonpans', yet at least 'All the Foot except two regiments were good old battalions from Flanders'.[59]

The relatively few men (25) who were later in receipt of pensions for wounds inflicted at the battle give less scope for analysis than is the case for those at Prestonpans. They were from 13 different occupations prior to enlistment, with a preponderance of weavers, labourers and farmers. The overwhelming majority were English, though one was Scottish and two from Ireland. The years served varied between one and 21, with an average of between 6-8, and they were aged in their late twenties on average, with a few being in their thirties. However, Hamilton's Dragoons was a predominantly Irish regiment, with nine out of ten men from it who received wound pensions being so.[60]

---

53   TNA, SP54/27, 22A.
54   RA, CP9/91.
55   TNA, SP54/27, 22A.
56   TNA, SP54/27, 22A.
57   Blaikie, 'Origins', p.362.
58   RA, CP9/81.
59   RA, 7411-101-11, p.24.
60   TNA, WO116/4-5.

Falkirk Moor; view west towards Jacobite line. (Author photograph)

Hawley had given some thought to defeating the Jacobites, for on 12 January he had drawn up a memorandum, expressing his contempt for their fighting abilities and outlining how they could be beaten:

> The Manner of the Highlanders way of fighting which there is nothing so easy to resist. If officers and men are not preposses'd with the Lyes and Accounts which are told of them…The sure way to demolish them is at 3 deep to fire by ranks diagonally to the Centre where they come, the rear rank first, and even that rank not to fire till they are within 10 or 12 paces but if the Fire is given at a distance you probably will be broke for you never get time to a load a second Cartridge, and if you give way you may give your foot for dead, for they being without a firelock or any load, no Man with his Arms, accoutrements &c. can escape them, and they give no quarters, but if you observe the above directions, they are the most despicable Enimy that are.[61]

Both armies began to march up the hill; neither side being able to see the other. The Jacobites hoped to gain the summit of the hill and then march directly on the

---

61    Elcho, *Short Account*, pp.459-460.

enemy if there was enough daylight remaining. Otherwise they would remain here overnight and then attack next morning. Whilst they were climbing they could see some dragoons at the top of the hill, which they first assumed was just a small party of scouts, but then numbers were rising. However, 'The sight of an enemy gave fresh spirits to the Highlanders and it was impossible to restrain their ardour, but they still kept their ranks and marched up in the finest order imaginable, though at a prodigious rate'.[62]

The dragoons were formed up as seven squadrons, and once Hawley had seen to his infantry, he returned to find Colonel Ligonier at the head of the cavalry. Hawley ordered him to go to the left of the dragoons to head Cobham's there, with Lieutenant Colonel Shugbrough Whitney of Ligonier's at the front of the adjacent squadron.[63] The three regiments of dragoons made feints towards the Jacobite right, trying to entice them into firing at long range so that they could charge safely home against troops who could not fire a second time. In this they were unsuccessful. Meanwhile the armies continued their march and when they saw one another it was clear that each flank overlapped the other; the Jacobites outflanking the British on the right and vice versa, so that the Jacobite left was opposite the British centre.[64]

Murray later wrote that this misalignment might have been remedied if two or three of the battalions in the Jacobite second line had been brought up to extend the front line to the left. However, battalion commanders and clan chiefs only commanded their own men and the latter would take orders from no one else. Furthermore, the left wing was leaderless: though Drummond was allegedly in charge there, the reality was that 'he had no directions to do it, and was not there when the battle began'.[65] Drummond had ridden at the head of the cavalry on the march, making a feint. When the infantry was crossing the Carron, he turned the cavalry towards the crossing and followed the infantry there. By the time the army had formed, he was in the rear and the he joined the troops on the third line.[66]

The three regiments of dragoons had formed up in front of the camp 'in a moment'. Hawley told Captain John Masterton, a staff officer, to have them 'march immediately to him which was on a hill and ordered Major General Huske to follow with the Foot in two lines'. This having been accomplished, Hawley's next instructions for Masterton was 'to go to Lieutenant Colonel Shugbrough Whitney, once major and then lieutenant colonel in Hawley's dragoons (who was on the left of the whole as all our dragoons were in two lines) to desire him to file more to the

---

62   Maxwell, *Narrative*, p.100.
63   RA, 7411-101-11, p.25.
64   Elcho, *Short Account*, pp.374-5.
65   Forbes, *Jacobite Memoirs*, p.84.
66   Forbes, *Jacobite Memoirs*, pp.84-85.

left than the rebels might not outflank us and make room for the Foot to march up the hill, upon wch ye sd colonel told me he could march no further for they were a morass on his left'.[67] Captain James Stewart MacKenzie, another staff officer, later wrote that 'the General imagined the enemy was more afraid of Horse than Foot'.[68]

The men on the Jacobite right had seen the dragoon regiments after the former had crossed the Carron. They marched quickly ahead to secure the advantage of terrain that their enemy sought. Yet they kept their ranks and gave time for the rest of the army to come up on their left.[69] Murray sent Colonel John Roy Stuart and Robert Anderson of Whitburgh, who were both on horseback, ahead to ascertain whether there were any infantry in support of the dragoons, which meant them riding close to their enemies. This they did and in answering Murray in the negative he continued his men's advance.[70]

The dragoon regiments were 'a good way before' their own infantry. They attempted to attack the Jacobite right wing in the flank. Murray realised their plan and then he and Stuart 'made a very quick motion till he gained a morass [Abbot's Moss], by which he saved being flanked'.[71] Once again the dragoon regiments attempted to unnerve the regiments opposite them. Elcho recorded their next move that they, 'at last came down in a line at full trot & attacked them sword in hand'.[72] However, as Hawley noted, the cavalry charge was uneven. Cobham's three squadrons and Ligonier's two 'went on very handsomely', but 'Hamilton's who were in the centre, never stirred'.[73]

John Daniel was initially overawed by the sight, later writing:

> Here I must acknowledge, that when I saw this moving cloud of horse, regularly disciplined, in full trot upon us down the summit, I doubted not but that they would have ridden over us without opposition (I mean the front line) and bear us down without difficulty in their impetuous progress.[74]

Apparently there was some nervousness among Ligonier's and Hamilton's, which had routed at Prestonpans, 'Dear brethren, we shall all be massacred this day'. Lieutenant Colonel Whitney saw John Roy Stuart among the Jacobites, a man he

---

67  TNA, SP54/27/55B.
68  HMC 14th Report, IX, p.139.
69  Forbes, *Jacobite Memoirs*, pp.83-4.
70  Home, *History*, p.171n.
71  Blaikie, 'Origins', p.411.
72  Elcho, *Short Account*, p.375.
73  RA, 7411-101-11, p.25.
74  Blaikie, 'Origins', p.195.

was acquainted with and cried out, 'Ha! Are you there? We shall soon be up with you'. To which Stuart replied, 'You shall be welcome when you come. You shall have a warm reception'.⁷⁵

Elcho recorded the Jacobite response to the attack: 'The Highlanders march'd up to them very slowly, with their pieces presented, every man taking his aim, and when the dragoons came within half pistol shot of them, gave them a full discharge, which kill'd a great many of them'. Elcho claimed 400 were killed but this is a huge exaggeration; about 160 of the cavalry became casualties but only a fraction of these were deaths.⁷⁶ Much of the credit for this, according to Alexander McNab of Keppoch's, was due to Lord George Murray: 'He showed both courage and good conduct, being placed in the right wing, standing himself in the front line, he put his wig in his pocket, and scragging his bonnet, gave orders not to fire till the dragoons had fired first, as they made several attempts to make us dislodge first'.⁷⁷

Johnstone wrote that there was then hand to hand fighting:

> The cavalry…rushed upon the Highlanders at a hard trot, breaking their ranks, throwing down everything before them and trampling the Highlanders under the feet of their horses, the most singular and extraordinary combat immediately occurred. The Highlanders, stretched on the ground, thrust their dirks into the bellies of their horses. Some seized the riders by their clothes, dragged them down and stabbed them with their dirks, several again used their pistols, but few had sufficient space to use their swords.

MacDonald of Clanranald found himself trapped under a dead horse and was unable to extricate himself. He saw a Highlander struggling with a dismounted dragoon. The former was triumphant and then aided Clanranald. Johnstone concluded, 'The resistance of the Highlanders was so incredibly obstinate that the English, after having been for some time engaged pell-mell with them in their ranks, were at length repulsed and forced to retire'.⁷⁸ Among the dead was Whitney, who had escaped the debacle of Prestonpans, albeit being wounded, of whom Hawley later wrote, 'poor Whitney had devoted his life to redeem the character of his men and I saw him lose it, just by me, a gallant good man, and he the only one I would have recommended [for promotion]'.⁷⁹ Others received severe wounds; John Kirkland,

---

75   Robert Chambers, *History of the Rebellion*, p.231.
76   Elcho, *Short Account*, p.375.
77   Atholl, *Chronicles*, p.153.
78   Johnstone, *Memoir*, p.87.
79   TNA, SP54/27/38a.

a 30 year old private of Hamilton's Dragoons was 'disabled by several stabs and bruises'; John Kerny of the same regiment was 'disabled in both hands, stabb'd in the back'. Others in that regiment received severe wounds to the hands and fingers, suggestive of fierce hand to hand fighting. Patrick Barnet was 'cut across the nose'.[80] Corse, who, as a member of the Glasgow Militia was stationed behind the cavalry, had a good view point, wrote that he could see daylight between the cavalry.[81] Yet as the Duke of Perth remarked, 'Although the horse has given way, yet the work is not yet accomplished'.[82]

The dragoons who remained alive, fled, 'who in their flight run down all along the Princes first line and got the fire of the whole line'. This was because their own infantry had by now advanced close to them and so they could not go straight back without breaking their own lines. Captain Masterton was shocked, 'for such pannick God keep me from ever seeing again that our forces was in'. Hawley tried to rally them. He drew his pistol, 'but threats and fair words would not do for they never stopped till they got to camp wch was a good mile distant'. He was almost run over by the fleeing horsemen.[83] Hawley himself later wrote:

> 'The Lieutenant General in trying to stop the dragoons was beat downe, him and his horse, by them twice and bothe times was very near being killed or taken by the Highlanders…He was at last forced along with the crowde to the bottom of the hill'.[84]

The cavalry had failed to defeat the Jacobite right. John Home later attributed the decision to use the cavalry thus to Hawley's experiences at Sheriffmuir in 1715, where Home noted that the cavalry of Argyle's right wing routed the Jacobite infantry opposite to them. It is not known if this experience led to a similar tactic being used in 1746. However, Lieutenant Colonel Hepburn later related that when Hawley heard the news of the defeat at Prestonpans, he told those around him, 'that he knew the Highlanders were good militia, but he was certain that they could not stand against a charge of dragoons who attacked them well'.[85] We should also note Hawley's disparaging comments about the Jacobites as 'scum' and 'rabble' and also his remarks in his writings about the ability of the British cavalry. However, of the three regiments, two had behaved abysmally at Prestonpans, so to think they

---

80   TNA, WO116/4.
81   Forbes, *Culloden Papers*, p.271.
82   Metcalfe, *Life of John Metcalfe*, p.89.
83   TNA, SP54/27/55b.
84   RA, 7411-101-11, p.25.
85   Home, *History*, pp.176-177.

would have done better against a formed enemy was optimistic at best.[86] Hawley's first thrust, bred from overconfidence bordering on arrogance, had been an utter failure.

The Glasgow gentleman wrote, 'Hawley did what he could to rally the Flyers, but in vain, had either he been able to effectuate that' he could have won the battle.[87] Apparently some fled to Linlithgow where they reported that they were all that remained of Hawley's forces.[88] Some even rode as far as Edinburgh, bearing similar news and causing panic there.[89] The cavalry's flight also disordered the infantry battalions on the left and the Glasgow Militia who were to their rear, some of whom were in some farm houses.[90] John Metcalfe wrote, 'the horses did great mischief, by breaking through their own foot'.[91] However, as a Jacobite wrote, 'This beginning greatly inspired our men, as it had a contrary effect on the enemy'.[92]

The only mishap from the Jacobite point of view was that Major MacDonald of Keppoch took a dragoon horse, mounted it and was then carried away by the horse with the rest of the dragoons and was thus made a prisoner.[93] MacDonald, however, later found himself looking at the artillery which was stuck in the mud and asked about it, 'I am diverting myself looking at these pieces of cannon'. He was then warned that the Argyll Militia might arrive and so he decided to return to the nearest Jacobite unit. Looking for one, he saw red coated infantry and assumed that these were the Irish Picquets. Walking amongst them, his white cockade in his hat denoted he was a Jacobite and the men of Barrell's Regiment cried out, 'Here is a rebel'. Huske had him take his sword from the scabbard for examination and there was blood and hair on it, which sealed his fate. He then ordered his men to shoot him, but his life was saved by Captain Rich of that battalion who stopped his men from firing on him. MacDonald then drew his sword and pistol to give to Rich as part of his surrender, but Huske feared that this was a prelude to an attack, so once again wanted the man killed but again Rich prevented this and led him away to captivity.[94]

After the melee, the MacDonalds then charged with Murray, who was on foot, at their head. They pursued the dragoons in disorder and failed to keep their ranks. Murray wrote, 'it was not in my power to get them rallied so as to carry them

---

86   Anon, *A Letter from a Gentleman*, p.4.
87   Anon, *A Letter from a Gentleman*, p.4.
88   Ray, *History*, p.242.
89   Henderson, *History*, p.94.
90   Henderson, *History*, pp.94, 92.
91   John Metcalfe, *Life of John Metcalfe* (York: E. and R. Peck, 1795), p.89.
92   Blaikie, 'Origins', p.411.
93   Elcho, *Short Account*, p.375.
94   Paton, 'Lyon', Vol.II, pp.727-728.

down in the enemy's foot regularly'.[95] It was not only the infantry that pursued the fleeing dragoons, but a detachment of Jacobite cavalry also did so and were rebuked by Stuart, 'Gentlemen, keep your ground, these are only Cope's dragoons: You have the battle yet to fight'.[96]

Hawley found himself in a mixture of cavalry and infantry. He found the company of Edinburgh Volunteers, standing alone behind Fleming's Regiment. William Macghie, captain of the former, had been in search of Hawley for instructions and so was not with his men. Lieutenant Home was in temporary command and having met Hawley several times in Edinburgh, asked him if there were any units standing and, if so, where. Hawley was unable to answer him, but suggested the volunteers take cover in a nearby cattle fold. Hawley then rode down the hill, apparently in confusion.[97] Hawley's role in the next phase of the battle is unknown. He was certainly absent from the scene of the fighting as infantry took on infantry. It is presumed that he was attempting to rally the cavalry as Cope had similarly and equally fruitlessly tried at Prestonpans. It was left to his subordinate infantry officers to do what they could.

Yet the success on the Jacobite right wing resulted in 'there was no possibility of making the MacDonalds keep their ranks; many of the first line of the right, pursued the horse and fell in with some of the enemy's militia.'[98] O'Sullivan noted that 'our highlanders according to their usual custom, pursued them sword in hand, & destroyed as many as they cou'd overtake'.[99]

Apparently, Lord Hume, commander of the Glasgow Militia, ordered some of his men to fire and they did so, 'and brought down some of their horses'. Presumably this is a reference to the fleeing dragoons. Thornton's company of Yorkshire Volunteers was clearly nearby for he later wrote, of the said militia, 'they stood and maintained their ground most heroically, so as to secure in a great measure, the retreat of the army at the hazard of their lives and liberties, many of them being cut in pieces'.[100]

The next stage of battle was confusing because the irregular terrain made it impossible for anyone to have a grandstand vision as to what was happening. Andrew Lumisden, Charles' secretary, wrote of 'the inequality of the ground, being interspaced with risings and hollows, whereby there was no seeing from

---

95  Forbes, *Jacobite Memoirs*, p.94n.
96  Henderson, *History*, p.94.
97  Home, *History*, p.172n.
98  Forbes, *Jacobite Memoirs*, p.85.
99  Tayler and Tayler (eds.), 1745, p.118.
100 Blaikie, 'Origins', p.433; William Thornton, *The Counterpoise* (London: Unknown Publisher, 1754), p.40.

right to left what was doing'.[101] The other issue was that many of the men were less than rigorous in the pursuit as John MacLeod noted: 'When they came to the brow of the hill, they then stop'd their pursuit, and walk'd about, talking with each other and telling what marvels they had perform'd, with the same unconcern as if no enemy had been near'.[102]

It was now past 4:00 p.m. and the skies were darkening, not just with impending nightfall but with foul weather which was to play a decisive part in the battle. Daniel wrote, 'there blew such a storm of wind and hail; which was before on our side, and now turned miraculously, as we turned on our backs; and notwithstanding that almost disabled us to bear up against them, it so harassed the enemy'.[103] Corse wrote 'Had it been fair weather, I believe the Troops would have beat them at last…The great storm of Rain & Wind wch began about 10 minutes before the action had rendered their arms useless, & wet all the soldiers' cartridges'.[104] The British infantry were disordered by the weather.[105] Cholmondeley also noted, 'as we march'd, all the way uphill, and over very uneven ground, our men were greatly blown'.[106]

The British infantry were 100 yards apart from the Jacobites.[107] According to Maxwell, 'the left of the Prince's army having spent their fire upon the dragoons, found the enemy's whole foot before them, and by this time, the rain, which had begun with the battle, was become so violent, that it was impossible for the Highlanders, who do not use cartridges, to load again; nevertheless, they drew their broadswords and went on with abundance of resolution'.[108] Meanwhile, the clans on the Jacobite right 'as usual Threw down their Guns and advanced very quick sword in hand'. Some fell on the Glasgow Militia who were to their front. However, because the Jacobite right outflanked that of their opponents, most found no enemy before them, 'made a Stop and went into the greatest confusion'.[109] Others met some opposition, as O'Sullivan related:

> Our left in pursuing the horse, met with the four or five battalions yt I spoke of before, recd their fire, for the highlanders had non to oppose 'um, & rished in upon them sword in hand, immediately after the enemy's

---

101 Blaikie, 'Origins', p.411.
102 William Fraser, *The Earls of Cromarty: their Kindred, Country and Correspondence* (Edinburgh: Unknown Publisher, 1876), Vol.II, p.392.
103 Blaikie, 'Origins', p.195.
104 Forbes, *Culloden Papers*, pp.271-2.
105 Douglas, *History*, p.114.
106 Anon, *Eglinton*, p.441.
107 Douglas, *History*, p.116.
108 Maxwell, *Narrative*, p.102.
109 Elcho, *Short Account*, pp.375-376.

discharge, & cut them to pieces. This was perhaps one of the boldest and finest actions, yt any troops in the world cou'd be capable of.[110]

Captain George Fitzgerald was grenadier captain of Munro's Regiment and he wrote how part of the front line collapsed, 'Blakeney's regiment being put into some disorder on the left of ours by being attacked on their flank by the rebels, occasion'd ours likewise to give way'.[111] At least three junior officers from Blakeney's fled the field and arrived in Edinburgh. Ensign Eyre Coote did so because, bearing the colours as he was, he feared for their safety. Apparently 'He shew'd great joy… as if he had done a very meritorious action. "I've saved the regiment's colours"'.[112] Lieutenant Baldwin Leighton fled, but claimed that he first 'used his utmost endeavours both during the time of the Action and after the Break to rally the men'. In any case, as paymaster of the battalion he thought the next priority was to save the regimental money and the accounts.[113] Another reason for the flight was exhaustion and bad weather; that the infantry had been 'marching against the wind (which then began to be pretty violent and up the face of a steep hill…The Foot, out of breath with the Quickness of their March'.[114]

Infantry fire was limited. There was some Jacobite musketry; Roger Cane of Wolfe's Regiment was shot in the left arm, for example, but it was limited.[115] Cholmondeley wrote that they gave but a 'faint fire'.[116] Many of the British infantry merely fled without firing, Hawley writing 'the whole second line of Foot ran away without firing a shot'.[117] A private from Barrell's Regiment in the second line stated, 'at the running of –'s regiment, like a catching infection, the whole front follow'd, and likewise the rear, not one regiment being left in the field but ours'. It is worth noting that these battalions had a great deal of battle experience, as Sir John Penicuik wrote, 'whole regiments ran off without firing or receiving fire from the enemy…who had behaved well in Flanders'. Cumberland later noted, 'they did not use to run away formerly'.[118]

As with Prestonpans, sometimes officers found themselves abandoned by their men, hence a large proportion of casualties among them. Captain George Fitzgerald of Munro's was knocked down by a musket ball, which went through

---

110 Tayler and Tayler (eds.), *1745*, p.118.
111 RA, CP9/110.
112 National Army Museum, 7607-83.
113 RA, HT, 7411-24-108, 44.
114 Anon, *Letter from a Gentleman*, p.4.
115 TNA, WO116/4.
116 Anon, *Eglinton*, p.441.
117 RA, CP9/99.
118 *Gentleman's Magazine*, 16, pp.41-2; J.M. Grey (ed.), 'The Memoirs of the Life of Sir John Clerk of Penicuik', SHS, 1 series, 7, (1892), p.195; RA, CP9/141.

his hat and wig and grazed his forehead, stunning him and knocking him to the ground. He was soon attacked by a 'party of the rebels who cut me in the head and knock'd me down a second time, when they began to rob me'. Fortunately, a French officer, on hearing his cries, intervened and saved his life.[119] Worse was to come for the battalion's commander, Sir Robert Munro of Foulis (1684-1746). In a letter by a relation, it was claimed that he was deserted by his men and:

> was attacked by Cameron of Lochiel's regiment & for some time defended himself with his half pike. Two of the six, I'm informed, he kill'd, a seventh coming up, fired a pistol into my father's Groin, upon him falling, the Highlander with his sword gave him two strokes on the face, one over the eyes & another on the mouth, with instantly ended a brave man. The same Highlander fired another pistol into my uncle's breast & with his sword terribly slashed him; whom he killed, he then despatch'd a servant of my father.[120]

Some British soldiers were killed in the pursuit, Daniel writing, 'We pursued them sharply for about sixty paces, and fetched down a good many of them'. Apparently, Munro, 'who was heard much to blaspheme during the engagement and as a punishment, for which, his tongue was miraculously cut asunder by a sword and that struck him directly across the mouth'.[121] Munro was shot in the breast; on falling he was joined by his brother in law, a Dr Duncan, who rode unarmed to his assistance. Both were killed. Contemporary historians elevated these two deaths to the status of atrocities, 'they were both miserably slaughtered' and then mutilated.[122] The Glasgow gentleman noted, 'Some of the private men were killed in the Fight, or butcher'd, afterwards in cold blood, for the Highlanders gave very little Quarter in the Field, and discovered a particular thirst after the Blood of our Townsmen. The tempers became dayly more soured and violent'.[123]

A number of other infantry officers stood more or less alone, abandoned by their men, and were killed or wounded. These included, among Munro's Regiment, his lieutenant colonel, Biggar, and three captains, Hall, Fitzgerald, and Witherall. Blakeney's also resisted the Jacobites, with Captains Tod, Kellet, Dalrymple and Edmondson falling, along with six lieutenants, Fairfield, Garing, Hamilton, Launders, Hele, and Kirkson. Howards' Regiment lost two captains and

---

119  RA, CP9/110.
120  Forbes, *Culloden Papers*, pp.267-268.
121  Blaikie, 'Origins', pp.196, 198.
122  Henderson, *History*, p.95.
123  Anon, *A Letter from a Gentleman*, p.5.

Cholmondeley's and Wolfe's one officer each; in the former case it was Lieutenant Colonel Powell.[124]

There were probably some of the rank and file of the battalions on the left who stood and fought, for over half of the casualties (151 out of 271) came from Cholmondeley's, Wolfe's, Munro's, and Blakeney's.[125] Samuel Jordan of Battereau's, a 25 year old from Manchester, was disabled in his left arm and Griffith Williams, a Welshman twice his age, of Blakeney's, lost an eye.[126]

The left wing of the Jacobite army fell against Hawley's centre and leftwards battalions, attacking sword in hand, without recourse to musketry which would only slow them down and expose them to greater firepower. In any case, many of the men had already fired their guns. The British battalions broke, probably after minimal resistance ('irregular fire') at best.[127] Hawley went with these retreating infantry.[128] The Glasgow gentleman observed of the flight: 'Such a scene of confusion and Dismay I never beheld! Horse-men and Foot, Red-Coats and militia, coaches, chaises, and horses with empty saddles, all tumbling and jostling one over another'.[129]

As with Prestonpans, it had taken little time for the Jacobites to rout the British line. Officers who had taken part in it discussed its length thereafter. They concluded that the time between the first firing and the retreat of the British army's right wing, was about 20 minutes.[130]

There were some attempts made to rally the troops. Of Ensign Coote of Blakeney's, it was claimed:

> When the regiment was broke he hurry'd on, by the regiment and had the misfortune to be thrown into a dike of water, when he got up and recovered himself he saw a standing making at the bottom of the hill by different regiments and he immediately made towards that party, but before he could come up they were dispersed by running different ways.[131]

Lieutenant Colonel Jackson rallied between 30 and 40 men and they marched to the army's right, where they could see friendly troops holding their ground, but

---

124 Ray, *History*, p.249.
125 TNA, SP54/27/22D.
126 TNA, WO116/4.
127 Elcho, *Short Account*, p.376.
128 Henderson, *History*, p.93.
129 Anon, *Letter from a Gentleman*, p.5.
130 Home, *History*, p.174n-175n.
131 NAM, 7607-83.

'fire coming on close to them, some threw down their arms and went away and others dispersed'.¹³²

However, on the British right the advantage lay with them inasmuch as that they had no Jacobites to their front to directly threaten them. Furthermore, there was a 'ravine or gulley' separating them from their nearest enemies and there was a small farm house securing their left. Barrel's and Ligonier's, in the first rank, under Brigadier Cholmondeley, stood firm. The latter wrote that the battalions' officers 'deserve the greatest praise, for the spirit they shew'd'. Cholmondeley wrote 'I got the men to be quite cool, as cool as ever I saw men at exercise; and when the rebels came down upon us, we not only repulsed them, but advanced, and put them to flight'.¹³³

The ravine on the British right flank at Falkirk. (Author photograph)

One commentator reported that the Atholl men that were fired upon fled after the first volley and did not return to the field that day.¹³⁴ This may seem strange, as the brigade were on the Jacobite right, but could be accounted for if they were

132  NAM, 7607-83.
133  Anon, *Eglinton*, p.441.
134  Anon, *Letter from a Gentleman*, p.4.

marched over to shore up the Jacobite left. Meanwhile, Ligonier's and Barrell's men sustained minor casualties; one man from the former was killed and six in total were wounded; but 30 were missing, which suggest additional losses. However, compared to those four battalions on the left these were light.[135]

Other infantry under Huske, St. Clair's and Howard's (moving up from the third line), joined them. They began by firing in platoons against small bodies of Jacobites. Cholmondeley told them 'if they will keep their ground I will go back and rally the dragoons'. They did so, and 100 men of Cobham's Dragoons were added to the force. Cholmondeley addressed them all:

> I told them that I had repuls'd the Enemy, with two weak battalions and that if they would march up, I would beat them, and that I would order the two battalions, to march up Briskly at the same time, & give them their Fire, and that they should fall in, sword in hand, they were greatly pleased with this, and with many oaths and Irish Exclamations, swore they would follow me.[136]

The dragoons marched 100 yards behind the infantry battalions as they advanced. They found some Jacobites formed behind houses and barns. Cholmondeley fired his pistol to have the men form for action. Cholmondeley remarked that if he and Huske could gather more troops, they could drive the Jacobites off the field. Nightfall, however, brought their venture to an end.[137] Furthermore, the weather led to only one musket in five being able to fire. Nor was there any artillery support. When Huske's forces retreated they found the British artillery abandoned and stuck in the mud. Grenadiers from Barrell's Regiment drew one away and horses were taken from the camp to drag another two away.[138] A private from Barrell's later wrote, 'Brigadier- [Cholmondeley?] was pleased to express his satisfaction at our Behaviour, by kissing our men and making us a present of 10 guineas'.[139]

The artillery had played no part in the battle, as was the case with the Jacobites' guns. Yet there had been an expectation that it would have done so. Mackenzie later wrote that this 'was a great disadvantage to us especially as we had to do with the Highlanders who don't at all like cannon'.[140] Hawley had not given Cunningham any orders, presumably due to the haste that he gave orders to the rest of the army. Cunningham rode up and down the line to find him but was unable to do so. He

---

135 TNA, SP54/27/22D.
136 TNA, SP54/27/22D.
137 TNA, SP54/27/22D.
138 Douglas, *History*, pp.117, 124.
139 *Penny London Post*, 25-27 January 1746.
140 HMC 14th Report IX, p.140.

asked Huske, but Huske only told him that he had to see Hawley. Eventually a staff officer eventually told Cunningham to 'march the artillery up to an adjacent hill in the rear of the front line of the army'. It seems that the mortars were never moved from the camp. Yet the road that the train had to take was 'very bad and intricate'. Speed was slow and they fell behind the second line of the infantry as it moved forward. Two of the heavy guns became stuck in the mud and so were abandoned. With only three guns left (two 4-pounders and a 1 ½-pounder) they carried on, but on seeing retreating infantry, the civilian drivers deserted with the horses and the majority of the men left, too. A soldier noted that 'the carelessness and cowardice of the people belonging to the horses, who cut the traces and made the best way to save themselves'. Cunningham later observed, 'In such a situation, deserted by his men and the rebels within 20 paces of him, it was impossible for him to do any service with three guns, he thought it most prudent to order them down the hill'.[141] Accompanying the guns were the men of Thornton's Yorkshire Blues volunteer infantry company, but, dismayed by such inaction, Thornton had ridden off to join the cavalry charge, crying out 'Damn this accident! We shall see no sport today'.[142]

Meanwhile, Huske's force was faced by a body of 400 Jacobites returning from the pursuit, but lacking muskets; having thrown these away, the latter were unable to stand up to them in a fire fight. John Roy Stuart thought that this might be an ambush, so called out to the men to stop their pursuit and the call 'flew immediately from rank to rank and there the while army into disorder'. He later wrote, 'The Highlanders were in complete disorder, dispersed here and there with the different clans mingled pell-mell together'.[143] Macleod wrote, 'if they [the British] return'd to the charge, he was afraid that they wou'd still take the victory out of our hands, considering the great confusion we were in'.[144]

This trio of officers won plaudits from contemporary historians. Cholmondeley's activity was particularly praiseworthy because he was 'dangerously wounded, and contracted a palsy from the cold he caught in the field'. Huske had shown 'great vigilance and Presence of Mind [and] acquired the Highest Reputation'. Brigadier John Mordaunt (1697-1780) 'was allowed to have done all that could be expected from the most knowing and experience Officer'.[145] However, Hawley had played no part in this successful rearguard action. As noted, he had been carried away with the rout of the troops he was trying to rally and was at the camp before any other of the senior officers. Hawley knew nothing of the whereabouts of Cholmondeley, Huske, and their four battalions as all firing had ceased. Hawley feared that the

---

141 RA, CP9/102; *Penny London Post*, 25-27 Jan. 1746.
142 Metcalfe, *Life*, p.88.
143 Johnstone, *A Memoir*, p.88.
144 Fraser, *Earls of Cromarty*, Vol.II, p.392.
145 Ray, *History*, p.247.

Jacobites might march to Linlithgow to cut him off from Edinburgh so when the rearguard did arrive, had Mordaunt take some of the men and march to Edinburgh to secure the city.[146]

Meanwhile, the Argyllshire Militia, stationed to the right of the army to the east end of Callander Park, saw no action. As night fell they marched back to Linlithgow and arrived at Edinburgh on 18 January, in an orderly manner.[147]

Huske's and Cholmondeley's counter attack also had an effect on the second line of the Jacobite army. They did not move further to left to face these battalions head on, nor did they stand still and wait for new orders, but rather crowded in with the first line. Those that did, 'went down upon the enemy with them; the rest of the second line fell into confusion with their ranks, being thinned by those who had run in with the first line'. They fell back to their initial positions on the battlefield.[148] Some went back to Bannockburn or even Stirling, 'where they gave out yt we lost the day'.[149] When Farquharson's men heard firing they left their artillery and rushed forward, but were met by 200 or 300 men flying westwards, though he forced them to turn back.[150] MacDonald claimed that the Lowland battalions in the second line 'smitten apparently with terror took to flight' and he and O'Sullivan managed to rally them.[151]

According to Murray, O'Sullivan was the man to blame. He should have brought up troops from the second line or the reserve to have extended the first line. Murray wrote, 'nothing was more easy; but that gentleman had certainly no knowledge in these affairs, nor was he ever seen to do any thing in the time of action'.[152] Eventually Murray tried to take charge. He had his Atholl battalions, 'who kept their line in perfect good order'. Seeing the enemy's confusion, he resolved to exploit it to the full. Marching down the hill, he attempted to rally the MacDonalds. This was difficult because there were none to play the bagpipes; the pipers having already thrown away their pipes and taken part in the charge. He sent Colonel Henry Ker of Graden, a Jacobite staff officer, to plead that the reserves might advance to their left. Ker brought up the Irish Picquets and Royal Ecossois. Drummond and other officers accompanied them. Marching forward to the foot of the hill they passed the abandoned cannon. It was then realised that there were four British infantry battalions and a regiment of dragoons intact and now to the Jacobites' rear. The remainder of their opponents, though, was long

---

146  Henderson, *History*, p.94.
147  RA, 7411-101-11, p.25.
148  Forbes, *Jacobite Memoirs*, p.86.
149  Tayler and Tayler (eds.), *1745*, p.118.
150  Home, History, p.175n.
151  Tayler and Tayler (eds.), *1745*, p.115n.
152  Forbes, *Jacobite Memoirs*, p.91.

gone. 'The other part of their army were in the utmost confusion, running off by forties and fifties to the right and left to get into Falkirk, so that their line was in the greatest disorder'.[153]

According to some Jacobites the battle represented a lost opportunity. Daniel wrote, 'we let an opportunity slip out of our hands, which never afterwards presented itself again'. He blamed this on Murray, 'who would not permit the army to pursue any further'.[154] John Macleod wrote, 'Had our army been disciplined or have been commanded by experienced generals, I am fully convinced that we would have cut the King's army to pieces'.[155] At least one of their opponents thought so, too, Corse writing:

> Why they did not use their advantage, & enter when the troops were broke, sword in hand, as is their way; & in the next place, why they did not pursue when the army marched to Linlithgow, when all firearms were useless is not to be comprehended. They cant [sic], in all human probability, ever have such another opportunity.[156]

According to Elcho, 'all the generals & their aid de camps were on foot, whereas they ought to have been on horseback, for Generals' business in a battle is more to command than to fight as common soldiers'.[157] Murray stated that at this point he only had 600-700 men 'the rest being all scattered on the face of the hill, he judged it would be risking all the advantages they had gained'.[158] Drummond suspected an ambush. On seeing St. Clair's Regiment file away he remarked, 'these men behaved admirably well at Fontenoy, and yet they are flying; I fear there is an ambuscade'.[159]

In fact, the British army had left the field once it was dark. It was a full hour since the last shot had been fired. It was not possible for them to return to the fray because the rain had spoiled their arms and ammunition, and so lacking provisions and ammunition, and finding that their horses had been taken from the camp by the drivers, orders were sent to burn the tents. The army then retreated to Linlithgow, then to Edinburgh on 18 January.[160] Some fleeing troops had already arrived at the Scottish capital with tales of being defeated, but shortly afterwards Grosett was sent there to give Lord Chief Justice Fletcher an alternative version of

---

153 Forbes, *Jacobite Memoirs*, pp.86, 88.
154 Blaikie, 'Origins', p.196.
155 Fraser, *Earls of Cromarty*, Vol.II, p.392.
156 Forbes, *Culloden Papers*, p.272.
157 Elcho, *Short Account*, p.376.
158 Forbes, *Jacobite Memoirs*, p.87.
159 Henderson, *History*, p.94.
160 Douglas, *History*, p.117.

events. He told him that 'the Kings Troops had at last beat the Rebels from and kept the Field of Battle 'till obliged to leave it for want of Provisions, and leave seven of their Cannon on the Field for want of Horses to carry them off'. This dissipated the alarm that was becoming widespread among Edinburgh loyalists.[161]

Yet the Jacobite victory was far from complete, 'The honour of remaining masters of the field was of little avail to us. We had no reason for believing that we had lost the battle as the English army had retreated, but as we supposed them still in their camp, we considered it at most as undecided'.[162] However, Lumisden put the delay down to the need to re-order the army in order to defeat the British at their camp, for which only half the army could be got together. They then saw the camp being burnt and the men retreating to Falkirk. Three officers went forward, disguised as peasants, to reconnoitre. On their return, they told how the enemy was in full retreat to Linlithgow. Lumisden deemed that this was an error:

> a few men properly posted could have hindered the highlanders from entering that night, and obliged us either to have abandoned the field of battle, or to have stood all night under arms, wet and fatigued as we were, and exposed to the inclemency of the weather, a thing impossible.[163]

There was even the suggestion that at this point the Jacobite army should retreat towards Dunnipace and places nearby. This was because of the weather, 'it being a prodigious rain', and the men needed to be under cover. There was a great deal of confusion among the Jacobite army. Many did not know what had happened on either wing of the army. Bad weather and poor light did nothing to help.[164]

In the evening the Jacobite army were permitted to take hold of the town of Falkirk. According to Murray, 'he would either lye in the town or in paradise' and strongly advocated marching towards the town. Charles, who rode up to him, agreed. Murray advised him to stay in a house at the foot of the hill until word could reach him that Falkirk had been secured.[165] As they marched towards it they found the guns which had been abandoned by Cunningham's men earlier that day. Drummond, Murray, and Lochiel led the column entering the town by three different routes. They had but the Atholl men and the Irish Picquets with them and a handful of men from the MacDonald regiments and from those of Ogilvy, the Appin Stewarts, Cameron, and John Roy Stuart, headed by their colonels. There was little opposition. The army was merely 1,500 strong in Falkirk, the remainder

---

161 Blaikie, 'Origins', p.362.
162 Johnstone, *A Memoir*, p.88.
163 Blaikie, 'Origins', p.412.
164 Elcho, *Short Account*, p.376.
165 Forbes, *Jacobite Memoirs*, p.87.

Falkirk battle monument. (Author photograph)

Tomb in Falkirk churchyard of Captain William Edmundstone (or Edmundson) of Blakeney's Regiment, killed at Falkirk. (Author photograph)

being scattered throughout the district, with some back at Bannockburn.[166] Daniel and seventeen men were told to take a house three miles away which housed some of the enemy. The door was shut against them. They surrounded it and made a summons to surrender. On the first refusal, the Jacobites opened fire and then the inhabitants gave in. There were 54 in all.[167] A few other prisoners were taken and by the day's end, Charles arrived, too. It was 8:00 p.m.[168] In the town were found many of the supplies belonging to Hawley's army, especially those of his officers, especially 'hampers of good wines, & liquors & other provisions'. O'Sullivan, wrote, 'The Prince profited of General Hally's supper wch he wanted very much, for he had not a bit of his own, nor either did he eat a morsel yt day'. He also had 'a great quantity of bread found, wch was distributed' among the men. He stayed at Falkirk that night and the next two days.[169]

Inclement weather persisted until the night. Daniel wrote that 'we went thoroughly wet and cold, to repose ourselves a little while on straw, and some in the open fields or air, so that it was impossible to find any resource or ease for our excessive hunger, wet and cold'.[170] Yet some men did take shelter, 'every one putting himself under cover to dry his cloaths and refresh himself after the fatigue of the day'. This meant that the intended 1,000 men who were to pursue had been whittled down to a mere 50 and so these were insufficient to do much apart from mounting sentries that night, though some cavalry did pursue and rounded up a few stragglers. Hawley's army, elements of which had been departing Falkirk from the east as Drummond's column arrived at the other end, got clean away. The Jacobite army's behaviour was allegedly due to their being irregular troops.[171] Elcho wrote, 'Had the Prince's army been able to have followed them, the same night to Linlithgow there is no doubt he would have destroy'd them'.[172]

Murray wrote about why the army's behaviour went awry;

> Had the MacDonalds on the right either not broke their ranks, or rallied soon after, they , with the Atholl men, would have cut the whole enemy's foot to pieces, for they were close at them , and must have drove them down the hill before them; and by speed of foot, not a man of them would have got off from them.

---

166  Blaikie, 'Origins', pp.412-3; Forbes, *Jacobite Memoirs*, p.88.
167  Blaikie, 'Origins', pp.196-197.
168  Forbes, *Jacobite Memoirs*, p.88.
169  Tayler and Tayler (eds.), *1745*, pp.119-120.
170  Blaikie, 'Origins', p.197.
171  Blaikie, 'Origins', p.413; Elcho, *Short Account*, p.378.
172  Elcho, *Short Account*, p.379.

Had there been any officer on the left, to have ordered two or three battalions from the second line, or reserve, to have faced those of the enemy that outflanked them, they would have had a complete victory. Most of the officers were with his Royal Highness in the reserve; had they come up, and with the left of the second line followed the first, extending a little farther to the left, the enemy's whole army, or at least the foot, must have been taken or killed, and, in that case, even but few of the horse would have escaped.[173]

He also listed the enemy's failings. They were unready and so failed to reach the summit of Falkirk Muir first. Later, they could have lined the camp or the town and repulsed the Jacobite attack, assuming the Jacobites would have ever attacked.[174] Johnstone wrote that if this had happened the Jacobite army would have had to have retreated because they 'could not pass the night in the open air, during such a terrible tempest' and so this would have 'been a sort of victory for General Hawley'.[175]

On the following day the field of battle was surveyed by the victors. Numbers were counted; apparently there were 600-700 British and 50 Jacobite dead. The corpses of both armies were buried. Social distinctions were maintained in death as those men identifiable as officers were brought down to the town and were buried there, and these included Munro and Whitney.[176] Johnstone recounts the reality of seeing corpses on a large scale, 'the horrid spectacle I had witnessed was for a long time, fresh in my mind…when we coolly proceed over a field of battle, we are seized with horror at the sight of dead bodies, a spectacle repugnant to human nature, though when living, they may have been perfectly unknown to us'.[177] The men took the belongings of the dead. O'Sullivan wrote of 'Gold watcheses were at a cheap reat'.[178] Officer prisoners were housed in Stirling town house and the men in the church; later they were rehoused in Down Castle. They included a number of Presbyterian priests and hangmen.[179]

Daniel wrote, 'But this cheap bought victory, you will say, merited a better exit!' There were about 100-700 prisoners and one remarked, 'By my soul, Dick, if Prince Charles goes on in this way, Prince Frederick will never be King George'.[180]

---

173 Forbes, *Jacobite Memoirs*, pp.89-90.
174 Forbes, *Jacobite Memoirs*, p.93.
175 Johnstone, *A Memoir*, p.93.
176 Blaikie, 'Origins', p.413.
177 Johnstone, *Memoir*, p.95.
178 Tayler and Tayler (eds.), *1745*, p.120.
179 Elcho, *Short Account*, p.380.
180 Blaikie, 'Origins', p.198-9.

Johnstone was certain it was a Jacobite victory, writing, 'Mr MacDonald of Lochgarry…revived our spirits by announcing for certain that we had gained a most complete victory'.[181] Lord George Murray had no doubts and his correspondence immediately after the battle was full of such; writing to his wife, 'We have gott a most compleat victory: cannon, stores, camp, tents &c all our. The enemy made the most confused retreat that could possibly be seen. Night coming on hinder'd the utter slaughter of the enemy' and to his brother, William, Jacobite Duke of Athol, he wrote 'His Royal Highness has obtained a compleat victory over his Enemys'.[182] However, there were too few Jacobites to exploit the victory. According to Daniel, only 3,000 remained to hand, 'many of them having loaded themselves with booty, returned up to the hills'.[183]

Jacobite loses were light. Lumisden counted them as three captains, four lieutenants, and 40 privates dead, with double that wounded. This was a little more than at Prestonpans, but far fewer proportionately.[184] Elcho counted 50 dead and 60 wounded including Cameron of Lochiel and his brother being slightly injured.[185] Of the senior officers, Drummond had been shot in the fleshy part of his arm.[186]

Jacobite estimates of the number of the enemies who had become casualties varied; Johnstone wrote that 600 had been killed and 700 made prisoner; Elcho that there were 500-600 dead and 600 taken and Maxwell gave lower figures; 400-500 killed and hundreds taken captive.[187] The reality is that all these figures were wild exaggerations. The official list of the British casualties was as follows: 14 officers and 69 other ranks, killed, totalling 83, with 83 wounded and 289 missing (many of which may have been killed or died), totalling 455. These casualties broke down as follows:[188]

---

181 Johnstone, *Memoir*, p.89.
182 Atholl, *Chronicles*, pp.157-158.
183 Blaikie, 'Origins'. p.197.
184 Blaikie, 'Origins'. p.411.
185 Elcho, *Short Account*, p.379.
186 Henderson, *History*, p.95.
187 Johnstone, *Memoir*, p.92; Elcho, *Short Account*, p.378; Maxwell, *Narrative*, p.105.
188 TNA, SP54/27, 22D.

## Officers Killed

| Unit | Field Officer | Captain | Lieutenant | Ensign/Cornet | Staff/Quartermaster | Total |
|---|---|---|---|---|---|---|
| Barrel | | | | | | |
| Cholmondeley | 1 | | | | | 1 |
| Munro | 1 | 2 | | | 1 | 4 |
| Wolfe | | 2 | | | | 2 |
| Blakeney | | 4 | 1 | | | 5 |
| Battereau | | | | | | |
| Pulteney | | | | | | |
| Price | | | | | | |
| St. Clair | | | | | | |
| Howard | | | | | | |
| Fleming | | | | | | |
| Ligonier | | | | | | |
| Cobham | | | | | 1 | 1 |
| Ligonier | 1 | | | | | 1 |
| Hamilton | | | | | | |
| Total | 3 | 8 | 1 | | 2 | 14 |

## Officers Wounded

| Unit | Field Officer | Captain | Lieutenant | Ensign | Staff | Total |
|---|---|---|---|---|---|---|
| Barrel | | | | | | |
| Cholmondeley | | | | | | |
| Munro | | | | | | |
| Wolfe | | | | | | |
| Blakeney | | | | | | |
| Battereau | | | | | | |
| Pulteney | | | | | | |
| Price | | | | | | |
| St Clair | | 1 | | | | 1 |
| Howard | | | 1 | | | 1 |
| Fleming | | | | | | |
| Ligonier | | | | | 1 | 1 |
| Cobham | 1 | | | | | 1 |
| Ligonier | | | | | | |
| Hamilton | 1 | | 1 | | | 2 |
| Total | 2 | 1 | 2 | | 1 | 6 |

## Officers Missing

| Unit | Field Officer | Captain | Lieutenant | Ensign | Staff | Total |
|---|---|---|---|---|---|---|
| Barrel | | | | | | |
| Cholmondeley | 1 | | | | | 1 |
| Munro | 1 | | | | | 1 |
| Wolfe | | 3 | | | | 3 |
| Blakeney | | | | | | |
| Battereau | | | | | | |
| Pulteney | | | | | | |
| Price | | | | | | |
| St. Clair | | | | | | |
| Howard | | | | | | |
| Fleming | | | | | | |
| Ligonier | | | | | | |
| Cobham | | | | | | |
| Ligonier | | | 2 | 2 | | 4 |
| Hamilton | | | | 1 | 2 | 3 |
| **Total** | 2 | 3 | 2 | 3 | 2 | 12 |

## Other Ranks Casualties

| Unit | Sergeants killed | Sergeants wounded | Sergeants missing | Others killed | Others wounded | Others missing | Total |
|---|---|---|---|---|---|---|---|
| St. Clair | | | 2 | 6 | 1 | | 9 |
| Howard | | | | 1 | | 12 | 13 |
| Barrell | | | | | 1 | 11 | 12 |
| Wolfe | | | 1 | 5 | 9 | 20 | 35 |
| Pulteney | | | | 1 | 3 | 10 | 14 |
| Blakeney | 1 | | | 39 | | | 40 |
| Price | | | | 1 | 2 | 31 | 34 |
| Cholmondeley | | 1 | | | 9 | 7 | 19 |
| Fleming | | | | | 4 | 7 | 11 |
| Munro | | | | | 11 | 28 | 39 |
| Ligonier | 1 | | | 1 | 5 | 11 | 18 |
| Battereau | | | | 2 | | 35 | 37 |
| Cobham | | | | 9 | 11 | 18 | 38 |
| Ligonier | 1 | 1 | 1 | 1 | 15 | 28 | 47 |
| Hamilton | | | | | 4 | 59 | 63 |
| **Total** | 3 | 2 | 4 | 66 | 75 | 277 | 429 |

Material losses include seven brass cannons, three iron ones, several mortars, ammunition for these, wagons, tents, three standards and two colours, a kettle drum, some muskets and baggage.[189] Hamilton's Dragoons also lost 79 horses, presumably some being killed, others taken, and some running off, but there are no equivalent figures for the other two cavalry regiments.[190]

Casualties were far fewer, both numerically and proportionately, than they were at Prestonpans. In part this was because many men fled immediately, because there were no barriers to escape as there had been at the earlier battle and because some of the British battalions stood and repelled their adversaries. Most of the army fled, but lived to fight another day. A muster roll taken 11 days after the battle gave 6,755 infantrymen present.[191]

Colonel Ligonier died ten days after the battle, not by wounds, but because he had been unwell prior to the battle, but could not be persuaded not to lead his men. Despite being bled and blistered beforehand, he was drenched to the skin by the rain on the day of the action, contracted a cold and quinsy and died.[192]

There is no record of how many of the militia and volunteers were killed, wounded or captured. Many fell into the latter category, however. Yet, at least nineteen Glasgow Militia privates lost their lives and their widows later received £5 each.[193] Apart from these men, some of the volunteers present were also taken prisoner. Prisoners were held in Falkirk and Stirling church and Castle Down. These included 20 of Thornton's Yorkshire Volunteers, (one of whom had 84 out of the 90 guineas on his person taken by his captors) though most escaped fairly quickly afterwards, as did another 25 detainees.[194] One of them, John Metrcalfe, was asked by a dragoon officer how he found his own way back, being blind, and replied, 'I found it very easy to follow the sound of the dragoon horses, they made such a clatter over the stones'.[195] A number of the Glasgow Militia, perhaps 25, were also taken, as were some of the spectators.[196] The lot of the prisoners was dismal, with most of the provisions intended for them eaten by their guards. When those remaining marched north in early February they were described as being 'in a miserable condition, some wanting shoes and stockings'.[197]

---

189  Blaikie, 'Origins', p.411.
190  RA, CP16/223.
191  TNA, SP54/27/55C.
192  Ray, *History*, p.248.
193  Blaikie, 'Origins', p.433.
194  Ray, *History*, p.250; *Glasgow Courant*, 3 February 1746.
195  Metcalfe, *Life*, p.96.
196  Henderson, *History*, p.95.
197  *Glasgow Courant*, 3 Feb, 1746; *Stamford Mercury*, 20 February 1746

Despite Hawley writing, 'I flatter myself that nobody will lay many faults to my charge', they did so.[198] After the battle the recrimination began. On 28 January Walpole told Mann:

> you will find there [in the newspapers] an account of another battle lost in Scotland – our arms cannot succeed there. Hawley, of whom I said so much to you in my last, has been as unsuccessful as Cope, and by almost every circumstance the same, except that Hawley had less want of skill and much more presumption. The very same dragoons ran away at Falkirk, that ran away at Prestonpans.[199]

Private Enoch Bradshaw of Cobham's Dragoons had no love for his commander, writing 'General Hawley who does not love us because our regiment spoke truth about Falkirk job' and he was sorrowful over 'the brave Englishmen that are now in their graves had not been lost'.[200] An officer wrote to Lady Elizabeth Hastings thus:

> I am alive and well at present though, it is only by God's blessed will than our general's conduct. For he drew only 400 dragoons, sword in hand, up against 1,000 of our enemy and we had orders not to draw a pistol or fire and as soon as he had given these orders to the rest of the officers he moved away from us and we never saw him move until the next morning. We lost the day for we were all sold to our enemies by treacherous general Hawley, for we could have got the day if he had done us justice or let us fight like Englishmen as we are. I wish the Duke had been with us'.[201]

Richard Glover wrote that the battle was lost due to Hawley's 'beastly ignorance and negligence'.[202]

Contemporary historian, John Marchant, writing in the same year as the battle wrote:

> What was the real occasion of our Miscarriage, and how our men came to lose that spirit and Vivacity for which they were ever famous in an Engagement, is hard to account for: And yet perhaps if one was to canvass this affair thoroughly, one wou'd not be so much at a Loss for the cause, as

---

198 RA, CP9/134.
199 Lewis (ed.), *Walpole*, Vol.19, p.203.
200 Paton, 'Lyon', Vol.II, pp.380-381.
201 Anon, *Hastings*, p.54.
202 Richard Glover, *Memoirs by a Celebrated literary and political figure* (London: John Murray, 1814), p. 40.

one at first might Apprehend. If a General would have his men fight well, he must use them well; bad Usage will make the Brave turn Cowards; as, on the Contrary, Kindness, Civility, and courteous Behaviour, will inspire the most dastardly with a Resolution and Firmness they never felt before. If a General has not the Love and Good Opinion of is soldiers, he will be very rarely successful in any of his Enterprizes.[203]

Marchant then cited Marlborough and Cumberland and two soldiers who were respected by the troops and concluded, 'To what then must we impute our ill Success under other Generals? Can it, in Reason, be ascrib'd to any other cause, but the want of those gracious Qualities in some of their late commanders, which are so conspicuous'.

An unknown contemporary, who has been identified as Major General Joseph Wightman, who shared the long-deceased general's surname, saw Hawley shortly afterwards and wrote, 'Hawley seems to be sensible of his misconduct…he looked most wretchedly; even worse than Cope did a few hours after his scuffle'. Like others he was critical of the general's conduct, 'Hawley is in much the same situation as General Cope; he was never seen in the field during the battle'. Wightman thought it could all have been much worse 'if General Huske had not acted with judgement and courage, and appeared everywhere'.[204]

Yet even if the Jacobites had been defeated, the British army would probably have had to fall back. The Glasgow gentleman noted of Hawley's advance, 'and what surprizes every body, without having made any preparation for provisions'. Indeed, at Falkirk itself, most of the available supplies had been eaten up by the spectators. He wrote 'the Army, without a new Miracle, must have been obliged to retire back again'.[205]

News of the battle reached the Jacobite court in Rome and the French court as one Brown, an Irish officer, was sent from Scotland to Louis XV, where it was presented as a great victory (Brown was awarded the Cross of St. Louis). The Jacobite account included the line, 'After a compleat Victory, gained by 8000 over above 12,000, we remained masters of the field'.[206] According to Lord George Murray, 'The accounts sent to France put me quite out of continuance; my name is on evert paragraph'.[207] Mann despairingly reported to Walpole. He wrote, 'Hawley's affair for example frightened us out of our Senses. The French accounts magnified it an hundred

---

203 John Marchant, *History*, pp.324-325.
204 Forbes, *Culloden Papers*, p.267.
205 Anon, *Letter from a Gentleman*, p.4.
206 Douglas, *History*, p.155. Lewis (ed.), *Walpole*, Vol.19, p.217.
207 Atholl, *Chronicles*, p.159.

fold'. He could not believe that an outnumbered army of '6000 Vagabonds' could defeat 18,000 troops.[208]

Hawley realised that, like Cope, he needed to defend himself and wrote to Cumberland on the evening of the battle thus:

> My heart is broke. I can't say we are quite beat today, but our left is beat, and their left is beat. We had enough to beat them, for we had 2000 men more than they. But such a scandalous cowardice I never saw before…I must say one thing, that every officer did his duty, and what was in the power of man, in trying to stop and rally the men, and they led them on with as good a countenance, till a Halloo began.[209]

Mackenzie agreed, writing that the men 'seem to have lost all spirit, and sense of honour'.[210]

In another letter of the same evening, after noting that there had been a battle, he wrote, 'Butt not neare so bad as I guess you may have heard from some hasty ones; we did retreat and so did they butt we lost the field, allmost all ye King's Troops ran away' but that apart from losing most of the artillery there had been very little loss.[211]

Yet Newcastle, as well as Cumberland, was very solicitous towards Hawley, writing on 24 January:

> His Majesty was extremely concerned for the unfortunate event of the Engagement on Friday last near Falkirk: But I have the satisfaction to answer you, that the King is persuaded you did everything in your power to prevent the misfortune that happened; and will not fail to do your utmost to retrieve it in the best and most expeditious manner possible.[212]

Argyle was also sympathetic, writing to Hawley after the battle, 'I don't wonder at your being affected with your Troops having deserted you in so unaccountable a manner…I don't find that it has lessen'd you in the esteem of anybody'. Likewise Lord de La Warr wrote, 'I wish with all my heart I have congratulated you on a victory that is not to be obtained if the Troops run away'.[213]

---

208   Lewis (ed.), *Walpole*, Vol.19, p.214.
209   RA, CP9/99.
210   HMC 14th Report, IX, p.140.
211   NLS, Mss 16625, 105.
212   TNA, SP54/27/40.
213   RA, HT, 7411-24-112, 28, 29.

Other reasons were ascribed for the defeat, with Miss Gertrude Saville (1697-1758), a well-to-do London spinster, recording in her diary, 'The reasons given are, the same cowardly dragoons who ran away when Cope was beat, did so again; also a storm of hail, rain and wind not only blinded our men…but wet their powder, so that most of their guns would not go off'.[214]

However, in recent years, a revisionist account of Falkirk suggests that this battle was not a defeat for the British army.[215] This is, in part, because of comments made by Major James Wolfe, who wrote, 'twas not a battle as neither side would fight…possibly it will be told you in a much worse light than it really is. Though we can't be said to have totally routed the enemy, yet we remained a long time masters of the field of battle and of our cannon'.[216] A private from Barrell's Regiment was not at all downcast, writing after the battle that 'We expect in a few days time to give them another meeting which I pray God it may be attended with a better opportunity'.[217]

Yet Mackenzie was in no doubt, writing:

> this unfortunate affair which does us very little honour, for they were inferior to us in numbers, had no artillery and made but very little use of their broadswords, which is the weapon they rely most upon, and yet notwithstanding all this, if the victory was to be given to either side, it certainly was theirs, rather than ours.[218]

A French officer in the Jacobite army was under no doubts, either, writing:

> *je regarde comme une bataille de Fontenoy, en petit, par rapport a 'l'effet qu'elle produit. Les Ennemis ont ete arretes dans leurs projects comme a Fontenoy, & et le siege de Sterling est continue, comme celui de Tournay.*
> [I compare it to the battle of Fontenoy, in small scale, by the effect it produced. The enemies were stopped in their aim just as at Fontenoy and the siege of Stirling continued, just as that of Tournai did].[219]

---

214 A. Saville (ed.), 'Secret Comment: The Diaries of Gertude Saville, 1722-1757', *Thoroton Society Record Series*, 42, (1997), p.266.
215 Reid, *1745*, p.100.
216 Beckles Willson (ed.), *Life and Letters of James Wolfe* (London: Heinemann, 1909), pp.56-57.
217 *Penny London Post*, 25-27 January 1746.
218 HMC, 14th Report IX, p.140.
219 Anon. *Lettre d'un Officier du Regiment Royal Ecossois* (Paris: Unknown Publisher, 1746), unpaginated.

One contemporary newspaper likened the battle to that of Sheriffmuir, in that both armies saw their left wing rout from the field of battle. Yet, as with most comparisons, the differences are also evident on closer examination. At Sheriffmuir, Argyle's army held the field and their enemy retreated back to Perth. Their march south has been thwarted. In this instance the Jacobite army held the field and had prevented their enemies' march to Stirling and so had won the battle. Neither battle ended the campaign, though.

Falkirk was therefore not a decisive Jacobite victory as Prestonpans had been. Hawley had been defeated but they had caused only minimal casualties; a roll call of the 12 battalions engaged taken ten days after the battle showed a greater number of men in the ranks than before the battle. Bad weather, nightfall and a lack of formed troops under orders had prevented a rigorous pursuit on 17/18 January. Yet they had retained command of the field of battle and had prevented Hawley from relieving the siege of Stirling Castle, or from destroying the Jacobite army or forcing it to retreat. The campaign was not at an end and so the fighting would continue as both sides' armies were mostly intact.

The reasons for the battle's result can be stated as follows. Hawley was overconfident, relying on his previous experience of dealing with the Jacobite army at Sheriffmuir. He was convinced that an unsupported cavalry charge would rout the Jacobites. In this he was wrong. Because of this reverse, much of the infantry's morale collapsed and many of them, mostly those on the left wing nearest to the cavalry, fled. Hawley was then unable to take control of the battle which was rapidly becoming very chaotic with some troops fleeing and others standing. The lack of co-ordination of all three arms of the army led to them being unable to support one another, as they were to at Culloden. The artillery was unable to come into action at all, such was Hawley's rush to battle. Finally, the bad weather made an effective stand at the camp impractical. Yet the Jacobite leadership was also at fault and collapsed after their initial repulse of the dragoons. This loss of control of the battle combined with bad weather and darkness to prevent any successful pursuit.

7

# The End of the Jacobite Campaign

Most generals who are defeated in battle are disgraced and are never given a battlefield command again, as with Cope after Prestonpans, but by no means all; Cumberland after Fontenoy and Mackay after Killiecrankie, for example, were both employed again. Hawley was fortunate, too. Cumberland did not blame Hawley for the debacle at Falkirk, writing from St. James's, on 23 January 1746:

> General Hawley,
> I have deferred answering your two Letters, the one before the other after your affair, till we had received another account how matters stood & today the desired account arrived which has eased people's minds vastly. I sincerely congratulate you on the King's being entirely satisfied with your conduct on that disagreeable occasion. I can assure you that I think that you have done wonders in coming off so after such a Pannick was struck in the Troops. On the allarm that your first letter gave, I was ordered for Scotland but no way because of the least Dissatisfaction of you, but thinking the éclat necessary, & the King objected to Ligonier when proposed, because it might be construed superceeding of you. If you should have the success I believe you will have, before I may get to you, then I flatter myself that I shant unfit you.
> 'As to the Behaviour of the Irish Dragoons, I am not surprised. For, escaping the first time, made them like safe methods. But I hope that the orders the Duke of Newcastle sends you this Post will hinder such Proceedings for the future. Officers should especially be made examples of. Pray make my compliments to all your little staff, to everyone in particular. Nobody was better able to feel for you than I was, having felt such a distress myself. For God's sake, purge the Foot, for they did not use to run away formerly. Whenever you may want any particular orders or send a publick narrative let it be to the Duke of Newcastle, but I beg

you would continue your correspondence with me, as the times are so interesting. I remain your affectionate friend, (William).[1]

Hawley put the outcome of the battle down to the behaviour of those under him. He made no distinction between officers and men in this, writing on 20 January to Newcastle, regarding 'the genll good behaviour of the officers, except a few, who require some scrutiny'.[2] He downplayed the battle's effects, writing to Major General John Campbell that it was 'a very trifling loss on our side', writing of 100 British and 1,000 Jacobite dead'.[3] As noted this was to exaggerate both; Hawley lost far more men than the Jacobites did. Campbell evidently agreed, telling him of 'the foolish, ignorant and impertinent letters I have seen on this subject'.[4]

Perhaps one of the latter might have included an anonymous note, undated but presumably written about this time, which denounced Hawley, 'who's misconduct lost us ye battle of Falkirk, is most unluckily the Duke's first favourite. He is despised by the army who call him Jack Catch, hated by ye Country for his misconduct & Blunderer'.[5] The reference to Jack Catch, meaning Jack Ketch, a notorious late seventeenth century hangman, is an early reference to Hawley's alleged predilection for hangings, but the term did not immediately catch on.

Yet the battle had been a setback for the British army. Had it been otherwise, the Jacobite army would have been in retreat or rout. Cumberland would not have needed to travel to Scotland. Yet Hawley was not in disgrace, despite his many critics. Cumberland recognised in him military ability and so he retained a role in the army, albeit not as commander.

Meanwhile, Hawley held court martials on those deemed to have misbehaved during the battle. In this he had been sanctioned by Newcastle. On 19 January a summons was issued for Cunningham, 'who ran away with the horses… there was such strong proofs against him' to attend, though surgeons feared he would die as he had opened an artery to bleed to death. Hawley announced to Newcastle on 20 January:

> The Court Martials are going on with the tryall of two officers of Blakeney's and one of Flemings, another court martial tomorrow to try some men of several regiments, who were in here in some hours. I will send the court martial of the officers to the Secretary at war to lay before His Majesty, as

1    RA, CP9/141.
2    TNA, SP54/27/34.
3    NLS, MS.3734, 111.
4    NLS, MS. 3734, 120.
5    NLS, MS.16639, 152.

to the others, some casting of lots may serve for examples, as I have many things to write upon.[6]

The courts martial sat for at least five days. One of the findings was that some of the men had run five miles from the battlefield, having thrown their weapons away and never once looked about themselves. Hawley wrote, 'I believe many of them will be condemned I will proceed with the advice and proper caution, but some examples are requisite'.[7] On 26 January he sent an express to Sir William Yonge, secretary at war, regarding the court martial proceedings.[8]

The first hearings were on 20 January on the three officers from Blakeney's who were accused of cowardice for having fled the field of battle. All three gave their reasons for having done so and were found not guilty. However, they were all felt to have been guilty of an error of judgement and were suspended from the service, with suspensions dating from 15 February.[9]

Others tried were three army deserters taken aboard a privateer, though there were fourteen more found. Hawley asked Cumberland for instructions, 'may I beg to ask shall they all be hanged, there's one of Hamilton's hanged for deserting to the rebels, theres 2 of our Foot to be shot for cowardice, running in here, before they stopt, theres some dragoons tried yet for the same crime and worse, I have acquainted the Duke of Newcastle…re officers'.[10] The four men found guilty were Francis Forbes of St. Clair's, John Irvine of Ligonier's, David Welsh of Pulteney's and Henry Macmannus of Hamilton's. All were Irishmen and the first three had deserted on the Continent but had been captured aboard the *Louis XV*, a French ship carrying troops to aid the Jacobites in Scotland. The fourth man had joined the Jacobites after having been made prisoner at the Battle of Prestonpans.[11] Those were four were hanged at noon on 24 January and remained on the Grassmarket gibbet for 24 hours. Two captains, one lieutenant and six privates of Hamilton's Dragoons were found guilty and sentenced to death by shooting, to take place on 27 January. Hawley also found a further 14 men among the 'French' troops to be British army deserters and wrote to Cumberland 'may I beg leave to ask shall they all be hanged?' However, they were reprieved. Two men, though, were 'punished by severe whipping' for 'running in here before they stopt'; they were to have been

---

6   TNA, SP54/27, 35.
7   TNA, SP54/27, 41.
8   TNA, SP54/27, 46.
9   RA, HT, 7411-24-109, 44, 56.
10  TNA, SP54/27, 48.
11  Douglas, *History*, p.128.

shot. Dragoons had been tried for the same offence.[12] Another man hanged was not a deserter but a spy, one Macgan.[13]

In these punishments, Hawley had been well within his rights. Army commanders had been given permission to hold courts martial where necessary and desertion in war time was a capital offence under the Articles of War. It had already occurred during the campaign and was to recur. For example, when Cumberland had taken Carlisle on 31 December 1745, four dragoons who had deserted to the Jacobites following the Prestonpans battle had been apprehended and were hanged there and then (Ligonier wrote 'I wish the vermin at Carlisle hang'd'). On 19 September 1746, in Perth, a captain who had deserted in Flanders was hanged and two deserters were shot. Others had been executed after Culloden.[14] Hawley had ordered nothing that was unexceptional for the time but he seems to have been singled out for opprobrium, perhaps because he had lost a battle and so any circumstance that could possibly be used against him, was. The need for strict discipline was widely held by army officers at this time. Major Samuel Bagshawe wrote in 1747 'Those who treat them with the greatest severity are best served by them'.[15]

Hawley was probably also influenced towards moderation by a letter of Fletcher's in which the Lord Chief Justice suggested that 'it may not be for the general good, that the execution of these private men be delayed at least for some little time'.[16] He replied on 27 January to justify his actions. As to one unstated event, presumably a hanging, he wrote, 'it shall be delayed, but it must be…justice is blind, theyr carse is the strongest of a hundred who were all condemned and pardoned by me and theirs near a hundred more'. He also expected more hangings would be demanded, 'I expecte ane order for decimation'.[17] The courts martial ('the tyrall of the cowards') continued and on 28 January Hawley reported that they had sat every day and were still ongoing, for Cunningham had yet to face them.[18] Hawley complained that Cunningham was 'not yet well enough to stand his tryall'.[19] Cunningham, who had already earned Hawley's annoyance, survived his suicide attempt, was found guilty and cashiered before the whole army on 24 February, at

12   TNA, SP54/27, 187.
13   *Derby Mercury*, 24 January 1746.
14   Douglas, *History*, pp.98, 266.
15   A.J. Guy (ed.), *Colonel Samuel Bagshawe and the Army of George II* (London: Bodley Head, 1987), p.65.
16   Home, *History*, p.351.
17   NLS. MSS16625, 107.
18   TNA, SP54/27, 51a.
19   RA, CP10/15.

Montrose: his sword was broken over his head and he was forced out of the army for cowardice.[20] He died later that year.

Andrew Henderson, as we have seen, clearly felt some animosity against Hawley, for he wrote about him at this stage in a derogatory fashion, 'some severity had been used by Hawley, which tended to discourage those under his command. Many of the private men were whipped in a terrible manner, the shrieks and cries of their wives and children were too piercing to be related'. Apparently, some men who had been taken prisoner after Fontenoy and who had been forced into Lord John Drummond's Royal Ecossois in the French army, left at the first opportunity in Scotland and arrived in Edinburgh 'and gave the King's troops the best intelligence in their power, their services were ungratefully received by General Hawley'.[21]

However, morale was beginning to improve, for on 20 January, Hawley wrote 'The Foot recover their spirits, they owne to their officers they all deserve to be hanged, some Regts have shooke hands and vowed all to dye next time'. Hawley repeated that he noted these sentiments on the following day. However, he retained his impression on the worth of the cavalry, writing 'as for the dragoons, I have done wt them' and later wrote 'the men are so bad and so cowed' so did not know what to do with Ligonier's and Hamilton's.[22] Apparently 31 dragoons had been tried and Hawley was predicting that 32 men would be shot and another 47 hanged for cowardice and desertion respectively.[23] All were pardoned on Cumberland's arrival, however. He wrote, 'As Hawley communicated to me copies of the infamous sentence that are passed on our cowardly officers, I thought it better to pardon the private men, to give a sort of mark of favour to the corps. If I might venture to give my opinions of the officers, I wish the King to supercede them all, since they are not hanged'.[24]

A more benevolent side is shown to Hawley's character in a letter to Fletcher written on 2 February, when he asked for a favour for one William Gardener who had 'served many years in a regiment of Foot which I once commanded'. Gardener was clearly an old soldier and Hawley stated 'I know him to have been a good soldier and an honest fellow. I shall be obliged to you if you'l recommend him to be one of the soldiers in the castle of Edinburgh'.[25]

A few days after the battle, Hawley addressed Edinburgh's civic dignitaries in sharp tones: 'Gentlemen, you pretend to have an extraordinary zeal for His

20   *Stamford Mercury*, 6 February 1746; *Glasgow Courant*, 27 January 1746; Douglas, *History*, p.153.
21   Henderson, *Cumberland*, pp.224-225.
22   TNA, SP54/27, 35, 38a, 41.
23   TNA, SP54/27/48.
24   TNA, SP54/27, 55a.
25   NLS, MSS16625, 109.

Majesty's service, and seem to be very assiduous in promoting it, but let me tell you, you have either been mistaken in your measures, or have been betraying the cause'. This was by their misrepresenting the Jacobite army as 'a despicable pack of herds, and a contemptible mob of men of desperate fortunes', giving them low numbers and exaggerating the number of loyal Scots, leading him to think that they would be easy to beat. As he said, with all the wisdom of hindsight, 'I never saw any troops fire in platoons, more regularly, make their motions and evolutions quicker, or attack with more bravery and better order than those Highlanders did at the battle of Falkirk last week'.[26] He continued, 'you represented [them] as a parcel of raw and undisciplined vagabonds. No Jacobite could have contrived to hurt the Kings faithful friends, or done more service to his inveterate enemies' and he assured them that he would inform the Court of this unless they had any defence to make. This was published in a pamphlet circulated in London, *A Few Passages showing the sentiments of the Prince of Hesse and General Hawley*.[27]

Additional forces arrived in Edinburgh. On 22 January the artillery from Newcastle finally arrived, but the train lacked powder. Others were on their way, with Kerr's Dragoons arriving at Kelso en route to the Scottish capital. Preparations for the continued campaign went ahead. Hawley and Huske negotiated a contract with a Mr Dundas, a wine merchant from London, for forage for the horses. They advanced to Dundas £1,000 and he agreed to supply one million rations of forage at four and one half pence per unit, each unit to be of 18 pounds of hay.[28] Some of the officers were not well; Cholmondeley was 'layed up lost the use of one side' and Hawley claimed, with some exaggeration, 'We have no officers at all hardly'.[29] There were more mundane matters to be dealt with. Hawley was dealing with applications about junior officers' commissions. Fletcher lobbied on behalf of one Robert Campbell to be an ensign and for Robert Hamilton, who had performed well at Falkirk, to be an ensign in Barrell's. The question of Cornet Creighton, raised a few months ago, was still not resolved, as Henry Liddell wanted his post for a friend of his. Cumberland was asked about these matters.[30]

Hawley informed Richmond that he 'expresses the greatest joy upon the Duke's going to Scotland'.[31] He wrote similarly to Newcastle on 28 January, 'I had rather serve under him than have the command, the pleasure I have in it, and my personal love for him, by farr overbalances any vanity I may be tainted with'. He thought

---

26    Dalton, *Army of George I*, Vol.I, pp.46-47.
27    Dalton, *Army*, I, pp.46-47.
28    TNA, SP54/27/41, 41f.
29    RA, CP10/15.
30    TNA, SP54/27, f187
31    McCann (ed.), *Correspondence*, p.202.

that Cumberland being in command 'will have a very good effect'.[32] Hawley told Cumberland that his anticipated arrival 'has given the greatest pleasure to every body'.[33] Cumberland arrived at the Scottish capital on 30 January. He met the generals immediately and they provided him with news of the military situation, 'and these threw no blame on each other. Hawley's conduct was approved, and yet it was judged, that he was more proper to obey than to command'.[34]

Cumberland wrote:

> Holyrood House
> 30 January 1745
> My Lord Duke of Newcastle,
> This morning about three I arrived, having met on the Road with all manner of civilities & Respect. Everything here was in readiness to move, & after the state of things had been well considered, I thought it of the utmost importance to move to the relief of Stirling Castle, which we are under some pain for, tho' the Rebels have as yet mounted but three Guns, they have made a seeming disposition for saving their Baggage in case of another affair, but I believe they propose to themselves to retire to Perth without coming to Blows, if they can take the castle before we come up.
>
> As we shall march as far as Lithgow tomorrow, this Town will have all their own Regiment left & many of the county militia call'd in, besides about 400 of the broken Regiments in the castle, the two Irish Dragoons (which will be left here) & on Saturday Bligh's will come in here to remain; we shall take with us fourteen Battalions, and Cobham's and Lord Mark Kerr's dragoons enough to drive them off the Face of the Earth, if they will do their Duty which we must expect.
>
> I send enclosed a copy of our new order of Battle, & of Mr Hawley's late one, in the last unhappy affair; I put all the cavalry in the third line, because by all accounts, the Rebels don't fear that, as they do our fire, & on that alone I must depend.
> I am your affectionate friend,
> William[35]

On 1 February the army under Cumberland's command marched northwards. The Jacobites began to fall back, much to Cumberland's displeasure as he sought

---

32   TNA, SP54/27/51a.
33   RA, CP10/18.
34   Henderson, *Cumberland*, p.224.
35   TNA, SP54/27/55a; the enclosures mentioned seem no longer to exist.

a decisive battle. He was concerned that the Jacobites might simply disperse as they had done in 1716, but they did not in fact do so and made their base in late February around Inverness where they undertook aggressive operations against loyalist forts and outposts, with a degree of success.

Initially, Hawley was confident of an early victory. He wrote to Campbell on 3 February, 'the rebels seem now to be entirely disconcerted, there remains for us only to pursue and punish them in the manner they deserve'.[36] Likewise, he wrote to Newcastle on 9 February when at Perth, 'I think our affairs in these parts seem to be in a very good posture and I hope soon to see an end to this wicked rebellion, especially as the Hessian troops have now arrived'.[37] Dunkeld and Castle Menzies had been occupied and there was to be another advance. Yet only a week later, matters were far less rosy as the campaign had ground to a halt. Hawley wrote to Ligonier, 'as to use we are all becalmed here, and dare not yeat move forward for fear of starving'. A few detachments of troops were pushed forward, but the bulk of the army remained at Perth, needing magazines of meal and corn. Hawley thought that in the short term the Jacobites were triumphant, they 'may indeed laughe at us, for a time because we cant follow them, but then they will starve soon for they have no meal'.[38]

Hawley was doing his best by arranging hand to mouth contracts for meat for the army, but the main work was undertaken by Cumberland in Edinburgh. Hawley wrote 'I wishe I was off'. In the meantime, with annoyed soldiery, 'the Duke keeps up their spirits by a little plunder he gives them now and then'. This was not something Hawley could order, 'unless I have an indemnification for what I may do against law, as the late Duke of Argyle and Mr Wade had'.[39]

The British army marched along the east coast of Scotland so as to maintain their supply lines by sea in the unconventional winter campaign in which they found themselves. Civilians suffered at this time. On 23 February the army reached Aberdeen and was based in and around there for the following six weeks. Officers needed quarters in the city. Lieutenant Colonel George Watson (1718-1780) was one of Hawley's aides de camp and he, together with a Mr Thomson and Provost Robinson visited a Mrs Gordon, who was told that her house would be needed.[40] She was initially assured that 'they would not let me be a sufferer in any respect'. China, linen and kitchen furniture was to be locked away in the cellar, and that the house would only be needed for two days. This inconvenienced her as she had to find alternative accommodation for herself and her maid at short notice. This

36   NLS, MS.3734, 127.
37   TNA, SP54/28, f50r.
38   TNA, SP87/28, f.95r.
39   TNA, SP87/28, f.95r.
40   Forbes, *Jacobite Memoirs*, pp.212-213.

she did. Yet on the following morning, Hawley sent two messengers to her, to command that she gave them all her house keys. This she did, 'thinking that when he had satisfied his curiosity he would send them to me again'. However, at six that afternoon, Major James Wolfe, the future conqueror of Quebec, but now another of Hawley's staff officers, and in a bad temper, 'was come to let me know, that by the Duke and General Hawley's orders [she] was deprived of everything I had but the clothes on my back'.[41]

Apparently Hawley 'had been very strict in his inquiries about me, but could not find anything to lay to my charge'. She petitioned Cumberland for clemency and to have her goods returned and a favourable reply was forthcoming. Actions, however, did not match words, for:

> General Hawley, who lived in my house, took care to prevent that, for he packed up every bit of china I had, which I am sure would not be bought for two hundred pounds, all my bedding and table linen, every book, my repeating clock…my worked screen, every rag of Mr Gordon's clothes… twelve tea-spoons, strainer and tongs, the japanned board on which the chocolate and coffee-cups stood, and put them on board a ship in the night time, directed himself at Holyrood House, at Edinburgh.

He also gave away her flutes, music and cane. The food and drink in the house and even her empty bottles 'he kept for himself'. When the unwelcome guest left on 8 April he took the bed clothes, 'in short he left nothing behind him but the beds without coverings'. Chairs, tables and cupboards were damaged, locks removed, 'in short a house so plundered, I believe was never heard of. It is not six hundred pounds that would make up my loss'.[42]

Andrew Fletcher remarked on the above, 'I really wish it had not happened; for it occasions a great clamour, & I doubt it can be well justified in law'. Mrs Gordon's husband was an officer in the Jacobite army and this may well have influenced Hawley in his decision to plunder the place. Sir Edward Fawkener, Cumberland's military secretary, was unhappy with Hawley's action, writing, 'The things might as well have been left, and I am sure the Duke would have been better pleased if they had'.[43] Yet he did not think that a legal action could be made against Hawley, 'his prudence or humanity may be called into question, but I don't see the case is

---

41 Forbes, *Jacobite Memoirs*, pp.213-214.
42 Forbes, *Jacobite Memoirs*, pp.251-216
43 RA, CP13/75.

actionable'. Those men in open rebellion, as Gordon was, could have their property seized without the legal niceties being observed.[44]

Hawley was also responsible for having a spy hanged in Stirling. There was a complaint made to Fletcher about this at the end of March, but this time Fletcher dismissed it: 'I never heard of any prosecution threatened against General Hawley for hanging the spy, nor do I believe it and if there were, the great law of necessity, would probably justify what was done, because without such severitys, it would be difficult to carry on any war, foreign or civil'.[45]

It is probable that this spy is the man referred to in a letter from Archibald Campbell of Strathbogie, who sent the man to Hawley. He was 'a spy from the rebels called Donald Campbell born in Argyleshire who was apprehended yesterday [25 March]…I am informed since, by Captain Campbell at Inverack, that he is a notorious villain, who he often wished to catch for what he has been concerned in the rebellion from the beginning of it. He would have been hanged here, but could not find an executioner'. John Gordon, who was 'very active in soliciting men for the Pretender' was also sent to Hawley.[46]

On the eve of what was to be the campaign's final battle, Walpole retailed another anecdote about Hawley, 'General Hawley has been tried, (not in person, you may believe) and condemned by a Scotch jury for murder, on hanging a spy. What do you say to this?'[47] This may have been the spy hanged on a tree near to Strathbogie bridge with 'this Writing fixed on his Breast, A Rebel Spy', which, it was thought, would 'hinder Crows from building Nests in that Tree for a Season'.[48] It was not a unique event to hang Jacobite spies; in April, at Banff, a man was seen making notches on a stick to note the number of the British army; one was hanged in a nearby tree and the other on part of a house which projected out, 'All you that does pass by, Take warning by me, a Rebel Spy'. According to James Ray, 'which, with the Addition of good Entertainment, might have been a very famous sign'.[49]

On 1 March Hawley was briefly back in Edinburgh and wrote to tell Fletcher that 'my time has mostly been taken up in obeying the Duke of Cumberland's commands conveyed to me by Sir Everard Fawkener and in keeping things right with the Hessians in many different ways'. The latter was a reference to the Hessian corps under Prince Frederick of Hesse which had arrived in early February to supplement the British army in Scotland, but given Hawley's earlier dealings with

---

44   NLS, MS16621, 91r.
45   RA, CP13/74.
46   RA, CP12/346.
47   Lewis (ed.), *Walpole*, Vol.19, p.241.
48   Ray, *History*, p.300.
49   Ray, *History*, pp.313-314.

the prince must have been fraught with difficulty. It is noteworthy that Captain Toovey was on Hawley's staff at this time.[50]

Hawley's responsibilities included dealing with issues of supply. In March he corresponded with Major General Crawford, in the Lowlands as liaison with the Hessians, whose role was to prevent the Jacobite army slipping past Cumberland's forces around Aberdeen and into the Lowlands. On 23 March he told Crawford that the army needed forage and, if need be, he was to send out troops to enforce its collection. On the next day he asked that Colonel Napier acquire horses to transport the baggage of the recently-arrived Bligh's Regiment. A week later he asked Blakeney about the need for horses. He also had to deal with the supply and payment of a consignment of 1,300 pairs of shoes made in Edinburgh for the army at £132 1s 6d. Clearly he had his hands full, telling the latter, 'as I am very busy I have employed another to write for me, wch you will excuse'.[51] However, he was also unhappy with the campaign, writing to Crawford, 'How do you like this way of making war, I am weary of it but not while the Duke stays. We have as many alarms and as good intelligence here as in other places, but I learned many years ago here never to believe what is told'.[52]

Hawley's actions are but little known, until the army left its quarters on 8 April, on news that the last physical barrier between them and the Jacobites, the River Spey, was now fordable. It is probable that there was no need for Cumberland and Hawley to write to one another as they could now converse; and as Hawley was no longer commander, he did not need to write to Newcastle or others at a distance. It is possible that he offered his advice to Cumberland, for he had previous experience of fighting the Jacobite army. He may even have advised him on how to deal with the enemy.

Other good news was that the Jacobites' supplies were exhausted and men had begun to desert. On reaching the Spey on 12 April, 'the Scotch assured him; the rebels would make a stand and he would find a bloody piece of worke'. Cumberland crossed one ford at the head of the infantry whilst, a half a mile to the left, Hawley crossed it at the head of the three cavalry regiments; Cobham's and Lord Mark Kerr's Dragoons and the newly-raised Kingston's Light Horse.[53]

After the army passed the Spey they marched to Alves and then to Nairn. En route, towards Forress, they crossed the stream of Findhorn. Apparently when one of the baggage carts became stuck fast in the stream bed, 'Hawley came up immediately, and fell to lashing the waggoner' and when Cumberland heard this,

---

50   NLS MS 16625, 119
51   NLS, MS 16625, 119; ADV.MS.23.3.28, 78, 153, 288.
52   NLS, ADV.MS.23.3.153.
53   RA, HT, 7411-24-101-1, p.26.

he rode to the scene 'and checked Hawley for his impatience: '"Fye upon it, Hawley, to use any person thus, the man is my friend, and do you not see he is assisting us"'. Henderson alleged 'Hawley became every day more hated'.[54]

The British army camped near Nairn on 14-15 April, the Duke allowing the men a day's rest after a week's hard marching. He also provided brandy on the 15 April so the men could celebrate his 25th birthday. On the night of the 15 April the Jacobite army attempted to surprise the British camp and to kill the men whilst asleep. They turned back before they could do so because the march had taken longer than planned and so were not in position at dawn as envisaged. So on the next day the British army marched towards Inverness for what Cumberland believed would be a decisive battle. By noon the two armies were facing each other across Drummossie Moor. With just over 7,000 men Cumberland had the advantage in numbers as the 5,000 Jacobites lacked the men who were not present either due to men looking for food or sleep after the abortive night march or because units had not arrived.

At Culloden, Hawley and Bland were given command of the five squadrons of cavalry on the army's left flank, which were two squadrons of Cobham's Dragoons and three of Lord Mark Kerr's. This was an ideal command for Hawley as he had commanded cavalry in battle at both Dettingen and Fontenoy in recent years, as well as at Sheriffmuir 31 years ago. Using the men of the Argyllshire Militia to break down the walls of the Culwhinniac enclosure, they were able to move to the Jacobite flank and then to threaten their rear.[55]

Hawley's command stood thus:

## Officers

| Unit | Field Officers | Majors | Captains | Lieutenants | Cornets | Others* | Total |
|---|---|---|---|---|---|---|---|
| Cobham | 0 | 1 | 3 | 2 | 2 | 5 | 13 |
| Kerr | 1 | 1 | 2 | 6 | 6 | 5 | 21 |
| **Total** | **1** | **2** | **5** | **8** | **8** | **10** | **34** |

*indicates adjutants, surgeons and quartermasters: none had a chaplain

---

54  Henderson, *Cumberland*, pp.245-246.
55  Yorke (ed.), *Hardwicke*, Vol.I, p.523.

## THE END OF THE JACOBITE CAMPAIGN 159

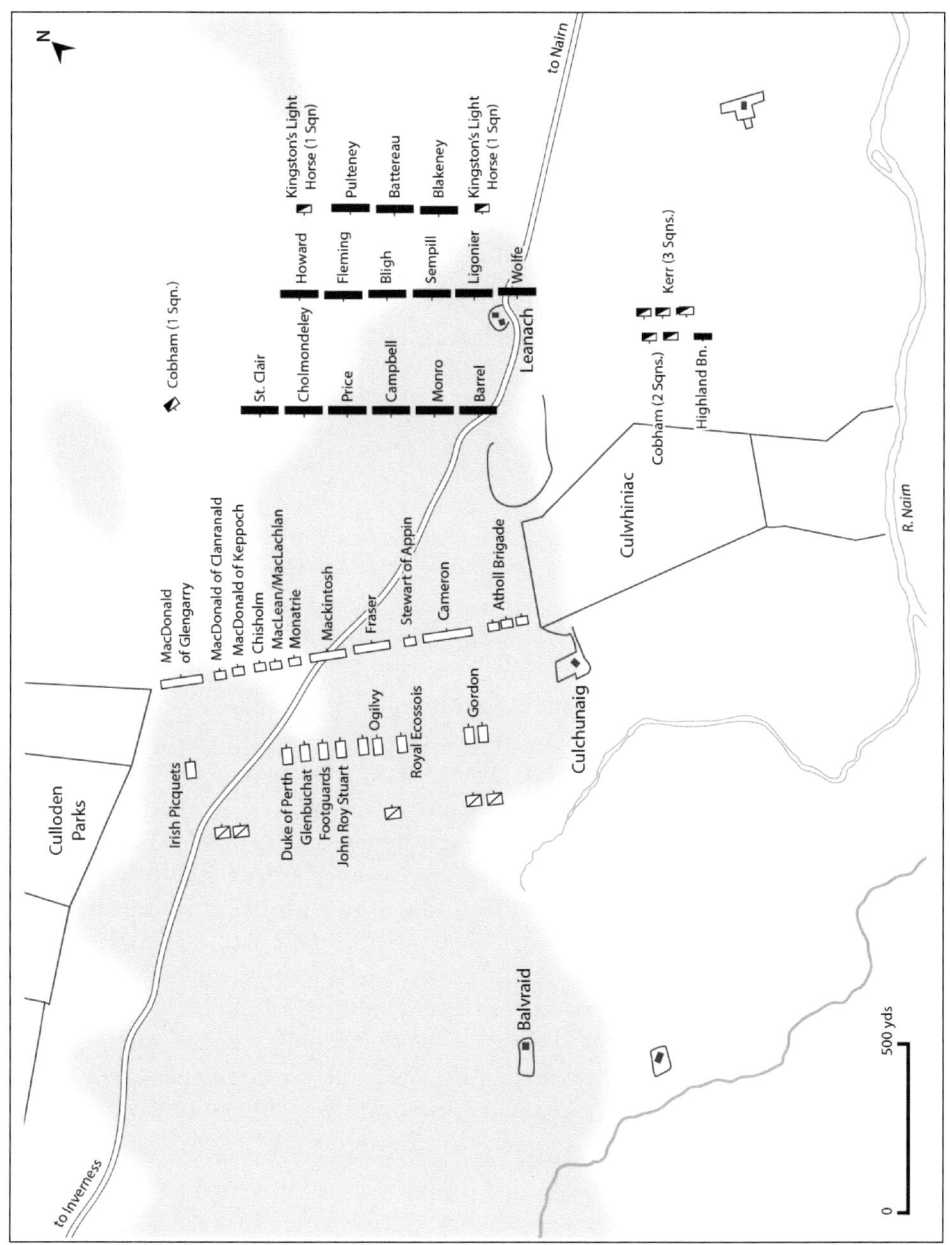

The Battle of Culloden, 16 April 1746.

## Other Ranks

| Unit | Sergeants | Drummers | Troopers | Total |
|---|---|---|---|---|
| Cobham | 12 | 8 | 219 | 239 |
| Kerr | 13 | 12 | 249 | 274 |
| **Total** | **25** | **20** | **468** | **513** |

Total cavalry strength: 34 officers and 513 men (547 total).[56] The number given above for Cobham's includes the third squadron which was posted on the army's right wing and so Hawley's actual command was perhaps just under 500 men.

Hawley had apparently been reconnoitring the Jacobite position, 'having been some time before to see the ground, had been up near the right of the enemy'. Cumberland expressed to him the concerns he had over his left flank. Hawley said, 'Sir, if youle give me the conducting of the dragoons, I'll answer for your left flank'. Cumberland answered, 'Do so: I depend on you'. Hawley then had Bland divide the dragoons on the left (Cobham's and Kerr's) into 'as many little squadrons as there were troops' and put them in two lines of two men deep, which made 12 small squadrons. He did this 'knowing they had no cavalry to deale with worthe thinking of'.[57] This seems an unusual arrangement, as a cavalry regiment was usually made up of three squadrons, so, with a detached squadron of Cobham's, this would make five squadrons in the command. Sub-division into two troops per squadron would make '10 small squadrons' not 12, so either Hawley was incorrect or some of the men were formed into two additional squadrons.

Apparently Cumberland was not entirely sure what to do next and sent an aide to Hawley, as a more experienced general, for his opinion, and Hawley sent a message back, 'twas his opinion to attacque immediately and that he would very soon be in upon their flanque with the dragoons, that he saw nothing but what he liked for they seemed to be all in confusion'.[58] Cumberland sent Lord Bury, a young aide, forward to see what he could of the Jacobite position. Shortly afterwards the Jacobite artillery began to open fire, though with minimal effect, and then there was returning fire from the Royal Artillery. The latter was more effective, though was not devastating, as these were small calibre guns firing roundshot at long range. Eventually the units on the Jacobite right began to move forward and attack the two battalions on the left wing of the British front line. They took heavy casualties from cannister and musketry but the survivors kept charging and a melee ensued.

---

56 RA, CP14/7.
57 RA, HT, 7411-24-101, p.28.
58 RA, HT, 7411-24-101, p.28.

Meanwhile, on the left of the British infantry, the dragoons were moving away from them, Hawley planning to move towards the river and out of sight of both armies, in order to attack the Jacobite right flank. Learning of the walls ahead, it was thought that they could be 'tumbled down in a minute' and the Argyll Militia did so. On the Jacobite right, 500 yards beyond the first wall on the left was another, eight feet high, which was taken down and the British squadrons marched through 'as soon as possible and upon a trot in two lines'. Yet the last wall was held by the two Jacobite battalions 'drawne up with their noses close to this eight foot high wall' posted on the right to defend the flank against any such attack.[59]

Charles, mounted on horseback on an eminence, saw the destruction of the walls and sent repeated orders to Murray to attack them, but apparently 'Lord George paid no attention to this order'.[60] The units posted to prevent any further attack were John Gordon of Avochie's Battalion, Elcho's Lifegaurds, and a squadron of the French Régiment de Fitzjames, who prevented any further advance.[61] Apparently 'They seemed quite astounded and never faced nor fired one shott'.[62]

Wolfe, seeing how the infantry conflict was progressing following the repulsion of the Jacobite charge, described Hawley's response: 'as soon as the rebels began to give way to the fire of our own foot…he ordered General Bland to charge the thickest of them with three squadrons and Lord Ancrum to support him with two. It was done with wonderful success and completed the victory with great slaughter'.[63] Hawley had Bland take eight of the twelve 'squadrons' of dragoons that had been formed and 'who went all along theyr rear and tooke all the runaways in the flanque and made great havock'. Meanwhile Hawley with the remaining four had them wheel against the flank of the two battalions posted by the walls, whilst the Argyll Militia engaged these two battalions in musketry from the rising ground on the other side of the wall. The Jacobites broke and were pursued, though not before causing some fatalities and other casualties among the militia. According to Hawley, the cavalry were 'killing them, to a pass by the river where they made a short stand, the dragoons being all dispersed in the pursuit and not there together'.[64]

---

59   Forbes, *Jacobite Memoirs*, p.142; RA, HT, 7411-24-101-1, p.28.
60   Johnstone, *Memoir*, p.123.
61   Elcho, *Short Account*, p.432.
62   RA, HT, 7411-24-101-1, p.28.
63   NRS, GD45/1/229.
64   RA, HT, 7411-24-101-1, p.28.

Culloden Moor battlefield, from an old postcard. (Author's collection)

Elsewhere, the other British cavalry could be used to their full effect, as Argyle had done at Sheriffmuir. O'Sullivan recorded:

> The cruelty of the enemy cant be imagined. The Dragoons & Horse yt follow'd the McDonells, MccIntoshes & another clans of about a hundred & twenty that joined some time before the battle, as they were the last yt staid upon the field, what slattor they made of them, & if it was not for the Parks & inclosiers of Castle Hill, where the horse cou'd not follow them, not a man would wou'd escape.[65]

According to John Marchant, a contemporary historian, 'the cavalry cut down great numbers, without the least opposition'.[66] Wolfe wrote, 'It was done with a wonderful spirit and completed the victory with much slaughter. We had an opportunity of avenging ourselves, for that and many other things, and indeed we did not neglect it. As few Highlanders were taken prisoner as possible'.[67]

The cavalry which had charged from the 'right, & left met in the centre, except two Squadrons of Dragoons which we miss'd, & they were gone in pursuit of the

---

65 Tayler and Tayler (ed.), *1745*, p.165.
66 Marchant, *History*, p.400.
67 Willson, *Life and Letters*, p.63.

Runaways; Lord Ancram was ordered to pursue with the horse as far as they could & which he did with so good effect, that a very considerable number were killed in the pursuit'.[68] Bland had also 'made great slaughter, & gave quarter to none but about fifty French officers, & soldiers he pick'd up in his pursuit'.[69] Kingston's Horse 'galloped up briskly, and falling in with the fugitives, did excellent execution'.[70] James Ray referred to 'there was much knapping of Noddles' and claimed 500 were killed in the pursuit.[71] Three former Nottinghamshire butchers in Kingston's later bragged of having killed 14 Jacobites each. According to Yorke, 'Had not fear added wings to their feet, none would have escaped the edge of the sword'.[72]

The Jacobites streamed away. Those who fled downhill towards Inverness were unfortunate, as James Johnstone wrote, 'Having been pursued by the English cavalry, the road from Culloden to that town was everywhere strewed with dead bodies'.[73] According to Hawley, 'The dragoons had cleared all the country for three miles before them and had made great slaughter every way, even downe to Inverness'. They took no prisoners.[74] Some arrived in Inverness, 'There were vast numbers ran thro' the Town, some crying, others mourning, some stood astonished and did not know whither to turn themselves'.[75] Meanwhile, the British infantry switched from line into two columns and marched to the Highland town.[76]

Slaughter by pursuing troops who are faster moving than their victims is commonplace after battles. It had happened after Killiecrankie and Prestonpans where the Jacobites slew their routing enemies; it had happened after Sheriffmuir when Argyle's dragoons struck down Jacobites from the defeated left wing. The cavalry's actions after Culloden was not a unique 'war crime' therefore, but the bloody reality of the cavalry's business.

There is an allegation that in the battle's aftermath, that Cumberland, or perhaps, Hawley, was riding over the battlefield with Wolfe and saw a wounded but defiant Jacobite. Hawley told Wolfe 'shoot me that Highland scoundrel, who dares to look on us with such contempt and impudence!' The junior officer replied, 'My commission is at your disposal, but I can never consent to become an executioner'.[77] However, the story post-dates the battle by several decades, Wolfe's attitude towards the Jacobites was anything but merciful, writing to a friend two

68 TNA, SP54/30/21a.
69 TNA, SP54/30/21a.
70 Marchant, *History*, p.393.
71 Ray, *History*, p.337.
72 Yorke (ed.), *Hardwicke*, Vol.I, p.514.
73 Johnstone, *Memoir*, p.126.
74 RA, HT, 7411-24-101-1, p.28.
75 *Newcastle Courant*, 26 April 1746.
76 RA, HT, 7411-101-11-1, p.28.
77 Blaikie, 'Origins', p.99n.

days afterwards to that effect, as noted previously, and finally to disobey a direct order from a superior officer on the battlefield was to risk a court martial, but there is no evidence of any such occurring. The story must be deemed apocryphal, part of the corpus of pro-Jacobite material which came into being following their defeat in 1746 and of the need to establish Wolfe as a hero following his victory and death at Quebec in 1759.

There is another story from this time by a Jacobite source about Hawley's behaviour. On the evening after the battle, the senior officers were assembled in Inverness, where the magistracy assembled to wish them well. Provost Frazer and former Provost John Hossacks were among this number. There are two accounts about what happened, one crediting Hawley with the following actions and the other being unsure whether Hawley or Huske was to blame. Apparently some of the soldiers were engaged in killing Jacobites, although it is hard to accept that this happened in the city itself. Hossacks, who was loyal to the Hanoverian dynasty, remonstrated, 'making a low bow to General Hawley or General Husk, he said, "I hope your excellency will be so good as to mingle mercy with judgement". Upon this Hawley or Husk cried out, in a rage, "Damn the rebel-dog. Kick him down stairs and throw him in prison directly". The orders were literally and instantly obeyed'. The other version is very similar, but apparently 'Hawley bawled out "Damn the puppy! Does he pretend to dictate here? Carry him away"' and the unfortunate councillor was thrown down the stairs.[78]

Apparently at Inverness, Hawley also caused the ports to be closed to prevent Jacobites from escaping there and had a meeting house burnt down (if this was an Episcopalian one then he was acting within the law, these being deemed illegal in 1690, and the same was done elsewhere by the army in 1746). He also thought that giving the Jacobite prisoners half a pound of oatmeal a day was too much.[79]

Jacobite propaganda made Hawley into one of the major villains of the '45. There was a verse written about the British army after Culloden and it features Hawley, Cumberland, Huske, and Major Lockhart shortly after the battle. Hawley is given the following lines:

> Now we soldiers now we've put 'em to rout
> Kill all the wounded see their latest breath
> And let them feel our mercy by their Death.[80]

Another verse about him at this time reads as follows,

---

78 Paton, 'Lyon', Vol.I, pp.218-219; Vol.III, p.73.
79 Paton, 'Lyon', Vol.III, pp.54, 155.
80 BL.Add.Mss. 33954, f.82r.

And Hawley joys his mandates to perform,
To whom compared an Alva's name is sweet
Brave in the field tho' cruel in the State.[81]

Another notes, 'A Hawley, a Husk, an Albermarle, or even a Scott or a Lockhart was preferred to the long-headed, sagacious Forbes', lumping Hawley with other characters who feature within the Jacobite bete noires. It is worth noting that Duncan Forbes believed that repression was crucial where it was necessary; he was no wholehearted lover of mercy as is often thought.[82]

Hawley had no doubt about the magnitude of the victory, writing from Inverness two weeks later, 'this rebellion is I think quite crushed and His Majesty's enemies quite dispersed for some years at least'. Yet he did not want to remain in Scotland for much longer, for there was 'not the least prospect of any more military action and since a different scene is now going to be acted here, in which I am not at all versed'. He went on to tell Newcastle that 'I do in the most humble and earnest manner beg of His Majesty…will be generously pleased to employ some other, who has more capacity for civil affairs I must beg your Grace to intercede for me in assuring His Majesty I am not fit for this employment now'. As with Wade in December 1745, he pleaded he leave on health grounds 'never to return hither unless there was occasion to draw my sword'.[83]

By 30 April Hawley was fed up with being in Scotland and appealed to Cumberland to be sent elsewhere. The latter wrote thus to Newcastle, that Hawley 'has asked leave to quit this command as he says he has neither temper nor cunning to live with them. Who can be in his room I know not but I believe it must be either Ld Albermarle Ld Tyrawley or L G Wentworth. I don't like either of them intirely but I like others worse'.[84] There was no immediate response from Newcastle, so Cumberland raised the issue with him again on 8 May:

> I am desired by General Hawley to ask his Majesty's leave for him to retire from this service as soon as ever the military affairs shall be quite over, he finding this climate was very contrary to his health. He has also desired me to mention again Mr Wiltshire Wilson to be a second Cornet in his Regiment, & that his commission may be given out, if his Majesty shall have been pleased to accept the Recommendation.[85]

81  Paton, 'Lyon', Vol.I, p.243.
82  Paton, 'Lyon', Vol.II, p.86.
83  TNA, SP54/30/34.
84  Henderson, *Cumberland*, p.267.
85  BL.Add. Mss, 32707, ff.128.

Some days after Culloden there were court martials held on those deserters who had joined the Jacobite army and had now been taken. According to Henderson, 'the Duke remonstrated with Hawley upon the impropriety of putting so many of the deserters to death, and in the most sympathising manner insinuated that men were not made to starve, "You may try an officer for surrendering up a fort, when under no necessity to do it, but let not the blood of the poor be spilt profusely"'.[86] Yet Henderson must be in the wrong here. Cumberland, as commander in chief, initiated the proceedings into actions against deserters. His orders on 17 April were issued to the sergeant majors of all the battalions present. They read that they were 'to visit all those prisoners taken and in doing so to be taking the names of those who had been in any of the Regiments in our service'. Two days later, the sergeants from each battalion were 'to visit the French prisoners who came in last'. Those which were found to have previously served in the British Army were then court martialled without much delay; a dozen were hanged on 20 April. Over the next few weeks another 17 men were hanged having found to have deserted. Many of these had deserted on the Continent and some were probably enlisted into the French army as prisoners after Fontenoy; others had joined the Jacobite army after Prestonpans. Yet many were not executed and were sent back to their battalions, on one occasion 11 men were reprieved by the intervention of a Scottish clergyman. Desertion was a capital offence and there is no doubt that these men were guilty; by the standards of the day, many were dealt with leniently, some men were executed as an example or because there were deemed to have been aggravating circumstances.[87]

On 18 April, Cumberland told Newcastle that he had 'ordered the Generals Hawley, Lord Albemarle, Huske, & Bland to enquire into the reasons of the surrender of Fort George, & as I fear he will not have any good ones to give, I shall order a Court Martial for his tryal, which I hope his Majesty will approve of'.[88] Major James Grant had surrendered Fort George, at Inverness, to the Jacobites, after a very short siege in February 1746. Although the guns in the fort were unable to be depressed sufficiently to have fired on the Jacobites, and despite no immediate prospect of relief, some of his subordinates had advocated fighting on and had criticised their commander for surrendering so quickly. Grant was found guilty and cashiered. Huske had been president. Cumberland wrote, 'I sent a copy of the sentence, which I have taken the liberty to approve. The proceedings of the court are so voluminous, that I have not time to get them copied, & it is necessary to keep the original here for the trial of Lieutenant Colonel Innings, who had also

86   TNA, SP54/31/9a
87   Arnot and Seton, 'Prisoners of the '45', Vol.I, pp.284-287.
88   TNA, SP54/30/21a.

been at Fort George'.[89] The same four officers examined Major Wentworth who had surrendered Fort Augustus after a brief siege in March 1746, and though they thought the fort was incapable of defence, did think it could have been held out longer and so recommended a court martial.[90]

Hawley's views on the suppression of the Jacobites were unambiguous, as a letter written by him at Fort Augustus on 16 June makes clear:

> If His Majesty would leave me the Foot here, and the Parliament give the men a guinea and a pair of shoes for every rebell's head they brought in I would still undertake to clear this country.
>
> As to Law & Politicks I beg to be excused, I have no Tallent that way. I have so many prisoners dayly coming in, old Lovett and above 50 more were brought in yesterday, there's still some hopes of theyr Prince Charley too, there's still so many houses to burn and I have still more to be put to death, tho' by computation there's about 7000 houses burn'd already, yeat all is not done.
>
> I won't, nor can't, stire, still the Duke does.[91]

The burning of civilian property which was the property of Jacobites who remained defiant was not untypical of warfare in contemporary Europe. In 1743 the French had burnt villages in Bavaria, so as to deny supplies to the Austrians, and, worse, the Croats in the latter army massacred civilians.[92] Yet the human cost of the destruction of Highland homes must be borne in mind, as a letter from a loyalist Highland clergyman in June 1746 noted:

> As the most of this parish is burnt to ashes, and all the cattle belonging to the rebels carried off by His Majesty's forces, there is no such thing as money or pennyworth to be got in this desolate place. I beg therefore, you'll advise me what steps I shall take to recover my stipend. My family is now much increased, by the wives and infants of those in rebellion in my parish crowding for a mouthful of bread to keep them from starving; which no good Christian can refuse notwithstanding the villainy of their husbands and fathers to deprive of our religion, liberty and bread.[93]

89 TNA, SP54/30, 24.
90 NLS, MS 3142, f97r.
91 Lennox, *A Duke and his Friends*, pp.511-512.
92 Reed Browning, *War of the Austrian Succession*, (New York: St. Martin's Press, 1990), p.136.
93 Douglas, *History*, pp.232-233.

In May, Wolfe wrote to Captain Hamilton about Hawley's instructions for Major Chaban, 'he is to receive and keep together all such accusations as shall be sent him from you, or any other officer under his command, that they be more conveniently had when called for'. As to property held by Jacobites, 'the manner of treaty the houses and possessions of rebels' was to be as always.[94] This meant that property belonging to Jacobites who had not surrendered was to be destroyed or seized.

As part of an attempt to alleviate the tedium of life at Fort Augustus, where much of the army was stationed in June, Cumberland organised horse races, in late June to be ridden by soldiers' wives on horses without saddles. One evening Hawley and Lieutenant Colonel George Howard had a match run for a 20-guinea prize, with the rider backed by Hawley winning by about four inches. Apparently 'there were three of the finest heats ever seen'.[95]

Eventually Newcastle gave him his consent to leave and so on 5 June Cumberland could write 'I have acquainted General Hawley with his Majesty's permission for him to retire from his command here, for which he is extremely thankful.'[96] Hawley did not leave, however, for some weeks hence, arriving at Edinburgh on 23 July and leaving for London two days later, a few days after Cumberland departed.[97]

Those in England who were still critical of Hawley used his defeat at Falkirk as a stick to castigate him. On his return from Scotland he travelled through Newcastle, where he was hissed by the crowd there.[98] As part of his comments on the trials of the Jacobite lords in London in the summer of 1746, Horace Walpole wrote to Mann on 12 August, 'Cope is actually going to be tried; but Hawley, who is fifty times more culpable, is saved by partiality: Cope miscarried by incapacity; Hawley, by insolence and carelessness'.[99] However, once in London, Hawley basked in Cumberland's and the army's glory.

Yet before Hawley returned to the Continent, he penned a memorandum to the Customs House in regard to his own regiment of Royal Dragoons,

> for the better encouragement of the officers and soldiers personally assisting the officers of the customs in preventing the running of the goods, the shares of seizure belonging to the forces should be divided amongst the troop or troops employed in the same service.[100]

---

94   Dalton, *Army of George I*, Vol.I, p.48.
95   Douglas, *History*, p.234.
96   TNA, SP54/32/4A.
97   Douglas, *History*, p.251.
98   *London Evening Post*, 2926, 5-7 Aug. 1746.
99   Lewis, *Walpole*, Vol.19, p.295.
100  TNA, PC1/5/111.

They had not been involved against the Jacobites, but had been stationed in Sussex and were engaged in a typical peacetime army role; combatting smugglers, the soldiers being led by Major Johnson. On 5 December, Hawley was displeased about how his regiment and his men were being treated by the customs officers. According to him, the customs officers made the soldiers drunk and bought their share of the smuggled goods for reduced rates. Riding horses whilst drunk led to horses being killed or injured. No allowances were made by the customs officers for this and so captains were half-ruined having to buy new horses. The soldiers were widely dispersed and this meant that they were not under the watchful eye of officers or NCOs and were susceptible to bribery. According to Hawley 'There may be a better and more military disposition of the quarters'. He also thought there should be an equal division of the prize money and Cumberland supported Hawley in this, as the latter noted. The report was sent to a committee of the Privy Council for consideration. Yet the customs officers did not uphold Hawley's complaints.[101] This episode shows Hawley's focus on the need for the soldiers to be under such authority, and that he still had Cumberland's support.

---

101 TNA, PC1/5/111.

# 8

# Back to Europe, 1747-1748

The war on the Continent had continued to go badly during Hawley's absence, maintaining the trend of the previous year. At Rocoux on 11 October 1746, a battle in which Ligonier served, de Saxe had secured another victory over the allies. However, with the end of the Jacobite campaign, those British troops sent to Britain could now return to 'proper soldiering'. Shortly after Cumberland was back in London, so too was Hawley. The former went to the Hague in November, but two days before he left he conferred with Hawley. He told him that he had not ordered Hawley's regiment to return to Europe because of the 'expense he had been at to put it in repair', but he asked him if he would go with him and Hawley 'assured him he was allways ready & desirous to do any parte of the world'.[1]

It was in January 1747 that Cumberland returned from the Dutch Republic and told Hawley to prepare to return there with the first embarkation, with Major General John Mordaunt under him. The troops not being all ready, Mordaunt went first with the infantry and a squadron. Five weeks later Hawley crossed with the rest of the cavalry, arriving at Willemstad. On the same day, Colonel George Keppell, Lord Bury (1724-1774, later Earl of Albemarle), arrived with troops from Scotland. Hawley went with the dragoons to 'Longestrate' (possibly Langestraat, a suburb of Bruges), where there were another nine squadrons which had been there since the previous year. They remained there until equipped with their new uniforms and then marched to the camp at Alphen. Hawley had the command of 36 squadrons of cavalry, which were to be on the right of the army on the march.[2]

The army marched towards the French, who were assembling at Louvain, though their designs were unclear. Hawley was detached with 20 squadrons and 20 battalions; the latter being under the command of the Hanoverian General

---

1  RA, HT, 7411-24-101, p.29.
2  RA, HT, 7411-24-101, p.29.

Sommerfeldt and were camped on the Nethe. Meanwhile, after Stair's death on 9 May 1747, Cumberland had written to the King about Hawley's wanting a governorship. Since Stair had been governor of Minorca, this seemed a possible opening, but Tyrawley was offered it instead and the younger man accepted. Hawley asked Cumberland about this being his last campaign. Cumberland acknowledged that this setback was an injustice and hardship to him, 'but that he thought 'twas a little hard on him to desire to leave him, since he knew it was not his fault and that he would still convince him upon the first of all occasions of his good intentions'.[3]

Hawley was again detached forward with the 10,000 men towards Tongres under the Austrian *Feldzeugmeister* Graf Leopold Joseph von Daun (1705-1766). There were over 20,000 French troops at Tongres, in two corps, but they only made a show of resistance in order to cover the march of the French army towards Maestricht in order to besiege this citadel. Cumberland brought up the remainder of the army towards Maestricht to prevent them from doing so.[4] They were about to fight the Battle of Laffeld; the war's largest battle in terms of manpower with over a quarter of a million troops involved, with the numerical advantage going to the French under de Saxe. On 2 July it was decided to attack the French on their left. Hawley was sent ahead to reconnoitre the ground as far ahead as he could between the two armies. A message arrived from Ligonier to tell him that the French were about to attack on the allied left, so Hawley returned and was ordered to march ahead with his cavalry. He had them formed behind the infantry just as the cannon began to fire. The British and Hanoverian infantry defended the village of Laffeld, repelling five attacks before the French took the village by 2:00 p.m. Fighting at the village took five hours. Ligonier than had the allied cavalry move against their French counterparts. This was where Hawley took his place, along with some of the Austrians and some of the Dutch.[5]

Hawley had brought up his British dragoons in three lines, fronting the village, just behind the infantry. There was no support from the Dutch and Austrians on the right. Hawley then ordered his squadrons to charge the flank of the nearest French infantry battalion, but at that moment, six Dutch squadrons were in full flight, pursued by two of French Carabiners.[6] Hawley had a squadron of the Scots Greys with him and they charged the pursuers in the flank 'and demolished them', but more French cavalry came into sight. Those British and Hanoverian cavalry units that had been disrupted by the flight of the Dutch were forced to veer off to the left, where they, and Hawley, were 'mixed up with the French squadrons'.

3   RA, HT, 7411-24-101, p.29.
4   RA, HT, 7411-24-101, p.29.
5   RA, HT, 7411-24-101, pp.29-30.
6   RA, HT, 7411-24-101, p.30.

Hawley shot at a French cornet bearing a regimental standard and the two troopers guarding it, and Hawley and his two aides took the broken banner and left the melee to take shelter with the Foot Guards.[7]

Hawley rallied the remains of the charging Scots Greys and put himself at the head of the British cavalry on the left wing. Ligonier and Cumberland arrived soon afterwards from the right. Putting themselves at the head of the line they charged the two lines of French cavalry and beat them back to some hedges. These were lined with French infantry who 'gave our squadrons such a fire they were forced to come back in great disorder followed by all the French squadrons'. Ligonier and Hawley attempted to stop the retreat and to rally their men, but found themselves engulfed by the French cavalry. Ligonier was taken prisoner, but Hawley escaped 'by the activity of his horse'. Thirty pistols were fired at him, but he rode to a little field and formed what squadrons he could find and then helped the army to make an orderly retreat towards Maestricht. Cumberland had Hawley take the cavalry through Maestricht that night and cross the Meuse.[8]

The French had suffered for their victory, according to Hawley, losing six standards, ten colours, and apparently 10,000 men and many officers, to the allies' loss of 4,000 men (an under-estimation by Hawley; allied losses were not much less than those of the French), seven guns and three standards. Hawley stated that the Austrians and Dutch were to blame; 'The Austrian Hussars and irregulars were of no use, good for nothing, the Austrian cuirassiers did not act and the Hessians were very shy and the Dutch Horse ran away and broke all the English and Hanovers that happened to be in their way'.[9]

For the rest of the summer, the army had the Meuse between themselves and the French. The latter took the fortress of Bergen op Zoom, though Maestricht was safe for the moment. Both sides went into winter quarters and Hawley recieved Cumberland's leave to return to England. The prospect of a vacant governorship came up again at the year's end, this time that of Tilbury. Yet, once again and unknown to Cumberland, the post went to another; Lord De La Warr, who was not even born when Hawley took up his first commission. This especially irked him, 'though it was a small thing he would not have accepted of it he tooke it so ill that he went off and acquainted the Duke that he was thoroughly convinced he must be in disgrace with His Majesty and that he being the only one who had never received any marke of Royall favour as almost everyone above him and below him in ranke had'.[10]

---

7   RA, HT, 7411-24-101, p.30.
8   RA, HT, 7411-24-101, p.30.
9   RA, HT, 7411-24-101, p.31.
10  RA, HT, 7411-24-101, p.31.

Hawley as Colonel of the Royal Dragoons c.1748, oil on canvas by David Morier (Courtesy of the Hawley family; image courtesy of Bonhams)

Because of the expense and because of the disrespect he felt that had been shown him, he thought that another lieutenant general should replace him in the staff that Christmas of 1747. Cumberland expressed his opinion of Hawley:

> in the kindest manner, that he was as sensible of the injustice done him as he himselfe and designed it might be left to him, that he tooke it upon himselfe to make him easy and hoped the first opportunity, which he beleaved would be soone, to tell him some good news, therefore designed he would relye at least in his sincere endeavours to serve him, but that it was not in his power to make him any promise of anythinge'.[11]

11  RA, HT, 7411-24-101, p.31.

On 24 December 1747, Hawley received word that the King wished to review his regiment, which had been in Sussex for the last 15 months, 'on hard duty against smugglers'. Honywood had reviewed them in September 'and made the handsomest report that ever was made', but some 'malicious court tatlers' had told the King and Ligonier that it 'was now the worst in the army'. As it was the regiment marched into London on Christmas day and the King 'made the most scutinous review that was knowne and at last was forced to owne that it was far from what he expected to have seen that he was thoroughly pleased and could find no one fault'.[12]

Cumberland then sent for Hawley and told him that the governorship of Kinsale would be vacant when Ligonier was promoted and so he could have that. Yet it was only worth a niggardly 20 Irish shillings a day, less tax. Hawley refused it. The next day he was told that the governorship of Fort St. Phillip on Minorca was vacant and had been for a while, worth 40 shillings a day. He need never go there. Hawley turned it down because the governor of Minorca itself and his lieutenant, Tyrawley and Blakeney, were younger than him. Cumberland went back to the Hague as the new year dawned and the matter was dropped.[13]

Hawley was very disappointed in the onset of 1748 and may have been considering standing down from active service. Richmond wrote to him on 31 January in an attempt to dissuade him from this course of action, writing, 'really for the sake of the service to which I am very sure you would be a loss, if you was to retire from it'. He strongly recommended that he return to the Dutch Republic for if he did not the King would never promote him. Richmond stressed Cumberland's support, 'he own'd you had not what you ought to have, but then added you certainly would have it, if you had a little more patience'. Cumberland was 'determined to do all he can for you'. Richmond claimed that instead of resigning, 'whereas if you was to be upon the staff now & have this next campagne, which in all probability might be the last, you could not fail of succeeding in what you justly wanted'.[14]

Henry Fox (1705-1774), secretary at war, by Newcastle's orders, proposed the governorship of Gibraltar for Hawley; this had been long vacant and was worth 40s per day. However, the King wanted the governor to reside there. The matter was unresolved as the army embarked for the Continent again. Wade died on 14 March 1748 and then Fox wrote to Hawley that the King wanted to divide Wade's appointments in Scotland (the governorships of Forts George, Augustus, and William, sinecures given to him in the previous decade), worth £800 annually in all. Fort William was designated for Bland and Fort George (worth £500) for

---

12   RA, HT, 7411-24-101, p.31.
13   RA, HT, 7411-24-101, p.31.
14   RA, HT, 7411-24-101, p.31.

Hawley. Kinsale was also offered and Hawley could choose which he wanted. He had already turned down the latter, and refused it again to Fox.[15] Hawley complained to Newcastle, 'severall of my juniors who have long had good governorships, while I had never had any mark of Royall favour' and he begged Newcastle to help, 'you will lay an eternall obligation' on him.[16]

Newcastle told Hawley he must take the Fort George posting, and that Hawley was put on the Irish staff as well. It was now time for him to return to the Continent. He intended to join Cumberland at Roermond. Yet on arrival at Willemstad, he was ordered by Cumberland to march with six battalions at Breda, which was the Dutch camp. It was here that a cessation of hostilities was announced and news arrived that Maestricht had fallen to the French at the last moment. William of Orange, the Dutch Stadtholder, talked to Hawley and was sympathetic to his plight and 'he hoped the King, would, when he had considered of it, for he concluded he should have seen him come over Genll of Horse'.[17]

Cumberland, in a letter to Newcastle on 19 March 1748, supported Hawley:

> I cannot refuse complying with his solicitations, as I know the justice and hardship of his case, he never having had those douceurs which other general officers have, and yet has been upon service since the beginning of this war, you will oblige me extreamly in interceding with the King in this affair.[18]

With Cumberland temporarily absent, Colonel Robert Napier, adjutant, wrote to Hawley, expecting him to be at Willemstad on 15 April, with Pulteney's Regiment and the new recruits. These, along with Skelton's and Leighton's Regiments, were, with Major General Fowke, to accompany Hawley to Breda. They would be joined by the artillery and Hawley was to remain at their destination until further orders from Cumberland. He was told to prevent any of his men from enlisting in the Prussian army.[19]

Even with the war apparently over, whilst at Breda, Hawley received orders in early May to join the British and Hanoverian camp at Hellenrouck with the seven battalions that were with him. He told Newcastle of the 'very disagreeable and cruell situation I am in here'. The four Dutch generals who were there were all younger than him. They were in command of the forces that Hawley had to command. Although he was just beneath Ligonier in the hierarchy of the British

15  RA, HT, 7411-24-112, p.8.
16  BL, Add. Mss. 32714, f.413r.
17  RA, HT, 7411-24-101, p.32.
18  TNA, SP87/24, f.31r.
19  RA, HT, 7411-24-128, p.323.

Army, he wanted equality in rank with the Dutch generals. It was also depressing; there was 'nothing but melancholy faces'.[20]

Hawley clearly thought that he had been treated in a beggarly manner. On 4 May 1748 he was at Breda with a command of the seven battalions of British infantry, 300 recruits and 300 dragoons, but there were 16 Dutch generals there, all junior to him in age but senior in rank and this clearly brought matters home to him. He complained in a letter to Newcastle:

> The very disagreeable, and cruell situation I am in here, commanded by so many Dutche Genlls: who are younger than me forces me to give your Grace this impertinent trouble…As I am nexte to Sir John Ligonier except Mr Handiside…I humbly beg of your Grace, to mention this to His Majesty, if he would be gratiously pleased, to give me my Ranke with them whiche is the ?? of May laste, it appears to me only a Piece of Justice and I cant see what injustice it can be…As I doubt this muste be the last campaigne, I shall never get my Ranke if His Majesty wont please to have some compassion for me now, I desire no addition of pay.[21]

On 9 May 1748, Cumberland wrote from Hellenrouck,

> We shall now in three or four days begin our long intended march towards Boisleduc, when I shall only consider my Camp with the price of convenience to the Troops, & this night send Genl Hawley orders to be ready to joyn me thereabouts with his seven Br Battns.[22]

He joined Cumberland at Eindhoven with the cavalry. Cumberland met him and told him that some of the younger lieutenant generals were eager to be made Knights of the Bath. He recalled that Hawley had turned this down before, but would he now like to reconsider the offer. He replied that 'he liked the title' but 'he would never give a thousand pounds for a bauble' so excused the 'empty honour'. He preferred 'His Majesty would please to give him his ranke of Genll of Horse… he should be very thankfull, a military tittle being the utmost of his ambition'.[23]

The war's end was dismal enough. With the Dutch and Austrians gone, the British and Hanoverians retired into cantonments. Hawley, with the British dragoons, remained there for four months, where fever struck and many died. Hawley had it 'amonge the rest'. Fortunately the Royal Navy's successes made

---

20  BL.Add.Mss. 32714, f.518r-519v.
21  Dalton, *Army of George I*, I, p.50.
22  RA, CP34/330
23  RA, HT, 7411-24-101, p. 32.

up for the military showing on the Continent: both Britain and France returned their conquests, but France again acknowledged the Hanoverian succession and agreed to expel Charles Stuart from France. At November, with the peace of Aix La Chappelle ending the war, orders were sent for Hawley on 26 November to march with the first division of the army, which was made up of the cavalry, to Willemstad and then for England. A yacht was sent for him, and after being delayed by storms, reached England on Christmas day, 1748.[24] This may have been the last time he ever went abroad.

Hawley was never made a full general (nor less a field marshal). He remained a lieutenant general as he had been appointed in 1743. It is possible that the debacle of Falkirk cost him further promotion, which was granted to other elderly senior officers not just Ligonier. Hawley seems to have thought that it was his right by seniority rather than merit and in this he was to be disappointed. However, as shall be shown, he was to receive additional posts and honours in later life.

24  RA, HT, 7411-24-108, p.64.

# 9

# Last Years, 1749-1759

Hawley's quest for preferment continued after the war was over. In April 1749 Parliament announced that there would be a British military staff of a lieutenant general and two major generals to inspect the troop encampments in Britain and to compile reports of what they saw. According to Hawley, 'Every body were told and believed' that Hawley would be the senior officer chosen and Cholmondeley and Mordaunt would be the other two. Hawley, working on this assumption, 'at great expense' assembled what he would need for this posting. Yet in June of that year 'to the surprise of moste people', Lieutenant General Sir Charles Howard was named for the senior role and he was Hawley's junior in seniority. Doubtless in disgust, Hawley left London and went to his country home, staying there until October, 'not a little out of humour'. Howard was 11 years his junior, though Hawley thought he was 16 years younger.[1]

Cumberland, had, that spring, asked Hawley if he would like 'to have a small mark of His Majesty's favour'. This was an offer of the governorship of Londonderry, now vacant on Lieutenant General Bowles' death. Hawley told him that 'he should allways be proude of any marke of Royall favour as he had received but few in comparison with many who were his junior, that as to this he was very indifferent'. He let Cumberland decide who it should be granted to. Hawley heard no more and it was given to another lieutenant general.[2]

On George II's return from Hanover, Hawley had cause to visit Cumberland about a cornet who wished to sell his commission. Cumberland asked if he would like to exchange the colonelcy of his current regiment for the Royal Horse Guards. He thanked Cumberland for thinking of him, and knew that this would bring him more income than his regiment, 'but, as he had never been voracious for money

---

1    RA, HT, 7411-24-101-p.33.
2    RA, HT, 7411-24-101-p.33.

when he was necessitous, he now thanked God he was not necessitous' and hoped that Cumberland and his royal father would excuse him for turning it down. He also liked his own regiment well enough, 'he had a regiment he liked and had made from nothing and a whole sett of officers who he had brought in and who he liked and that he ventured to say was the best regt then in the service'. What he would like, was not a governorship in Scotland or Ireland, which he had previously turned down, but an equivalent one anywhere else. This answer apparently amazed all who heard it.[3]

A fresh appointment did come Hawley's way, albeit a minor one. On 29 August 1751, Lord George Germain, first Viscount Sackville (1716-1785), an MP in Ireland, told Hawley that he was to be placed on the new staff for the Irish establishment as major general. This was an honorary post but worth to Hawley an allowance of £1 10s per day.[4] He accepted it.

When General John Murray, second Earl of Dunmore (1685-1752) died on 18 April 1752, Cumberland asked Hawley why he had never seen him at his principal residence, Windsor Lodge (Cumberland had been Ranger of Windsor Park from 1746). Hawley visited for a few days. He learnt that Cumberland had written to the King in Hanover about him, asking that he could offer Hawley the governorship of Plymouth and was expected an answer soon. However, there was a strong competitor for it; Ligonier. The latter was given it. However, on 17 June 1752, Sir Phillip Honywood, governor of Portsmouth, died. Hawley stayed at home and did nothing about this, but left anything that might happen in Cumberland's hands. Pelham suggested 'General Hawley might be contented with that of Guernsey'.[5] However, this was not to be. In July an express came to West Green Lodge and brought him news of his becoming the governor of Portsmouth (once held by his late kinsman and benefactor, Erle). He then rode to London and thanked Cumberland personally.[6]

In Chapter 3, we have noted Hawley's thoughts about civil government, indicative that he was not wholly taken up with military matters. Following the death of the Prince of Wales in 1751, there was concern by a number of Whig noblemen and gentry about the education of the heir to the throne, his eldest son, Prince George (1738-1820, later George III), that he be brought up with Whig principles and they drew up a Memorial to this effect. Two copies were made and one was given to Hawley. He gave it to Cumberland and it was then shown to the Prince's grandfather, George II. Horace Walpole wondered why Hawley had been chosen to

---

3  RA, HT, 7411-24-101-p.33.
4  RA, HT, 7411-24-119.
5  RA, HT, 7411-24-119; Rex Whitworth, *Field Marshal Lord Ligonier: A Story of the British Army, 1702-1770* (Oxford: Clarendon Press, 1958), p.188.
6  RA, HT, 7411-24-119.

be the conduit for this information and alleged that some claimed 'Hawley could not read', which is nonsense.⁷ Another report stated that the memorial was given by Hawley to Newcastle on 18 December 1752, not Cumberland, though it was believed it would be given to the latter.⁸

At the end of 1752, Hawley sent a copy of *The Penny Post* newspaper to Newcastle, for it contained 'objectional' reflections on the King and government. Newcastle thanked him for it and assured it would be laid before George II. Apparently, the King 'is sensible of the Regard, you shew'd to his Government'.⁹ Hawley wrote back on the next day, and after complaining of ill-health, noted that he would be spending time at home 'upon ane affair of some consequence to me' but that if needed he could be in London in six hours.¹⁰

Hawley clearly wanted to be remembered for posterity so had two paintings of himself made. One is of himself as cavalry officer, painted by David Morier (c.1705-1770), a client of Cumberland and best known for his painting of Culloden. He is shown in uniform on horseback, with a sword and facing to the right of the painting, his face obscure; very much a military pose. The second was by Christian Freidrich Zincke (1685-1767), known for his miniatures and here Hawley is portrayed out of uniform and this is now held at the National Portrait Gallery of Scotland. He is shown to have had a small facial blemish on the right side of the face. It was possibly painted, not for himself, but for a family member or friend, possibly female, as it is more intimate, emphasising his face and non-martial appearance, which the other does not.

In about 1752 Hawley decided to write a brief memoir of his life. He gave no stated reason why he should have wished to do so, but by this time he was about 67 so may have felt that with perhaps little time left to live, he should give an account of his military career. In it, he focusses on his early years, with very little to say about his role in the '15 or in the Spanish expedition of 1719; he is also very quiet about his role in the Highlands after Culloden, though gives reasonably lengthy accounts of both battles he fought in 1746. There is virtually nothing in his account about his personal life, nor about his family.

Hawley had one last military command bestowed on him. In November 1755, a letter from Fox gave him an appointment in the staff as principal general and ordered him to Canterbury to command forces appointed for defence against a feared French attack.¹¹ Hostilities between Britain and France erupted in the American colonies in 1755 as Major General Edward Braddock (1695-1755), one of

---

7   Horace Walpole, *Memoirs* (London: Henry Colburn, 1847), Vol.I, p.103.
8   HMC Var. Coll, VI, p.23.
9   BL. Add. Mss., 32714, f.413r, 415r.
10  BL. Add. Mss., 32714, f.440r.
11  BL. Add. Mss., 32714, f.440r.

Cumberland's protegees, was killed and defeated there. There was also perceived danger at home, too, and an invasion was feared. Given Britain's limited military preparedness, there was serious concern.[12]

Hawley wrote notes about how to deploy troops to repel them, titled, 'Dispositions for putting the Troops under cover to invest Dover'. These were to be that the infantry was to be in the first line and the dragoons were to be at a greater distance behind them. To be exact, the dragoons were to be in 18 villages, five-eight miles away from Dover, but that the infantry were to be housed in 17 villages one-four miles away.[13]

Hawley was not popular with his former subordinate, James Wolfe, now a colonel, who wrote thus from Canterbury on 5 November 1755, 'General Hawley is expected in a few days to keep us all in order; if there is an invasion, they could not make use of a more unfit person. The troops dread his severity, hate the man, and hold his military knowledge in contempt'.[14] It was also at this time, 21 August 1755, in a letter to Mann, that Walpole wrote about Cumberland's appointment of Braddock to lead the British army in the American colonies, 'This is not the first time, as witness in Hawley, that the Duke has found, that brutality did not necessarily consummate a general'.[15] Ligonier and the Duke of Montagu were in conference this month with Hawley about anti-invasion steps.[16]

Hawley then penned his 'Thoughts on possible invasion'. Customs and excise had riding officers in Kent, Sussex and Hampshire and should be stationed a mile from coast from Dover to Chichester 'to procure a quick intelligence of the place the enemy may land'. This was so that they could provide news of the enemy to the nearest troops. Major Batten, of the principal custom house in Sussex, was 'a very intelligent man' and he was to dispose these riders and to see that they do their duty, with patrols both night and day. He would need inspectors to ensure that night time duty in Kent took place. If the enemy were to land to the west of Lewes, troops there were to march to Arundel and Bramber and canton there until another regiment arrives at Lewes. If the enemy were at Arundel, which Hawley thought unlikely, the troops at Lewes were to stay and wait for the three other dragoon regiments. If the enemy were to be at Portsmouth, the four regiments of dragoons were to march in two columns and cut them down at the Downs, in the open. If the British cavalry must wait for their infantry, the cavalry were to wait on the Isle of Portsea if they were near Portdown, for there was sufficient forage and quarters there. Infantry in lower Kent were then to march to Portsmouth by

12   RA, HT, 7411-24-126
13   RA, HT, 7411-24-26.
14   Willson, *Wolfe*, p.280.
15   Lewis (ed.), *Walpole*, Vol.21, p.492.
16   *Oxford Journal*, 1 November 1755.

the main road, one column via Kingston, Guildford, Franham, Alton. Other forces were to march to Portsmouth at their commanders' discretion. If the enemy were aiming at Portsmouth, Selsey harbour, or Chichester were likely targets and so British forces should gather at Chichester.[17]

Hawley also seems to have been a conduit for intelligence. On 1 December 1755, Fox referred to an offer he had sent to Cumberland by a Mr Paris of 'giving usefull intelligence by the means of relatives in France'. Fox did not deem, in this occasion, that the intelligence was of use, but approved Hawley paying Paris either five or 10 guineas and assuring him that he would be rewarded if he was of use in the future. He also referred to Hawley rewarding one James Phone for remitting information. Fox asked Hawley if he could send information about Ferdinando Ferrari, a suspected spy currently held at Canterbury, and that he be sent to London for questioning.[16]

There were also military matters for the elderly general to contend with. At the beginning of 1756, there was an outbreak of smallpox among the troops at Canterbury. William, Viscount Barrington (1717-1793), secretary at war, instructed Hawley to 'provide an Hospital to receive all the soldiers that may fall ill of that Distemper, to prevent as much as possible, that Distemper from spreading'. Hawley was given no immediate funding for this, but was assured that he would be repaid.[18]

In May 1756, he was told to order Hay's, Skelton's, Honywood's and the King's Regiments to march from Canterbury and Maidstone for the West Country. Men who were ill were to be sent to Ashford and, when recovered, sergeants, and officers if need be, were to conduct them to their regiments. Pitt wanted Hawley in London, possibly to be in the command of cavalry forces there, fifteen squadrons in all, with a major general to be under Hawley's command.[19]

Much of Hawley's role was very much routine. He would receive orders from the secretary at war for the activity of troops under his command. These included ordering troops away from places where they had been stationed, but where sensitive civilian matters were to take place. These included an election in New Romney in December 1755 and assize courts being held in February 1756. In January 1756 troops were to be sent to the hospital at Deal to prevent any of the sailors there from deserting. In June of that year, smuggling in Kent was worrying the civil authorities, and so the army was to be 'aiding and assisting (upon application) to the civil magistrates and officers of the excise in preventing the owlers and smugglers from running goods and in apprehending the said owlers

---

17   RA, HT, 7411-24-120.
18   TNA, WO4/51, p.121.
19   RA, HT, 7411-24-122.

and smugglers and seizing their goods, but not to repel force with force, unless it should be found absolutely necessary or being thereunto required by the civil magistrates'.[20]

Later that year, Hawley was required to form part of a general court martial, along with a number of other senior officers including Ligonier and Huske. This was to try Lieutenant General Thomas Fowke, who, as governor of Gibraltar, had failed to send any of his men as reinforcements to the beleaguered garrison at Minorca, which had subsequently fallen to the French earlier that year. The court martial sat on 10 August 1756 and found Fowke guilty. He was suspended from all military appointments for a year.[21]

Hawley had decided on 29 March 1749, presumably because of his advanced age of 64:

> I being perfectly well both in body and mind now that I am writing this my last will by which I do hereby give order and dispose what is mine both real and personal that there may be no disputes after I am gone, therefore as I began the world with nothing and as all I have is of my own acquiring I can dispose of it as I please…as there is a peace I may die the common way.[22]

It was proved in May 1759, and extracts of it were published in several newspapers, caused somewhat of a consternation. This was because he made numerous statements of a controversial nature, as well as, more conventionally, giving some details about his private life, property and wealth. It was referred to as being a very 'particular will' and he was stated as being 'aged upwards of 80'.[23]

What probably shocked contemporaries most was his attitudes to the clergy, striking of atheism or agnosticism, and lawyers, which he expressed in forthright terms in his will, when it came to his burial, 'The priest I conclude will have his fee, let the puppy have it… I hate all priests, of all professions, and have the worst opinion of all members of the law'.[24] Conventionally wills, which were all proved in church courts until 1858, include references to commending the soul in the afterlife of the testator to Almighty God. Hawley did not do so. Given that Christian observance in the eighteenth century was almost universal, Hawley's remarks were eccentric at best and offensive at worst.

20  TNA, WO4/50, pp.97, 224, 116; WO4/51, p.64.
21  *London Gazette*, 9608, 10-14 Aug. 1756
22  TNA, PROB11/844.
23  *Oxford Journal*, 31 March and 12 May 1759.
24  TNA, PROB11/844.

The will also shows more positive sides to his nature, in his regard for the two important women in his life. Firstly, there was his sister, Anne, who had remained a spinster. She was to receive, as soon after his death as possible, £5,000 of the £7,500 he had invested in Bank annuities. As already noted, Hawley had given her a house to live in, at Charlton in north west Kent, as well as providing her with a sufficient income to live a respectable and comfortable, though not opulent, lifestyle as a maiden lady. He wanted her to have this as soon as possible after his death, not later than a month.

Throughout his life, Hawley had not been known to have had any dealings with women. His writings show that he was adverse to soldiers marrying and in this he practised what he preached. Many of his fellow generals, including Cumberland, Cope, Wade, and Ligonier, remained bachelors, so his choice was not uncommon. In part it may have been dictated by his relative poverty. Whether he indulged in any casual dalliances is unknown, but unlike Wade he is not known to have fathered any bastards. His will, however, showed that he was not wholly immune to feminine charms. The woman in his life was Mrs Elizabeth Toovey, described as a widow, 'for many years my friend and companion and often my careful nurse and in my absence my faithful steward she is the person I think myself bound in honour and gratitude to provide for as well as I can'. We do not know when she was born or when Hawley met her. She had certainly been married. It may have been after her husband's death she had met Hawley and became his housekeeper and mistress, though there is no suggestion the two were ever married. Probably she managed his properties when he was away at war. She was to inherit the bulk of Hawley's properties, for her lifetime (listed below), except the house his sister lived in. She also was to have his other 'goods and plate'.[25] Little is known of her, but her husband would appear to have been Caleb Toovey, a gentleman, who died in 1744, and left her lands in Henley upon Thames, Rotherfield Grey, Rotherfield Peppard, all in Oxfordshire, and in Chipping Wycomb, Buckinghamshire. In his will he refers to Elizabeth as 'my dear and loving wife'.[26]

The marriage had led to at least two sons. The elder was John, who became a lieutenant in Hawley's regiment in 1726. By at least 1744 his young brother William was also an army officer. It has been alleged that these two were Hawley's illegitimate sons and that he must therefore have met Elizabeth decades prior to her husband's death. There is no way to prove or disprove these allegations. Since John was a junior officer in Hawley's regiment in 1726 he may have known her by that date. But this does not mean to say he knew her years previously.

25  TNA, PROB11/844.
26  TNA, PROB11/844.

Hawley decided that 'as I never was married I have no heir. I therefore have long since taken it in my head to adopt one heir and son after the manner of the Romans'. Both of Elizabeth's sons were currently serving in Hawley's own regiment, the Royal Regiment of Dragoons. By 1759 John was the regiment's lieutenant colonel, appointed on 17 December 1754,[27] and William was a captain. It was William whom he chose to adopt, on the understanding that after Hawley's death 'he shall forthwith take upon him both my name and sign them either by Act of Parliament or otherways'. After his mother died, he would inherit all the properties given by Hawley after his death for her to enjoy in her own lifetime. He was also the sole executor of the will and had to look after the rights of Anne Hawley, Elizabeth Toovey, and his brother.[28]

John Toovey was to receive £1,000, plus Hawley's horses, arms and writings, and any money his younger brother owed him. Miss Elizabeth Birkett, 'having been a usefull agreeable handmaid to me' was to be given £100. She was Elizabeth Toovey's niece and presumably lived at West Green House. Yet Hawley continued his vendetta against marriage; if they (John Toovey and Elizabeth Birkett) 'be both fools and marry' the two would receive nothing from him and their inheritance would be transferred to Anne Hawley.[29]

There were a number of subsequent codicils made to the will. The first was on 7 November 1749. It gave William Toovey Harlebotts Farm, Hartfordbridge. The second was on 22 October 1750. This gave Dipley Mill to Anne Hawley and on her death to Captain William Toovey. The third was on 28 February 1752. This gave the Odiam estate to Anne, but transferred Dipley Mill instead to Captain William Toovey although he would have to pay Anne £50 per annum. He would also receive Blue House Farm. Mrs Toovey would give £1,000 of her share to Elizabeth Birkett and Colonel John Toovey would receive Hawley's arms, hoses, books and plans. The final codicil was made on 16 May 1753. It gave William Toovey Blowhouse Farm and Hillside Farm.[30]

These changes reflected in part Hawley's acquisition of land in later life. He also owned Exalls' Farm, adjacent to his house, and bought from Lord Castlemaine. Then there was the Paddock field, adjoining Exall's Farm, and bought from a farmer by the name of Bellhouse, as was the farm at the bottom of West Green and Little Meadow. He had the Great Meadow, also called Tilligany, bought from Thomas Ellis, a carpenter/wright. He also had land in adjacent parishes; the farm and barn at Birchen in Mattingley. He also owned a house, stables and outhouses

---

27  *London Gazette*, 9433, 17 Dec. 1754.
28  TNA, PROB11/844.
29  TNA, PROB11/844.
30  TNA, PROB11/844.

near Hyde Park, in the parish of St. George's, Westminster, bought from a Mrs Rooke.[31]

In later years he acquired Harlebotts, a farm with land in the parish adjacent to Hartley Wintney called Hartfordbridge, bought from James Hare, a yeoman. He also bought Dipley Mills and 92 acres of adjacent lands (including 12 of pasture and 12 of meadowland) in Phoenix Mill, Hartley Wintney, by 1752, bought from John Fly of Odiam.[32] He also bought a cottage and garden in Hartley Wintney known as The Sign of the Bull, from Edward Winter on 2 October 1754. A few days previously, William Winter sold Hawley land adjoining West Green House for £120 and a further eight acres adjoining Bell Wood for an additional £225.[33]

West Green House, Hartley Wintney, Hampshire. (Author photograph)

The will was brought to the attention of a lawyer, one Forrester, on 13 June 1759 for his opinion. Forrester was, unsurprisingly, scathing about Hawley, 'The high opinion the Testator seems to have entertained of his own talents and the prejudice he bore to those who might have given him effectual advice, have in

---

31   TNA, PROB11/844.
32   HRO, 25M87/11.
33   HRO, 79A08/2.

this instance, frustrated and determined intent of his, which was to prevent a marriage between the said Colonel Toovey and Miss Birkett'. Apparently the codicils to the will, which gave property to Colonel Toovey, were unaffected by Hawley's strictures to the contrary made in the main body of the will.[34] So John Toovey and Elizabeth Birkett did marry, by licence on 26 June 1759, and John became a major general in 1765. His younger brother married Jane Baker, a minor, at Heckfield on 17 June 1760.[35]

Hawley died on 24 March 1759 at his home at West Green; we do not know the cause of his death, but presumably old age or illness provided the reason. He was buried in the parish churchyard of St. Mary's Hartley Wintney, two days later. Presumably the Vicar, the Rev. Peter Smith, officiated, and the burial register simply notes, 'Lieutenant General Henry Hawley was buried 26 March'. Curiously, the register also reads 'Captain Tovey General Hawley's executor paid a mortuary of 10s 5 April 1759'. It is not known what this is a reference to. There is no monument or tomb stone standing to his memory, as would have been commonplace for a man of his wealth and social standing. Other senior generals such as Blakeney and Wade were commemorated at Westminster Abbey. This should be of no surprise, for Hawley wrote this in his will of 1749, 'my carcasse may be put any where tis equal to me, but I will have no more expense or ridiculous show than if a poor soldier (who is as good a man) was to be buried from the Hospital…pay the carpenter for his carcass box'. In some ways, Hawley was a modest man.[36]

Anne Hawley, Elizabeth Toovey, and her younger son sold the Mattingley property and several of those in Hartley Wintney shortly after Hawley's death, on 16-17 May 1759, to one George Rose.[37] William Henry died by 1763 and his brother by 1769, the same year that Anne Hawley died. However, the Toovey-Hawley family continued to reside in Hartley Wintney until at the end of the nineteenth century.

34  RA, HT, 7411-24-405.
35  Marriage Licences, www.ancestry.co.uk.
36  HRO, St. Mary Wintney Parish Registers; TNA, PROB11/844.
37  HRO, 50M63/B79/24.

# Conclusion

Contemporaries differed in their assessments of Hawley. Walpole wrote in his memoirs, in 1757, 'He despised money, fame and politics; loved gaming, women and his own favourites, and yet had not one sociable virtue'.[1] Cumberland had a diametrically different view, according to Richmond, summing up, in 1748, his senior officers thus:

> His Royal Highness expressed more regard for you than I think I ever heard him almost for any other military man…Ligonier is my right hand & next to him my principall reliance is upon Albermarle and Hawley, the first as a foot officer, and the second as a horse officer, & Hawley is the first I know in the whole allyed army for leading a line of cavalry.[2]

These comments tell us as much about the virtues admired by the writers as about Hawley, of course.

Hawley was a career soldier, the son and grandson of soldiers. In this he was a product of the new standing army, which offered careers to those of the middling sort. He was from gentry stock but needed a profession to earn a living. Fortunately for himself, Hawley was not an avaricious man, nor did he enjoy conspicuous consumption. His rise through the army was slow but sure, but he was probably disappointed to rise no more than to the rank of lieutenant general, which he reached at the age of 58.

There are two main charges laid against Hawley. The first concerns his conduct at Falkirk, which was the only battle in which he ever commanded an army and which was a defeat, though not a catastrophic one. There are some mitigating factors. The Jacobite army was at the height of its strength and the weather was against the British army with its reliance on musketry; furthermore the artillery was inadequate and never fired a shot, and the morale of two of the dragoon regiments was questionable at best. However, Hawley underestimated his enemy.

---

1   Walpole, *Memoirs*, Vol.I, p.103.
2   RA, HT, 7411-24-112, 8.

This led him to neglect the use of his cavalry in scouting in order to detect the Jacobite movements on the morning of 17 January, and then to thrust them forward, unsupported against formed ranks of infantry. Their rout helped sap the morale of the infantry, and exposed his battalions on the left, most of whom then fled. Had they not done so, the battle might have been a victory for Hawley. It is ironic that he had served as a cavalryman for decades yet failed to use his mounted troops to their best ability. However, he had the regular soldier's disdain for irregular forces, a prejudice that has led to disaster for generals both before and since. He did not learn from Cope's defeat, but Cumberland was able to learn from Hawley's (despite his contempt for his enemy).

The second charge relates to his predilection for executions. It is not known how justified the term 'Hangman' is, or even when the epithet was first employed (although it is regularly employed by historians from 1907). He was certainly in favour of discipline, but for an officer this was hardly unusual. All that can be said is that he did have five men hanged in Ghent in January 1745 and four deserters hanged almost exactly a year later after Falkirk. However, this is hardly excessive; far more deserters were hanged in the days after Culloden at Cumberland's behest and there were few officers who objected to having the Articles of War as laid down by Parliament carried out. Walpole was either unaware that hanging for deserters and spies was legitimate and usual or, as was more probably the case, he had an animus against Hawley personally.

Apart from these two facets of it, much of Hawley's career was steady if unexceptional. He seems to have been an ambitious young officer in the Spanish Peninsula, at Sheriffmuir, and at Vigo, and then a competent subordinate general in the War of the Austrian Succession and at Culloden. His writings were presumably unknown to others. Initial royal favour and then long service brought him promotions, but it was only in later life that he was awarded a governor's post, much to his annoyance. It is possible that there were no more promotions because of the failure at Falkirk which served to blight his career, as Prestonpans did for Cope.

As a private man, he was sociable with his hunting enthusiasm and in building up a household with Elizabeth Toovey and her sons and niece in Hartley Wintney. He cared for his sister and ensured that she was provided for. Yet he was also contemptuous of the niceties of polite society, with his hostility to both the Law and the Church, its two main civil pillars, leading him to an unmarked final resting place, which was his final desire.

However, it is as a soldier that his career must be judged. As a battlefield commander, Hawley had one chance to prove himself and in this he was found wanting. Nevertheless, the remainder of his career, both before and after was creditable enough, if not exceptional. As a subordinate officer he was capable and proved his worth, but this is usually overlooked in light of the defeat at Falkirk. Yet this was but one day in a career of decades and although significant should not cast an entire eclipse over his lifetime as a soldier.

# Appendix

# Casualties at Falkirk

This is a partial list of British casualties of the Battle of Falkirk, taken from the TNA, WO116/4, listing rank and file wounded who were discharged with pensions, and also some of those killed whose dependants received cash payments, taken from Blaikie, 'Origins of the Forty Five', pp.432-433. The officer casualties are taken from Marchant, *History of the Present Rebellion*, pp.318-319.

| Name | Rank | Regiment | Age/ length of service | Parish of origin/former occupation | Remarks |
|---|---|---|---|---|---|
| Armstrong, John | Private | Hamilton's | 23/6 | Menteith/farmer | Bruised |
| Barnet, Patrick | Private | Hamilton's | 28/3 | Durlevan, Wicklow/ shoemaker | Cut across the nose and lost his left eye |
| Barton, John | Private | Cobham's | 34/9 | Pershore/ Maltster | Shot in neck |
| Biggar | Lieutenant Colonel | Munro's | | | |
| Bland, Ambrose | Private | Blakeney's | 45/2 | Burnsall, Craven/wine cooper | Wounded |
| Blood | Private | Hamilton's | | | Killed, left a widow. |
| Bolton | Private | Blakeney's | | Near Wakefield | Killed; married to Mary (30). Awarded £10. |

# APPENDIX

| Name | Rank | Regiment | Age/ length of service | Parish of origin/former occupation | Remarks |
|---|---|---|---|---|---|
| Bourchier | Surgeon | Munro's | | Cardross* | Killed; left a widow and 5 small children. 'very poor'. Awarded £80. |
| Browne | Major | Fleming's | | Edinburgh* | Killed; left a widow. |
| Bullock, George | Private | Fleming's | 27/6 | Ashley, Gloucestershire/ Husbandman | Disabled in left hand |
| Cane, Roger | Private | Wolfe's | 25/3 | Stenoland, Donegal/Tallow chandler | Shot in left arm |
| Caufield, James | Private | Hamilton's | 39/4 | Stradbally, Queen's County/ Cooper | Disabled by several wounds |
| Clark? | Private | Ligonier's | | Salisbury* | Killed; married to Mary (38). Very poor. |
| Clarke, William | Private | Cobham's | 33/13 | Macclesfield/ Pedlar | Wounded in right hand |
| Craig? | Private | Ligonier's | | Edinburgh* | Killed; married to Jane (39); daughter Mary. Very poor. Awarded £15. |
| Crow | Cornet | Ligonier's | | | Prisoner |
| Cumpston | Private | Hamilton's | | | Killed; left a widow |
| Dalrymple | Captain | Blakeney's | | Marlborough* | Killed; married to Mary (45) |
| Dalton | Captain | Wolfe's | | | |
| Davidson, James | Private | St. Clair's | 50/24 | Pattie, Murray/ Labourer | Disabled in right foot |
| Edmundson | Captain | Blakeney's | | Canwallis, Stirling* | Killed, married to Mary (20), 'very poor'. Awarded £70. Buried in Falkirk churchyard. |
| Fanfield | Lieutenant | Blakeney's | | | |

| Name | Rank | Regiment | Age/ length of service | Parish of origin/former occupation | Remarks |
|---|---|---|---|---|---|
| Fitzgerald, George | Captain | Munro's | | | Wounded and captured |
| Fleming | Private | Battereau's | | Limerick | Killed; married to Catherine (26); 1 child, 'very poor'. |
| Frazer, Patrick | Private | Hamilton's | 21/3 | Dublin/linen draper | Lost his right arm and two fingers in the left |
| Garing | Captain | Wolfe's | | | |
| Gaven | Private | Blakeney's | | Westminster* | Killed; married to Elinor (36). |
| George, John | Private | Cobham's | 48/20 | Frome/shearman | Injured by fall of horse |
| Gibbins | Private | Hamilton's | | | Killed; left a widow. |
| Goodenough, Roy | Private | Barrell's | 39/4 | Demeran, Wiltshire/Collar maker | Wounded |
| Hacker | Captain | Howard's | | | |
| Hale | Captain | Wolfe's | | | |
| Hall | Captain | Munro's | | | |
| Hamilton | Captain | Wolfe's | | | |
| Huff | Private | Blakeney's | | York* | Killed; married to Grace (60). |
| Hutson? | Private | Ligonier's | | Norwich* | Killed; married to Ann (24). Very poor. |
| Johnston, Peter | Private | Hamilton's | 52/28 | Clayton, Yorkshire/brazier | Wounded in forehead, disabled in left arm |
| Jordan, Samuel | Private | Battereau's | 25/2 | Manchester/Woolcomber | Lamed in his left arm |
| Keandill, Thomas | Private | Hamilton's | 22/3 | Lisonkegh, Farmanaess/Confectioner | Disabled in left arm |
| Kellett | Captain | Blakeney's | | Kinsale, Ireland* | Killed; widow aged 38 |

# APPENDIX

| Name | Rank | Regiment | Age/ length of service | Parish of origin/former occupation | Remarks |
|---|---|---|---|---|---|
| Kerney, John | Private | Hamilton's | 31/5 | Armagh/weaver | Disabled in the hands, stabbed in the back |
| Kirkson | Lieutenant | Wolfe's | | | |
| Landers | Captain | Wolfe's | | | Killed, married |
| Lewisly | Private | Ligonier's | | Kelso* | Killed; left a widow and 1 child |
| MacKenny | Private | Hamilton's | | | Killed; left a widow. |
| McCann | Private | Hamilton's | | | Killed; left a widow |
| McCrea, John | Private | Hamilton's | 28/7 | Cookstown, Tyrone/farmer | Disabled in right hand, cut under the nose |
| McGlaudrey, Robert | Private | Hamilton's | 45/7 | Crookhill, Gavan/revenue collector | Disabled in both hands and lost his left eye |
| McGram, Roger | Private | | 28/5 | Killalan, Down/ Labourer | Wounded |
| McKennon? | Corporal | Ligonier's | | Salisbury* | Killed; married to Elizabeth (28) and 1 daughter, Sarah (6). Very poor. |
| McQuay | Private | Ligonier's | | Hadington* | Killed; left a widow and 2 children |
| Monk | Cornet | Ligonier's | | | |
| Montgomery | Private | Ligonier's | | Kelso* | Killed: left a widow and 2 children |
| Moore | Private | Hamilton's | | | Killed; left a widow. |
| Mounce | Sergeant | Blakeney's | | Tiverton, Devonshire | Killed; married to Esther (50). Very poor. Awarded £30. |
| Munro, Sir Robert | Colonel | Munro's | | | Killed; buried in Falkirk churchyard |
| Murray, John | Private | Hamilton's | 26/7 | Armagh/ Maltster | Disabled in right shoulder and other parts |

| Name | Rank | Regiment | Age/ length of service | Parish of origin/former occupation | Remarks |
|---|---|---|---|---|---|
| Nickle | Private | Ligonier's | | Stirling* | Killed; left a widow and a child. Awarded £30. |
| Ormsby | Private | Ligonier's | | Ireland* | Killed; left a widow and 3 children |
| Osrepo | Captain | Howard's | | | |
| Pearce, Charles | Private | Fleming's | 26/6 | Cambridge/ Shoemaker | Disabled in left hand |
| Pendleton, James | Private | Battereau's | 18/1 | Carymalden, Sligo/Weaver | Wounded in right arm |
| Powell | Lieutenant Colonel | Cholmondeley's | | | |
| Reilly | Private | Hamilton's | | | Killed; left a widow. |
| Robinson | Private | Ligonier's | | Fisheraw* | Killed; left widow and 2 children |
| Scott | Private | Hamilton's | | | Killed; left a widow |
| Shaw | Private | Hamilton's | | | Killed; left a widow. |
| Singleton, William | Private | Cobham's | 21/2 | Upton, Nottinghamshire/ Collar maker | Wounded in the hand |
| Smith | Cornet | Hamilton's | | | |
| Smith | Private | Hamilton's | | | Killed; left a widow |
| Spicer | Corporal | Blakeney's | | | Killed; married to Martha (20). Accompanied battalion. |
| Tamer, Robert | Private | Barrell's | 49/8 | Blessin, Devonshire/ Labourer | Lost use of right hand |
| Todd | Captain | Blakeney's | | Dublin* | Killed; married to Mary (40) |
| Vincent | Private | Ligonier's | | Edinburgh* | Killed; left a widow and 3 children |
| Whitney, Shugborough | Lieutenant Colonel | Ligonier's | /42 | Edinburgh* | Killed, left a widow. Awarded £100. |

| Name | Rank | Regiment | Age/ length of service | Parish of origin/former occupation | Remarks |
|---|---|---|---|---|---|
| Williams, Griffith | Private | Blakeney's | 50/13 | Lanuasbrimi, Carmarthenshire/ Husbandman | Eye knocked out |
| Williams, Thomas | Private | Fleming's | 27/7 | Brillay, Herefordshire/ Flax dresser | Disabled in right arm |
| Wilson | Private | Hamilton's | | | Killed; left a widow. |
| Wilson | Private | Hamilton's | | | Killed; left a widow |
| Witheral | Captain | Munro's | | | |

# Bibliography

## Manuscripts

### British Library

Additional Manuscripts, 32705-7, 32714, 32698, 33954, 35453, 61603.

### Hampshire Archives

20M50/194
25M87/11
55M90/512
79A08/2
St. Mary's Hartley Wintney Burial Registers

### Leeds University Library, Special Collections,

Townshend Manuscripts

### The National Archives

C8/539/14
PC1/5/111
PROB11/953/60, 418/451, 844/446, 684/66
State Papers Domestic, 36/76-80
State Papers Scotland, 54/8, 10, 11, 27-30
State Papers 87/11-24
War Office, 116/4-5
War Office, 4/513, 4/50-51.

### National Army Museum

7607-83

**National Library of Scotland**

Manuscripts, 3733, 7104, 16621, 16625, 16639

**National Records of Scotland**

GD220/5/787a.
GD45/14/263.
GD45/1/229

**Royal Archives**

Cumberland Papers, 3-13, 34
Hawley-Toovey Papers, 7411-24-100, 101, 105, 108-109, 111, 113-114, 119, 120, 122, 123-6, 128, 400

## Published Primary Sources

Anon, *A Letter from a Gentleman who was an eye witness of the late Battle of Falkirk* (Glasgow: Unknown Publisher, 1746).
Anon, *A Short Account of the Battle of Falkirk* (Bannockburn: Unknown Publisher, 1746).
Anon., *Report on the manuscripts of the Duke of Roxburghe…14th Report, Appendix III* (Royal Commission on Historic Manuscripts, 34, 1894).
Anon., *Report on the Manuscripts of the Earl of Eglington* (London: Eyre and Spottiswoode, 1885).
Anon., *Report on the Manuscripts of the late Reginald Rawdon Hastings* (Royal Commission on Historic Manuscripts, 48, 1928).
Anon, *Report on the Manuscripts of Lady Du Cane* (London: HMSO, 1905).
Anon, *Report on the Manuscripts of the Earl of Buckinghamshire…14th Report Appendix IX* (Royal Commission on Historical Manuscripts, 38 (1895).
Anon, *Report on the Manuscripts in Various Collections, VI* (Royal Commission on Historic Manuscripts, 55), 1901-1914.
Anon, *Ninth Report of the Royal Commission on Historic Manuscripts: Part II, Appendix and Index* (London: Eyre and Spottiswoode, 1884.)
Bell, Robert (ed.), 'Memorials of John Murray of Broughton', SHS, 1st series (Edinburgh, 1898).
Blaikie, Walter (ed.), 'Origins of the Forty Five', SHS, 2nd series, 2 (Edinburgh, 1916).
Blackburne Daniell, F.H. (ed.), *Calendar of State Papers Domestic series, of the reign of Charles II*, 1675-1676 (London: Longman, 1860-1947).
Blackburne Daniell, F.H. (ed.), *Calendar of State Papers Domestic series, of the reign of Charles II*, 1676-1677 (London: Longman, 1860-1947).

Blackburne Daniell, F.H. (ed.), *Calendar of State Papers Domestic series, of the reign of Charles II, 1679-1680* (London: Longman, 1860-1947).

Blackburne Daniell, F.H. and Bickley, F.C. (eds.), *Calendar of State Papers Domestic series, of the reign of Charles II, 1683-1684* (London: Longman, 1860-1947).

Blackburne Daniell, F.H. and Bickley, F.C. (eds.)., *Calendar of State Papers Domestic series, of the reign of Charles II, 1685* (London: Longman, 1860-1947).

Douglas, Francis, *History of the Rebellion in 1745 and 1746* (Aberdeen: F. Douglas and W. Murray, 1755).

Elcho, Lord (ed. Ewan Charteris), *A Short Account of the Affairs of Scotland, 1744-1746* (Edinburgh: David Douglas, 1907).

Evelyn, John, *Diary* (London: Everyman, 2005).

Forbes, Duncan, *Culloden Papers* (London: T. Cadell and W. Davies, 1815).

Forbes, Robert, *Jacobite Memoirs of the Rebellion of 1745* (Edinburgh: William and Robert Chambers, 1834).

Fraser, William, *The Earls of Cromarty, their Kindred, Country and Correspondence* (Edinburgh: Unknown Publisher, 1876).

Glover, Richard, *Memoirs by a Celebrated literary and political figure* (London: John Murray, 1814).

Grey, J.M. (ed.), 'The Memoirs of the Life of Sir John Clerk of Penicuik' SHS, 1st series (Edinburgh, 1892).

Guy, Alan J. (ed.), *Colonel Samuel Bagshawe and the Army of George II* (London: Bodley Head, 1990).

Hardy, William John (ed.), *Calendar of State Papers Domestic series, of the reign of William and Mary, 1689-1690* (London: Stationery Office, 1895-1906).

Hardy, William John (ed.), *Calendar of State Papers Domestic series, of the reign of William and Mary, 1691-1692* (London: Stationery Office, 1895-1906).

Hardy, William John (ed.), *Calendars of State Papers, Domestic series, of the reign of William III, 1694-1695* (London: Stationery Office, 1913-1937).

Henderson, Andrew, *The Life of William Augustus, Duke of Cumberland* (London: J. Ridley, 1766).

Henderson, Andrew, *History of the Rebellion* (London: Unknown Publisher, 1748).

Home, John, *The History of the Rebellion of 1745* (London: Cadell, jun. W. Davies, 1802).

Johnstone, James, *A Memoir of the Forty Five* (London: Folio Society, 1958).

Knighton, C.S. (ed.), *Calendars of State Papers Domestic series, of the reign of Anne, 1704-1705* (London: Boydell Press, 1916).

Lennox, Charles, *A Duke and his Friends* (London: Hutchinson and Co., 1911).

Lewis, W.S. (ed.), *Correspondence of Horace Walpole 1745-1748* (New Haven: Yale University Press, 1955)

Lodge, Richard (ed.), *Private Correspondence of Chesterfield and Newcastle, 1744-1746* (London: Royal Historical Society, 1930).

McCann, T.J. (ed.), *The Correspondence of the Duke of Newcastle and Richmond, 1724-1750* (Lewes: Sussex Historical Society, 1983).

MacKnight, J. (ed.), *Memoirs of Sir Ewan Cameron of Lochiel* (Glasgow: Maitland Club, 1842).
March, Earl of, *Records of the Charlton Hunt* (London: Elkin Matthews, 1910).
Marchant, John, *History of the Present Rebellion* (London: R. Walker, 1746).
Maxwell, James, *Narrative of the Expedition in Scotland of Prince Charles Stuart* (Edinburgh: T. Constable, 1841).
Metcalfe, Jack, *The Life of Jack Metcalfe* (York: E. and R. Peck, 1795).
Murray, Irene J. (ed.), 'Letters of Andrew Fletcher in 1715-1716', SHS 4th series, Miscellany, X, 1965.
Paton, Henry (ed.), 'Lyon in Mourning', SHS 22 (1894).
Ray, James, *A Compleat History of the Rebellion* (Bristol: S. Farley, 1754).
Saville. A. (ed.), 'Secret Comment: The Diaries of Gertrude Saville, 1721-1757', *Thoroton Record Society*, 42 (1997).
Tayler, Alastair and Henrietta (eds.), *1745 and After* (London: Thomas Nelson & Sons, 1938).
Thornton, William, *The Counterpoise* (London: Unknown Publisher, 1754).
Walpole, Horace, *Memoirs of the Reign of George II* (London: Henry Colburn, 1847).
Ward, W.R. (ed.), *Parson and Parish in eighteenth century: Replies to Bishops' Visitations* (Winchester: Hampshire County Council, 1995).
Willson, Beckles (ed.), *Life and Letters of James Wolfe* (London: Heinemann, 1909).
Yorke, Philip C. (ed.), *The Life and Correspondence of Philip Yorke, Earl of Hardwicke* (Cambridge: Cambridge University Press, 1913).

## Newspapers

*Caledonian Mercury*, 1745
*Gentleman's Magazine*, 16 (1746).
*Glasgow Courant*, 1746
*London Evening Post*, 1746
*The London Gazette*, 1685, 1689, 1715, 1719, 1730, 1735, 1739
*Oxford Journal*, 1759
*Penny London Post*, 1746.
*Stamford Mercury*, 1746

## Published Secondary Sources

Arnot, B.S. and Seton, A.G. (eds.), 'Prisoners of the Forty Five', SHS, 3rd series, 13-15 (1928-1929).
Bailey, Geoffrey, *Falkirk or Paradise! The Battle of Falkirk, 17 January 1746* (Edinburgh: John Donald Publishers, 1996).
Black, Jeremy, *Culloden and the '45* (Gloucester: Sutton, 1990).
Browning, Reed, *The War of the Austrian Succession* (New York: Sutton, 1994).

Charteris, Evan, *William Augustus, Duke of Cumberland, His early Life and Times, 1721-1748* (London: Edward Arnold, 1913).
Clark, George, *The Later Stuarts, 1660-1714* (Oxford: Clarendon Press, 1956).
Dalton, Charles, *English Army Lists and Commission Registers, 1661-1714* (London: Eyre and Spottiswoode, 1904).
Dalton, Charles, *The Army of George I* (London: Eyre and Spottiswoode, 1930).
Duffy, Christopher, *The '45: Bonnie Prince Charlie and the Untold Story of the Jacobite Rising* (London: Cassell, 2003).
Duffy, Christopher, *Fight for a Throne: The Jacobite '45 Reconsidered* (Solihull: Helion, 2015)
Duffy, Christopher, *The Military Experience in the Age of Reason* (London: Kegan and Routledge, 1987).
Gorsky, David, *The Old Village of Hartley Wintney* (Hartley Wintney: Hartley Wintney Preservation Society, 1973).
Gruber, Ira D., *Officers and their Books* (University of North Carolina Press, 2010).
Lenman, Bruce, *The Jacobite Clans of the Great Glens* (London: Methuen, 1984).
McLynn, Frank, *Bonnie Prince Charlie* (London: Routledge, 1988).
Oates, Jonathan, *Sweet William or the Butcher? The Duke of Cumberland and the '45* (Barnsley: Pen and Sword, 2008).
Orr, Michael, *Dettingen* (London: C. Knight, 1972).
Petrie, Sir Charles, *The Jacobite Movement* (London: Eyre and Spottiswoode, 1932).
Reid, Stuart, *1745: A Military History of the Last Jacobite Rising* (Spellmount: Staplehurst, 1996).
Riding, Jacqueline, *The Jacobites: A New History of the '45 Rebellion* (New York: Bloomsbury, 2016).
Speck, William, *The Butcher: The Duke of Cumberland and the suppression of the '45* (Oxford: Blackwell, 1981).
Tomasson, Katherine and Buist, Frances, *Battles of the Forty Five* (London: Batsford, 1962).
Whitworth, Rex, *William Augustus: Duke of Cumberland* (Barnsley: Pen and Sword, 1992).
Whitworth, Rex, *Field Marshal Lord Ligonier: A Story of the British Army, 1702-1770* (Oxford: Clarendon Press, 1958).

## Journal Articles

Dalton, Charles, 'Parentage of Lieut. General Hawley', *Notes and Queries*, 8th series, IX (1896), pp.121-122.
Dalton, Charles, 'Child Commissions, 1661-1714', *Notes and Queries*, 8th series, VIII (1895), pp.421-423.
Sumner, Rev. Percy, 'General Hawley's Scheme for Light Dragoons', *Journal of the Society for Army Historical Research*, XXV (1947), pp.63-66.

Rev. Percy Sumner, 'General Hawley's Chaos', *Journal of the Society for Army Historical Research*, XXVI (1948), pp.91-94.

## Electronic Resources

www.ancestry.co.uk

# Index

Albemarle, Lt Gen. Willem van Keppel, Earl of 166
Almansa, Battle of 28-31, 105
Ancram, Lt Col William Kerr, Earl of 163
Anne, Queen 21-22, 24, 38-39, 41, 54, 58
Antwerp 90-91
Argyle, Lt Gen. John Campbell, Duke of 38-45, 154, 162
Aschaffenburg 77

Bannockburn 106, 132, 136
Belford, Maj. John 104, 117
Berwick-upon-Tweed 38, 100, 102, 104
Blakeney, Maj. Gen. William 101, 103, 157, 174, 187
Bland, Maj. Gen. Humphrey 59-60, 92, 101, 105, 158, 160-161, 163, 166, 174
Bonnie Prince Charlie; see Stuart, Charles Edward
Braddock, Maj. Gen. Edward 180-181
British Army, regiments of: Barrell's Regiment of Foot 49, 52, 84, 97, 98, 115, 123, 126, 130, 139-140, 145, 152, 192, 194; Battereau's Regiment of Foot 97-98, 115, 128, 139-140, 192, 194; Berkeley's Dragoons 16-17, 25; Blakeney's Regiment of Foot 97-98, 105, 126-128, 139-140, 148-149, 190-195; Bland's Dragoons 78-79; Bligh's Regiment of Foot 75, 153, 157; Campbell's Dragoons 79; Campbell's Regiment of Foot (Royal North British Fusiliers) 98; Cholmondeley's Regiment of Foot 97-98, 115, 128, 139-140, 194; Cobham's Dragoons 97-99, 107, 114, 119-120, 130, 139-140, 142, 153, 157-158, 160, 190-192, 194; Erle's Regiment of Foot 21; Essex's Dragoons (late Berkeley's) 18, 24-25, 33-34, 39; Evans' Dragoons 41-44, 95; Fleming's Regiment of Foot 97-98, 115, 124, 139-140, 148, 191-192, 194-195; Gardiner's Dragoons 54; Hamilton's Dragoons 97-100, 106, 114, 117, 120, 122, 139-141, 149, 151, 190-195; Handasyde's Regiment of Foot 76; Hawley's Dragoons (late Gore's) 53; Hawley's Dragoons (late Harrington's; see also Gardiner's Dragoons) 54, 119; Hawley's Regiment of Foot 45, 52; Hill's Regiment of Foot 30, 41; Honywood's Dragoons 75; Honywood's Horse 78, 182; Howard's Regiment of Foot 52, 76, 83-84, 97-98, 111, 115, 127, 130, 139-140, 192, 195; Huske's Regiment of Foot (Royal Welsh Fusiliers) 75, 80; Kerr's Dragoons 152-153, 157-158, 160; Kingston's Light Horse 157, 163; Leighton's Regiment of Foot 175; Ligonier's Dragoons (late Gardiner's) 97, 99-100, 106, 114, 119-120, 139-140, 151, 191-194; Ligonier's Horse 78, 149; Ligonier's Regiment of Foot 97, 115, 129-130, 139-140, 191; Loudoun's Highlanders 115; Munro's Regiment of Foot 97-98, 115, 126-128, 139-140, 190-195; Onslow's Regiment of Foot 75; Ponsonby's Regiment of Foot 75; Price's Regiment of Foot 97-98, 115, 139-140; Pulteney's Regiment of Foot 97-98, 115, 139-140, 149, 175; Royal Dragoons (Hawley's 1740-1759) 71, 75-76, 78-79, 90, 168, 179; Royal Horse Guards (Blues) 178; Sempill's Highlanders (Black Watch) 79; Sempill's Regiment of Foot 98; Skelton's Regiment of Foot 175, 182; St. Clair's Regiment of Foot (Royals) 97-98, 115, 130, 133, 139-140, 149, 191; Temple's Regiment of Foot 22, 38; Wolfe's Regiment of Foot 97-98, 115, 126, 128, 139-140, 191-193; see also Foot Guards,

Volunteers, Militia
Bruges 75, 81, 170
Bury, Col George Keppel, Lord 160, 170
Byng, Admiral Sir George 33
Byng, Rear Admiral John 101

Cadogan, Lt Gen. William 18, 45
Cage, Capt. John, duel with Hawley 37-38
Callendar House 107, 111-112
Cameron of Lochiel, Donald 134, 138
Campbell, Lt Gen. Sir John 71, 76-77, 79, 81, 85-86
Campbell, Maj. Gen. John 103-104, 148, 154
Campbell, Lt Col John 115
Carlisle 40, 91-92, 94, 97-98, 104, 150
Carteret, John, Lord 76-77, 80-81
Charlton Hunt 54-55
Cholmondeley, Brig. James 97-98, 107, 111-112, 125, 129-132, 152, 178
Clayton, Lt Gen. Jasper 30, 74, 76-78
Clifton, Battle of 92
Cobham, Field Marshal Richard Temple, Viscount 22, 38-40, 46-48, 50-52
Cope, Lt Gen. Sir John 7, 12, 57, 76, 78, 87-88, 102, 117, 124, 142-145, 147, 168, 184, 189
Courts Martial 37, 46, 82-84, 102, 148-150, 164, 166-167, 183
Crawford, Maj. Gen. John Lindsay, Earl of 157
Culloden, Battle of 7-8, 11-12, 115, 146, 150, 158-166, 180, 189
Cumberland, HRH Prince William, Duke of 7-12, 71, 79-81, 86-98, 100-101, 104, 108, 111, 126, 143-144, 147-158, 160, 163-166, 168-176, 178-182, 184, 188-189
Cunningham, Capt. Archibald 115, 117, 130-131, 134, 148, 150

Dalzell, Lt Gen. Robert 74
Daun, *Feldzeugmeister* Graf Leopold Joseph von 171
De la Warr, Lt Gen. John West, Lord 144, 172
Deserters, executions of after battle 149-150, 166
Dettingen, Battle of 78-79, 93, 105, 158
Drummond, Lord John 84, 99, 106, 109, 111, 113, 119, 132-134, 136, 138, 151
Dutch Republic 14, 19-20, 22-23, 75, 170, 174

Edinburgh 37, 87-88, 91, 93, 95, 97-100, 102, 104-105, 107, 123, 126, 132-134, 151-152, 154-157, 168, 191, 194
Edinburgh Castle 86, 102, 151
Eindhoven 176
Erle, Lt Gen. Thomas, 17-18, 21, 23, 25, 27-34, 36, 38, 45, 54, 57, 179
Evans, Maj. Gen. William 40, 44, 85

*Falcon*, HMS 32
Falkirk 103, 106-109, 111-112
Falkirk, Battle of 7-8, 11-12, 64, 69, 97, 112-148, 152, 168, 177, 188-189; casualties at 139-141, 190-195; Orders of Battle for 97, 113-115
Farrar, Capt. John 40, 44
Fawkener, Sir Everard 98, 155-156
Fleming, Brig. James 97
Fontenoy, Battle of 85-87, 105, 133, 145, 147, 151, 158, 166
Foot Guards 14-15, 19, 22, 40, 172
Fort Augustus 167-168
Fort George 166-1667, 174-175
Fowke, Lt Gen. Thomas 175, 183
Fox, Henry 174-175, 180, 182
French Army, units of: Irish Picquets 102, 123, 132, 134; Régiment de Fitzjames 161; Régiment Royal Ecossois 81, 84, 106, 108-109, 132, 151

Galway, Lt Gen. Henri de Massue, Earl of 23, 26-29, 31-32
George I 22, 41, 45, 51, 53-54
George II 45, 54, 56-58, 60-61, 70-71, 73-83, 85-88, 92-96, 100, 144-145, 151-152, 171, 174-175, 178-180, 182; alleged paternity of Hawley dismissed 13
George of Denmark, Prince 21-22, 24-25, 34, 39, 54
Ghent 34, 75-76, 79-84, 189
Gloucester, HRH Prince William, Duke of 21-22, 39
Gordon, Mrs, Hawley plunders home of 154-156
Grant, Maj. James 166
Grosset, Walter 103, 117
Guest, Maj. Gen. Joseph 102

Hanau 77-78
Handasyde, Lt Gen. Roger 93
Hanoverian troops 75-78, 85, 170-171, 175-176

Hargrave, Lt Gen. William 74
Harrington, William Stanhope, Lord 81, 84-85, 89
Hartley Wintney 52-53, 186-187, 189
Hawley, Charles (brother) 17-18, 35
Hawley, Edward (brother) 17-18, 25, 37, 39, 57
Hawley, Lt Col Henry (uncle) 14, 18, 57
Hawley, Judith (nee Hughes; mother) 14, 19, 21-22, 58, 79
Hawley, Lt Col Francis (father) 14-18, 21, 57
Hessian troops: in Europe 75-76, 78, 90, 182; in Scotland 99, 174, 176-177
Hill, Maj. Gen. John 39
Home, Lt John 11, 102, 122, 124
Honywood, Lt Gen. Philip 48-49, 54, 71, 105, 174, 179
Howard, Lt Col George 112, 168
Howard, Lt Gen. Sir Charles 75
Huske, Maj. Gen. John 54, 93, 95, 97-98, 100, 103-106, 115, 119, 129-132, 143, 152, 164, 166, 183

Infantry weapons, Hawley's writings on 68-70
Inverness 154, 158, 163-166

Jacobite Army, units of: Atholl Brigade 113; Bagot's Hussars 114; Balmerino's Lifeguards 114; Cromartie's Regiment 113; Elcho's Lifeguards 114; Farquharson's Battalion 109, 113, 132; Fraser's Regiment 113; John Roy Stuart's Regiment 134; Kilmarnock's Horse 114; Lewis Gordon's, Regiment 106, 113; Lochiel's, Regiment 113, 127, 134; Lord Ogilvy's Regiment (including Kinloch's Battalion)106, 113, 134; MacDonald of Clanranald's Regiment 113, 123-124, 132, 134, 136; MacDonald of Glengarry's Regiment 113, 123-124, 132, 134, 136; MacDonald of Keppoch's Regiment 113, 123-124, 132, 134, 136; Mackintosh's, Regiment 113; MacPherson's, Regiment 113; Perthshire Horse 114; Pitsligo's Horse 114; Stewart of Appin's Regiment 113, 134; see also French Army, units of
James III; see Stuart, James Francis

Ker of Graden, Henry 132
Kerr, Lt Gen. Lord Mark 49, 86

Laffeld, Battle of 171
*Lennox*, HMS 26
Lerida 31
Lichfield 91-92
Light Cavalry, Hawley's proposals for 66-68
Ligonier, Col Francis 114, 119, 141
Ligonier, Field Marshal Jean, Earl 49, 57, 73, 75-76, 80-81, 83-84, 86, 88, 91, 93, 147, 150, 154, 170-172, 177, 179, 181, 183-184, 188
Linlithgow 37, 103, 106, 123, 132-134, 136
London 14-15, 21, 23, 33, 39, 45, 52-54, 66, 70, 77, 82, 87, 92-93, 100, 102, 145, 152, 168, 170, 174, 178-180, 182

Maestricht 171-172, 175
Mann, Sir Horace 82, 95, 99, 105, 142-143, 168, 181
Marlborough, Capt. Gen. John Churchill, Duke of 21-23, 34-35, 39-40, 45, 59-60, 143
Memorandum on defeating Jacobites, Hawley's, 118
Militia 41, 117, 128, 153: Argyllshire Militia 107, 123, 132, 158, 161; Glasgow Militia 106-107, 111, 122-125, 141

Monkey (spaniel), poem in memorial of 56
Monmouth, James Scott, Duke of 14-16
Mons 81, 89-90
Montague, John Montague, Duke of 100
Mordaunt, Maj. Gen. John 97, 131, 132, 170, 178
Murray, Lord George 92, 108-110, 112-113, 119-121, 123, 132-134, 136, 138, 143, 161

Nairn 157-158
Nairne, John Nairne, Lord 113
Newcastle 45, 91-92, 97-98, 104, 152, 168
Newcastle, Thomas Pelham-Holles, Duke of 54, 73-75, 88, 92-94, 98-102, 105, 117, 144, 147-149, 152-154, 157, 165-166, 168, 174-176, 180

O'Sullivan, John William 109-110, 113, 124-125, 132, 136-137, 162
Ostend 34, 75, 81

Pelham, Henry 54, 93, 179
Pitt, William 83, 182
Portugal 23, 51

Prestonpans, Battle of 7-8, 54, 88, 91, 99-101, 105, 117, 120-122, 124, 126, 128, 138, 141-142, 146-147, 149-150, 163, 166, 189

Rank and file, Hawley's advice to 61-66
Rich, Lt Col Robert 84
Richmond, Lt Gen. Charles Lennox, Duke of 54-55, 73-74, 90-92, 95, 152, 174, 188
Robinson, Lt Septimus 91
Rocoux, Battle of 170

Seven Years War 7, 12, 68; Hawley's service in 180-183
Seymour, Maj Gen William 34
Sheriffmuir, Battle of 8, 40, 44-45, 64, 85, 95, 105, 114, 122, 146, 158, 162-163, 189
Spain 12, 22-24, 26-27, 39-40, 46, 73, 81; See also Almansa, Battle of, Vigo, attack on
Spey, River 157
Stair, Field Marshal John Dalrymple, Earl of 75-77, 171
Stirling 41, 87, 97, 101, 103, 117, 132, 137, 141, 146, 156, 191, 194
Stirling Castle 99, 101, 103-104, 108, 145-146, 153
Stuart, Charles Edward 7-9, 87, 92, 108-110, 114, 124, 134, 136-137, 161, 177
Stuart, James Francis 41, 87
Stuart, John Roy 120-121, 124, 131, 134

Toovey, Maj. Gen. John 56-57, 75, 157, 185, 187

Toovey, Capt. William 57, 185, 187
Toovey, Elizabeth 56, 184-185, 187, 189
Torwood 108-109, 111-112
Tournai 81, 85-86, 145
Tweeddale, John Hay, Marquess of 85
Tyrawley, Lt Gen. James O'Hara, Lord 25, 77, 93, 165, 171, 174

Vigo, attack on 47-52, 189
Volunteers, 117, 141: Edinburgh Volunteers 102, 115, 124; Paisley Volunteers 115; Yorkshire Volunteers (Thornton's) 97, 115, 124, 141

Wade, Field Marshal George 7, 9, 13, 45, 51-52, 57, 70, 73, 79-80, 91-94, 96-100, 102, 104-105, 154, 165, 175, 184, 187
Walpole, Horace 8-11, 82-83, 95, 99, 105, 142-143, 156, 168, 179-181, 188-189
Walpole, Sir Robert 38, 53, 56, 58
Watson, Lt Col George 154
Wentworth, Lt Gen. Thomas 73-74, 93, 165
West Green House 52, 185-186
Whitney, Lt Col Shugbrough 119-121, 137, 194
Wightman, Maj. Gen. Joseph 143
Willemstad 170, 175, 177
William III 16-17, 20-22
Wills, Maj. Gen. Charles 31, 45
Wolfe, Col James 10, 145, 155, 161-164, 168, 181

Yonge, Sir William 75, 85, 149
Yorke, Col Joseph 91, 163

# From Reason to Revolution – Warfare 1721-1815
http://www.helion.co.uk/series/from-reason-to-revolution-1721-1815.php

The 'From Reason to Revolution' series covers the period of military history 1721–1815, an era in which fortress-based strategy and linear battles gave way to the nation-in-arms and the beginnings of total war.

This era saw the evolution and growth of light troops of all arms, and of increasingly flexible command systems to cope with the growing armies fielded by nations able to mobilise far greater proportions of their manpower than ever before. Many of these developments were fired by the great political upheavals of the era, with revolutions in America and France bringing about social change which in turn fed back into the military sphere as whole nations readied themselves for war. Only in the closing years of the period, as the reactionary powers began to regain the upper hand, did a military synthesis of the best of the old and the new become possible.

The series examines the military and naval history of the period in a greater degree of detail than has hitherto been attempted, and has a very wide brief, with the intention of covering all aspects from the battles, campaigns, logistics, and tactics, to the personalities, armies, uniforms, and equipment.

## Submissions
The publishers would be pleased to receive submissions for this series. Please email reasontorevolution@helion.co.uk, or write to Helion & Company Limited, Unit 8 Amherst Business Centre, Budbrooke Road, Warwick, CV34 5WE

## You may also be interested in:

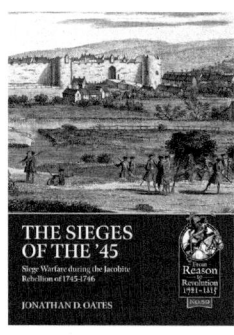

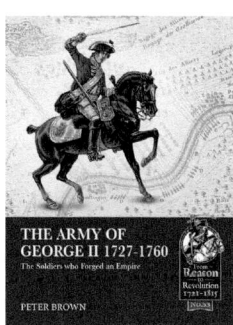

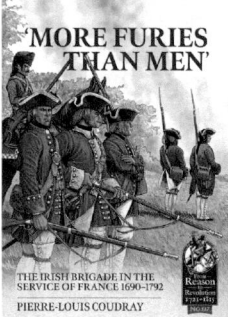
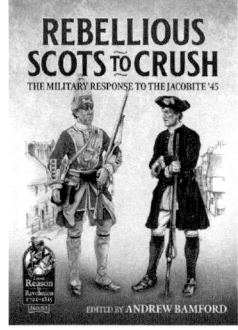